HOLISTIC PSYCHOLOGY OF ALEXANDER PINT

THERE ARE MANY OF US, BUT WE'RE ONE

Introduction to practical self-investigation

BY ALEXANDER PINT

Translated by Emin Kuliev, MD

www.pint.ru

https://caterpillartobuterfly.wordpress.com

skyrocket press

Visit www.SkyrocketPress.com

Cover art by Freydoon Rassouli
ISBN: 978-1-944722-03-6

What does each one of us needs to meet himself? What do we need for self-investigation? We need to meet with a direct mirror that would show us who we are in reality. This book is about one of those meetings.

Thank you for your direct and indirect participation in the process of creation of this book.

TABLE OF CONTENTS

A Short Introduction
to Holistic Psychology

•◆•◆•◆•◆•◆•◆•◆•◆•◆•◆•◆•◆•◆•◆•◆•◆•◆•

If you are not familiar with our approach toward knowing and realization of oneself, you probably want to understand what holistic psychology is.

HOLISTIC PSYCHOLOGY IS THE SHORTEST WAY TO SOLVE ALL YOUR EARTHLY LESSONS AND AN OPPORTUNITY TO PREPARE TO QUANTUM LEAP OFF THE EARTH TO THE NEXT VIBRATIONAL LEVEL OF CONSCIOUSNESS.

Holistic psychology offers you an opportunity to recall your life's major mission and to start solving it in a state of awareness.

We hope you understand that the shortest way is not the easiest way. Our approach toward the understanding of these earthly lessons and the meaning of human life is based not on "common values," but on a clear vision of the stages of the

i

evolution and this understanding must be tied to the lessons of the evolution of Human Consciousness.

What kind of experience do we receive on Earth at a given stage of our evolution, and what kind of puzzles or assignments do we solve during our lifetime? We are not discussing the questions that are considered common here, as the common, daily questions only create the context for us to solve our main assignments. **That's why when we don't know who we are in reality, our desires are just impulses that direct us to pass through the experience we have been incarnated on Earth to receive.**

What is this experience? This experience is born out of the illusion of our loneliness and the fight that we accept as our reality. It is precisely that illusion that gives birth to multiple lessons which appear throughout our lives, and the main reason that all these lessons happen is the **state of fear we live in.**

To see and to understand that the state of fear is the main reason that gives birth to all our earthly lessons and to the problems, conflicts, and hardships connected to these lessons is the most important thing for a human being who is ready to get to know himself.

What lessons happen to be the main lessons of your life today? Betrayal, dependence, oppression, poverty, unfairness, disease, suffering… What are the situations that show up in your life? They bother you and create strain or voltage that forces you to look for a way out of this intolerably heavy states. Perhaps you have already tried different methods to exit. How much did they help you? Most likely, that was just a temporary and partial escape. Otherwise, you probably would not be reading this text.

Holistic psychology is based on the revolutionary discoveries of Alexander Pint made during many years of his investigation of nature and the mechanisms of the human consciousness during a given stage of its evolution.

The main result of this investigation is a **discovery of the mechanisms of the dual nature of human perception and the characteristics of the personal program of a human being which provide an opportunity to exit into a qualitatively new level of consciousness.**

Perhaps you want to discover the difference between our approach to the transformation of personality and those that currently exist. The major difference is our discovery of the basic principles using which a Soul of a given human being creates specific circumstances in order to pass through its lessons on Earth. We review the dual mechanisms of these lessons, explore the ways they get realized in our life, and develop methods to solve them.

Our investigation was conducted through the Aware functioning and interaction of the three bodies of a human being: mental, emotional, and physical within the dual setting of human consciousness. Dualities happen to be the main principle that gives birth to the "sleep of consciousness" of a human being and one's lessons on the planet Earth. A complete, holistic review of the major mechanisms of the vital activity of any given human being has been provided, allowing one to open the basic principles of the accelerated passage of the Earthly lessons.

Are you ready for an accelerated movement toward yourself? This question can be answered only by you. If your answer is "YES," WE invite you embark on the most interesting journey—to become aware of your wholeness. Your first step will be to familiarize yourself with this and other books of our school, as well as other materials published on our site.

We want to remind you that "everything is not as simple and not as hard as it appears to you."

Recall who you are, where you are from, and why you are here!
As an incarnated body of a human being, do you remember why you are here on Earth and from where you came? Does this question interest you, or are you more concerned satisfying your personal desires?

What do you see as the meaning of your existence on Earth? In any case, you have a certain purpose, but from where did you get it, and why do you think it is the correct one?

"Why so many questions?" – you may ask. – "You had better answer them yourself and let us read the answers." If everything was so simple, I would do exactly that. But there is no sense in answering questions that have not been asked by you. At best, the answers would create an impression in you that the author knows something. But that is not what I want. And what do I want?

Transfer from consciousness of unity to consciousness of separation

I would like to pass on to you the state and the knowledge that comes from the WORLD of Unity, from the world of "WE." That is that WORLD out of which all of us—people incarnated on Earth—came from. That is the WORLD from which WE observe the WORLD of EARTH and many other worlds, experiencing the life of each human being as part of ourselves, i.e. WE. Over THERE WE are very interested in life on Earth, and WE incarnate on Earth in human bodies in order to satisfy this interest. But when we are born in a human body, we forget the consciousness of Unity we enjoyed THERE. On Earth, we enter into the opposite pole of Consciousness—Separation.

Earth is a scene for the game of Separation. It is here that WE learn this side of consciousness, the side opposite to UNITY. At the same time, in incarnating on Earth, we do not remember the Rules and the Laws of the game of separation; we cogitate them on our own. That is why every birth on Earth is a severe shock. From the world of Unity, WE get into the opposite world, the laws of which are different. From the energy of

Unconditional Love, WE get into the energies of Fear or Conditioned Love. From the state of Life, WE enter the state of Survival. From the state of timelessness, WE incarnate into the harsh limitations of linear time.

As the primordial impulse of our birth on Earth is OUR interest, we experience it in the highest degree in childhood. We are interested in our bodies and in everything that surrounds them. In childhood, we still remember the state of Unity. We feel it especially well with our parents. Observe children's relationships with their families, and perhaps you will recognize how that state, later on, leaves the majority of people, changing to disappointment, resentment, irritation, and pain.

Your personality represents a set of given conditions of your Earthly incarnation

Why does this happen? Because we come here to receive lessons in Separation, that we chose to receive previously, while in a World of Unity.

How is our program of scheduled lessons and experiences on Earth introduced and realized? Such a program is introduced at the level of the cells of our body and through the formation of our personality. That is precisely why the conditions of the puzzles and lessons of the Earthly incarnation of every human being are being given through the personality. Have you looked at your personality in this way? If you have not, you do not understand the main role it performs in the plan of your Soul.

Your personality represents **the given** of the puzzle you came to Earth to experience and solve. You need to understand your personality as **the given** of your puzzle. That understanding will allow you to solve the puzzle you were send here to solve.

Your interest in channeling, esoteric literature, psychology, philosophy, and religion represents the beginning steps in that direction. If you are already close to the end point of your holistic understanding of yourself, you will need the knowledge received in our Process. We call it holistic psychology.

In what way does the personality stimulate a human being to receive the necessary for his or her Soul experience? The perception of your personality is tuned in a precise way to receive the experience ordered by your Soul. During this process, the experience that we receive through our personality happens to be not fully encompassing, not whole. It is limited and conditioned by harsh beliefs or fixated on a one-sided point of view of oneself and the surrounding world. The personality of a human being represents a fixated and one-sided point of view or a certain angle of perception of oneself and the surrounding world. That is why it is so difficult for a human being to change the tuned-in perception. Personality resists that. That is why only through learning how to use the "knob" of the tuning dial of your perception or transformation of your personality can you obtain a holistic vision, which does not exclude completely different and opposite points of view, most importantly different views of yourself. It can be said that the supreme task of every human being incarnated on Earth is the transformation of his personality, which will allow him to exit out of the harshly fixated, unilateral perception of his ego or personality to a holistic, multidimensional perception of WE. During such a transformation, the human being receives an opportunity to view himself and the world holographically, simultaneously observing completely different possibilities of his movement through life. Only with such a perception would he receive the real opportunity of choosing the variants of his life journey.

Identification with the personality does not allow us to remember ourselves

Let us now review the major difficulty connected to viewing your personality as a given set of conditions of your earthly lesson. It consists of a human being's total identification with his body and personality. In other words, one considers himself to be a physical body and a personality that rules that body. That is why one cannot simply look at one's body from the side, as on the given conditions of one's task, because there is no one to take that look. One thinks there is no one else there. A human being can view certain tasks as his main life tasks. For example, to give birth and to bring up children, to achieve success in a certain profession, to make a lot of money, to move up the corporate or spiritual ladder, etc. But all those aims are dictated by the programs downloaded into his personality. By achieving them, he simply performs the requirements of his program. But he does not fully or holistically view his own program, i.e. his personality. He is unaware of it. **We call this state of consciousness of a human being sleeping or mechanical.**

While in this state of consciousness, the human being runs the program downloaded into him without seeing or understanding how it works. Meanwhile, the majority of people do not even raise questions regarding their program, i.e. the make-up of their personality. Those who raise those questions view the programs fragmentarily, only certain parts of it, without touching its essence—dual functioning.

Contemporary psychology does not view the personality of a human being as a set of given conditions of the task of his earthly lessons. That is why it cannot give holistic answers to these questions: "What is a human being, why is he born on Earth, and how is the scenario of his life given?"

How is your personality made?

So, what is the personality of a human being and how is it made? Personality gets installed into the mind of a human being as a program gets installed into a computer. We call it the conditioned mind, as it is conditioned by duality, and the principle of its action is based on the separation of opposite notions. The mind of a human being consists of two spheres separated from each other: consciousness and subconsciousness. This separation of a human mind into two opposite spheres gives birth to the duality of personality formed within it. So, the personality of a human being is also dual and has two opposite sides. We call those two sides the two directors that stage the show of one's life on a scenic stage that is called Earth. Both directors have equal capabilities and equal power but operate based on opposite tendencies. They embody the concept of a program contained in the personality of a human being. But this concept is realized in a way that the personality itself does not fully understand, as it is conscious of only the half that is being worked up by the conscious director. A subconscious director is acting in such a way that the personality perceives it as resistance, danger, oppression, evil, harm, negativity, and so forth. So, the tendencies of the conscious and subconscious directors are totally opposite. They create the duality, inconsistency, paradox, conflict, and drama of the lessons of a human life.

Duality is a basic condition of earthly lessons of a human being

Duality is a basic and major condition of all earthly lessons of a human being. Interestingly, the practical knowledge of the law and the mechanism of dual perception are concealed from a human being by a "veil of sleep" of his consciousness. That happens because the understanding of the law of dual perception would immediately provide ready answers to the lessons WE incarnate into the reality of Separation to solve. Therefore, the unaware Game in Separation would become impossible. But there is another quality of this game. It is an aware game in Separation. The transfer to this stage of the game becomes possible due to the appearance of the Knowledge of dual perception. Prior to the present time, this Knowledge was not accessible to human understanding. But it is open now and is the property of all humanity. But not all people are ready to meet it due to their own requests to receive the earthly experience. Having a request for mechanical acquisition of the earthly experience, a human being simply follows his personal program without seeing or becoming aware of his program, i.e. the personality itself. Another reason why that makes understanding this knowledge difficult or impossible is the harsh and one-sided attunement of perception of one's personality that blocks any information that does not correspond to one's views. You can only understand our Knowledge through the awareness and transformation of your own personality, i.e. through its practical application and by experiencing it yourself. It is a dual perception of a human being that gave birth to the idea of good and evil, God and Devil. The experience of Separation is living through a constant fight between good and evil, right and wrong, success and failure, positive and negative. This war is being fought within every human being. In the external world, we only see its reflection. Humanity would only be able to eliminate wars in the external world through the revolution of its own self-consciousness that would occur in the internal world of every human being. It is a transfer from a state of fight to a state of partnership of opposite sides of the personality of a human being. And this revolution is only possible through the New Knowledge of dual perception of the personality.

How is a program of our personality formed and how does it work?

We showed you a general scheme of a dual makeup of the mind, based on how the personality of every human being forms and crystallizes. But in what specific way is the personality formed and how does it work?

Depending on the request for an experience you intend to receive in a given incarnation on Earth, the time, place, and conditions of your birth are chosen. It is through them that the necessary context of the requested life experience is created. Social conditions and those chosen by your parents render the major influences on the formation of your personality.

It is your parents or the people that participated in your upbringing during childhood, who download the program of your personality. As a rule, it is your mother and father. They transfer their parts of the dual program of your personality to you. Therefore, you need to become aware of and accept those opposite parts in yourself. Father and mother are present in every human being as dual parts of a program of his or her personality. Their conflicts and problems became your conflicts and problems. You have the opportunity to solve these problems or to continue to suffer from not understanding them. If you don't solve these problems, you will transfer them to your children.

Let's take a look at how personality functions. The personality of a human being can be described as a collection of opposite qualities. In other words, they are dual. For example, smart – stupid, harsh – kind, strong – weak, etc. Such pairs of opposite qualities show a dual scale of a certain quality, marked by opposite notions.

If asked to determine one's own personality, a man names certain qualities. In the process of doing this, he chooses only one of their sides. Considering himself to be tidy, for example, he denies the presence of the opposite quality in himself. In this particular case, it is sloppiness. But, at the same time, he notices it in other people and gets irritated by it.

Because a personality is not aware of its duality, it is unable to see itself as a whole. Its perception of itself, of other people, and of the world is one-sided. That is the major reason for the "sleep" of human consciousness, which is necessary for one to receive the experience of Separation.

One-sided tune-up of personality's perception

What are the consequences of this one-sided tune-up of perception of personality? They can be described as a collection of major principles and mechanisms of human perception and reaction. Let's review them.

A personality fights itself, believing it is fighting with the outside world

A personality, representing a structure of dual qualities or a structure of dual parts, only identifies itself with one side of those dualities, projecting its opposite side onto the outside world and fighting it. That is why it happens to be in a constant fight with itself, believing it is fighting other people or life circumstances. That is how the program of personality survival is realized.

Fear—the main fuel of a "sleeping" man

Qualities with which personality identifies are appraised by it as positive and belonging to it. The opposite qualities are appraised as negative and are projected onto the outside world, i.e. onto other people and situations. Because a personality does not accept its negative qualities, it experiences negative emotions by perceiving them in other people.

The consequence of such unacceptable and hostile relationships of the opposite parts of personality is a state of fear, in which a human being constantly finds himself. All negative emotions, such as irritation, jealousy, depression and many others are variations of the state of fear.

Fear is the energy and the fuel on which ego-personality feeds during its passage through its lessons of the Game of Separation. You may not experience a state of fear, as it has become habitual to you, but you are unable to not be in it.

Internal stress or voltage is the result of an imbalance of personality

Fear is the energy of a personality, the magnitude of which is characterized by the level of voltage that appears between its opposite sides. The degree of such a voltage is determined by the magnitude of imbalance of its dual sides. The stronger you manifest a certain feature of your personality, the stronger the voltage that develops in you, aroused by the resistance of the part opposing it, which you do not accept or acknowledge in yourself.

Imbalance appears as the result of a personality's insistence on an exclusive righteousness of beliefs of only one of its dual parts. In this case, one stands upon one's one-sided belief as if this reflection of himself happens to be the only Truth.

At the same time, one suppresses the opposite of a given belief. In other words, one suppresses the opposite side of oneself. Projecting it onto another human being or onto a certain situation, one starts fighting it and experiencing the state of one's exclusive righteousness or pride.

The state of exclusiveness leads to exclusion

What is called pride here is a consequence of an imbalance of a personality. Pride appears in a personality as a result of its glorification of certain qualities or parts of itself. At the same time, the opposite qualities or parts are suppressed and not accepted by the personality. That leads to an increase of internal voltage.

Fear of being unable to justify its high self-assessment and the possibility of others revealing its bluff escalates in a personality. Concurrently, it experiences a state of exclusivity or pride that it does not want to refuse.

Pride is one of the key manifestations of a human being in a state of "sleep" of consciousness. Pride leads to experiencing a state of exclusion from other people. That is the main state experienced in the Game of Separation. The opposite of pride is a state of worthlessness, unimportance.

It is the fluctuations while experiencing those opposite sides of duality that happen to be fundamental for personality.

Blame and guilt as a mechanism of recharging the personality

Replenishing the energy of fear or nourishment of a personality happens mechanically in a "sleeping" man and without his awareness. Such a recharge appears every time one experiences a state of blame or guilt.

Blame can be manifested as a state of irritation, aggression, dissatisfaction, resentment, indignation, condemnation, anger, etc. Guilt can be experienced as depression, pity toward self or others, tearfulness, whining, etc.

Blame and guilt are dual sides that affect each other. When a man (or a woman) blames someone, in reality, he blames himself, projecting onto another his own side of a personality, of which he is unaware. Later on, he would feel guilty for this blame since he is really blaming himself, even though he does not understand it. His guilt appears as the result of blaming himself.

Inconsistency of one's personal desires

The development of a personality occurs in relation to the appearance of desires in it which it tries to realize. The desires of a personality are dual, even though it is unaware of this. Each opposite side of a personality has its own desires. The appearance of a desire of one of its parts leads to the appearance of an opposite desire in its dual part.

Therefore, the realization of every conscious desire meets the resistance created by its opposite part. The personality sees this resistance as external and experiences negative emotions toward it, while not understanding that these emotions come from the inside.

Role of the behavior of the personality

The personality program of a human being is similar to a scene in a movie. It presupposes a certain number of roles and their performers. The typical roles are father, mother, husband, wife, child, relative, director, subordinate, coworker, friend, etc. Each personality performs a number of roles with which it identifies.

Those role-type behaviors are determined by the laws and norms regulating them. They are based on duty and responsibilities. The performance of every role is regulated by certain rules which represent the limitations with which the personality should comply. Conflicts between these roles appear as the result of different understanding of rights and duties related to each role from the point of view of each personality performing it.

A man and a woman

A man and a woman are a dual pair with a very important meaning in the lessons in the world of Separation. The sex of a human being is determined according to the body into which one was born: male or female. The choice of sex during birth is a determining factor while passing through life lessons and the specifics of an acquired experience.

A man and a woman are opposites that are present in every human being, irrespective of the physical sex of his or her body. That is why conflict between man and woman occurs in the internal world of every human being. The external world shows only the reflection of this conflict. Interrelationships of man and woman are interrelationships of the mind and feelings.

Three bodies and the supreme task of a human being

Each human being occupies two worlds simultaneously. One's Soul, Spirit, or Supreme "I" is in That world. In This world, one is represented in the form of three bodies: physical, emotional, and mental. The main task during the passing of earthly lessons is to be aware and to harmonize these three bodies in such a way that they all submit to the Supreme "I" and not to the ego or personality. Then one finds the true Owner and becomes An Aware Creator, or a Whole Human Being.

In this world, one receives the experience of survival. Such an experience is created through the duality and separation to which all of three bodies are subject. Each of those three bodies perceives the world yet does not live in accordance with the two other bodies. Each pulls in its own direction. They are separate and uncoordinated, but the human being does not understand this. It appears to him that he is already whole, but his internal separation manifests itself through the external world, which happens to be a reflection of his internal world. By seeing separation in the outside world, the human being can become aware of his own internal separation. Duality pushes one towards working on and becoming aware of his three bodies. It is in this awareness that the essence of all the lessons in the world of survival, or separation, occurs.

Our passage through the experience of survival occurs in the following way. In the beginning, the physical body is being developed. Every one of three bodies of a human being consists of three components: physical, emotional, and mental. A Soul lives through as many incarnations as necessary in order to develop all of the three components of the physical body. When all three components are fully developed, a Soul harmonizes them. Afterward, it moves to develop the emotional body which also consists of three components: physical, emotional, and mental. The process is analogous. Then, the mental body gets developed in a similar way.

Working up in many incarnations, the experience of survival of each of the three bodies, during a certain incarnation, the human being approaches a possibility of their co-tuning. This process culminates in the formation of a whole Human Being as Three-in-One, i.e. total co-tuning and harmony of all his three bodies occurs.

Co-tuning the three bodies is the main task of our Process. We frequently view those three bodies as the physical body and the personality. Personality can be viewed as a combination of emotional and mental bodies. We view the mental and the emotional bodies as a Man and a Woman. In working with the personality, we harmonize mental and emotional bodies. The harmonization of one's physical body is the consequence of the harmonization of one's mental and emotional bodies.

This short introduction provides a general understanding of the direction in which we are moving, collecting and harmonizing ourselves into a Whole. But in order to really understand what is being transmitted here, you need to pass this Knowledge through yourself. In other words, you need to become a self-investigator.

SELF-INVESTIGATOR GUIDE BOOK

•◆•◆•◆•◆•◆•◆•◆•◆•◆•◆•◆•◆•◆•◆•◆•◆•◆•◆•◆•

While reading this book, you may come across some notions that are uncommon. To understand their meaning, you need to become familiar with the SELF-INVESTIGATOR GUIDE-BOOK. Come back to this during the process of reading in order to clarify the meaning of the new words you encounter.

Consider the notions brought up here as the markers leading you to a clearer vision of our world as a dual illusion, in which we receive the experience of separated existence. The exit out of this illusion is deep in your heart, where you connect with Unconditional Love. Unconditional Love can be neither described nor defined; it can only be felt. Therefore, while investigating the dual world of illusions, remember that we are not of This world.

THE WORLD OF UNITY AND THE WORLD OF SEPARATION
- **The World of Wholeness, The World of WE** – the world where unconditional love rules, timelessness, limitlessness, unconditional interest, and eternity.

- **The World of survival, The World of Separation** – the world where conditional love rules, fear, harsh restriction of time and space, the illusions of death, debt, and conditional laws, one-sided truth, the conflict of the opposites, and orientation on to have instead of on to be.

- **The Supreme "I", The Soul, Spirit, WE** – the part of a Human Being that happens to be in the World of Wholeness, in the World of WE.

- **The lower "i"** – the part of a Human Being that happens to be in the World of survival, in Separation.

- **Consciousness of the world of Wholeness** – the consciousness that accepts the opposite sides of duality while understanding their equal importance and necessity.

- **Consciousness of the world of Separation** – consciousness that denies one of the sides of duality.

- **The levels of being** – the worlds and realities that are characterized by different levels of consciousness.

- **The system of coordinates of reality** – the axioms upon which the make-up of a given reality and its perception are based.

- **The Matrix of survival, The Old Matrix** – a system of dual structure of the world in which the Lower "i" of a human being happens to be. It is characterized by the conflict of opposites and by the creativity that is based on fear.

- **The Matrix of Life** – a system of dual make-up of the world in which the Lower "i" transforms and becomes a partner of the Supreme "I" in the aware creativity. It is characterized by the equal partnership of opposites.

- **Three-dimensional reality** – reality that has only three dimensions: length, width, and height, where time is being measured linearly.
- **The linear time** – characterized by the past, present, and future. In the matrix of survival, future is a repetition of the past. One can only get to the present moment through the state of being Aware of oneself, i.e. through the connection with the Supreme "I".

DUALITY

- **Duality** – a unified scale of a certain quality of energy (level of vibration), perceived by the conditioned mind as two opposites. Duality is the basic condition of earthly lessons of a human being.
- **The law of duality** – the law of interaction of the polar, opposite tendencies. Everything that happens in the world of Separation obeys the law of duality.
- **The dual mechanism of perception** – the mechanism that provides a human being with the conscious perception of only one side of the duality of his external and internal world.
- **Duality, paradox, duality of the personality** – interactions of the opposite tendencies or parts of the personality. In the matrix of survival, such interactions always represent a conflict. In the matrix of life, they become an equal partnership.

- **Unconditional Love** – a state of gratitude for everything that happens around you, which comes out of understanding of its lawfulness.
- **God's Kingdom** – a state of a human being who is simultaneously aware of himself as the one who happens to be in the world of Separation and in the world of Unity.

THE SUPREME "I"

- **Awareness** – perception of the Lower "i" by the Highest "I", accepting its opposite sides with equal respect and unconditional love. The observer who clearly and holistically fixates on what he sees without experiencing condemnation and guilt.

- **Unconditional love** – emotional state of total acceptance, interest, and gratitude, which characterize the relationship of the Highest "I" toward Lower "i".
- **Intention** – goal directed, holistic (nondual) energy that has high vibrations coming from the Soul, the Supreme "I".
- **Aware creativity** – based on the power of intention and takes into account the actions of opposite dual tendencies.
- **The choice of the Soul** – aim, the action based on clear vision and total acceptance of the opposite tendencies of the Lower "i" of a human being.
- **The vertical perception** – perception that comes out of the world of Unity.

- **The third point of the triangle of perception** – the point of perception of the Lower "i" or a human being out of the world of Unity.
- **A state of awareness** – a state that appears during the observation of your Lower "i" out of Higher "I".
- **Contract (the request) to receive the earthly experience before birth** – an inquiry or a project of your Soul, its request to receive a certain experience in the world of survival.
- **The Program of receiving a dual experience** – is planned by the Soul prior to physical incarnation and is realized through the formation of the dual structure of the personality and of the peculiarities of the three bodies it incarnates into the physical reality, with a consideration of time, place, parents, and other peculiarities of birth.

A HUMAN BEING (THE LOWER "i")

- **The three centers or three bodies of a human being** – mental, emotional, and physical. The personality represents a mental-emotional constituent of a human being. The physical body is a physical constituent of a human being. The three bodies represent a space suit or an apparatus which a Soul uses to enter the reality of Earth in order to pass through its lessons, i.e. to receive a certain experience in survival. The presence of these three bodies allows a human being to perceive the world in three different ways.

- **The mental body of a human being** – the mind of a human being. It allows a human being to work with thoughts and images. It has a dual nature that is expressed physically in the presence of two halves of the brain separated by the corpus collosum. The duality of the mind is manifested metaphysically by the presence of two separated spheres: the conscious and subconscious.

- **The conditioned or dual mind** – another way to call the mental body of a human being or his mind, necessary for him to receive the experience of survival. The way the conditioned mind works is based on the formation of judgments. The opportunity to create a judgment is based on mind separation of the opposite sides of dual notions and identifying with one of them. It works based on the principle "Yes—No" and leads to hallucinations accepted by the mind as reality.

- **Judgment** – basic product of the mind's work. The pronounced judgment is made by comparison, which is based on the scale of dual notions.

- **The Conscious side of the mind, consciousness** – is what a human being is conscious of in his internal and external world. The light side of a human being.

- **The Sub-conscious side of the mind, sub-consciousness** – is what a human being is not conscious of in his internal and external world. The dark side of a human being.

- **The emotional body of a human being** – the body of emotional states. It allows a human being to experience feelings.
- **The physical body of a human being** - the body of a human being that can be perceived by physical vision. It allows a human being to manipulate the objects of the physical world and to experience and register multiple physical sensations.
- **The markers of the misbalance of the three bodies of a human being:** In the case of the physical body, it is diseases, traumas, and physical pain. In the case of the emotional body, it is suffering and emotional pain. In the case of the mental body, it is not-understanding.
- **Trinity** – attunement of three bodies or centers of a human being: mental, emotional, and physical.

PERSONALITY (THE LOWER "i")
- **The program of survival** – the personal program formed in a child as a method of his or her survival in the world of separation.
- **Personality, false personality, ego, personal program, personage** – terms used to define the personality of a human being.
- **Personality** – mental-emotional structure of a human being that has a dual structure and happens to represent the given conditions of the assignment of a human being in his current incarnation. It determines the peculiarities of the earthly lessons of a human being and connects to them dual experience. To investigate and to understand

one's personality is to understand the conditions of the assignment of one's current incarnation.

- **Personality or the personal program** – the summation of interconnected pairs of the opposite qualities. Every such pair shows a dual scale of a certain quality, expressed by the opposite notions. A personality that is not aware of itself only identifies with one side of its dual qualities, and as a result, only perceives itself from one side.

- **Formation of the personality** - download of the program of conditions of the assignment of a given incarnation of a human being. It occurs through the context of the place and time of birth of a child, his genetic make-up, and the people who participate in his upbringing. Situations that rendered a strong emotional influence on a child during his early formative ears are very important in the formation of his or her personality. As a rule, the paternal and maternal programs are the major components of the personality of a human being.

- **Formation of the personality** – acquisition of the experience of survival through activation of personal dualities.

- **Activation of personal dualities** – introduction of the dual notions of "bad" and "good" into the personal program through painful experience. In this way, personality becomes conditioned by duality.

- **Activation of dualities** – escalation of voltage or stress of the conflict between two opposite sides of duality in the personal structure of a human being.

- **The activated side of personal duality** – strongly manifested side of the personality.

- **The spreading of the opposite sides of duality of a personality** – occurs through the positive or negative reinforcement of the manifestation of personal qualities.

- **"Good—bad"** – the paradox of dual perception.

- **Relationships** – methods using which personality manifests itself.

- **Merits and shortfalls** – polar notions that describe the scale of duality. Shortcomings of a human being are continuations of his virtues. One cannot exist without the other. These opposites represent two sides of one coin.

- **Crystalized painful experience** – Similar painful experience repeated multiple times leads to the formation of non-healing "emotional wounds", which react sharply when touched.

- **Negative states** – different shades of condemnation and a feeling of guilt.

- **Blame and guilt** - polar states simultaneously experienced by a human being in respect to the same issue. In this process, a human being consciously experiences only one of these states. The opposite state is in the sphere of the subconscious. In time, they change their positions.

- **Aggression** – emotional experience of strong condemnation.

- **Guilt** – a state that appears as the result of experiencing one's own condemnation.
- **Misbalance of the personality** – caused by the conflict of opposite tendencies or parts of the personality (mental, emotional, and physical). It is characterized by the level of voltage or stress of the feuding relationships between the opposite sides. Personal imbalance appears as the result of the identification and assertion of personality on truth, the conviction of one of its dual parts and simultaneous suppression of the opposite part. This gives birth to the resistance of the suppressed side of the personality, which is equal to the strength of pressure applied to it.
- **Stress or excitation of the personality** – voltage that appears in the personality in connection to the suppression of its shadow sides. The power of this voltage is dynamic. At any given moment its cumulative effect is either "positive" or "negative". The sign, "positive" or "negative", depends upon which of the opposite forces is stronger—conscious (the power of a consciously set up goal) or subconscious (power of resistance to the aim).
- **Fear** – the state that reflects the conflict of the opposite sides of the personality. Fear is the fuel on which personality works while experiencing its lessons in survival.
- **Fear** – energy of the personality, the magnitude of which is characterized by the **degree of unacceptance** that appears between its opposite sides.

- **The old experience** – constant experience of fear in the states of condemnation and guilt.
- **Personal pride** – the illusory conviction in the truthfulness of one's one-sided, limited judgment. It appears as the result of the personality glorifying one side of its dual qualities while negating the opposite quality in itself. Pride, or a state of exclusivity, leads one to experience the states of exclusion, being forsaken, betrayal, and loneliness.
- **Convictions** – crystalized experience of one-sided perception.
- **The dual parts of the personality or sub-personalities** – parts of the personality that have opposite tendencies.
- **The conscious side, or conscious part of the personality** – the side or part of the personality that a human being consciously accepts in himself.
- **The sub-conscious side, or the sub-conscious part of the personality** – the side or part of the personality that a human being denies in himself.
- **Resistance of the aim or conscious desire of the personality** – counteraction of the subconscious part of the personality to its opposite conscious part that sets up a certain aim and tries to achieve it.
- **Suffering** – the state that appears as the result of unacceptance and conflict of the opposite sides of the personality.
- **Personal desire, tendency** – energy directed to seize something in order to have it. Every desire is born by

the personality and is therefore always dual, i.e. always appears with the opposite in its desired direction.

- **Desire, tendency of the personality** – has a dual nature. Any consciously appearing desire gives birth to its opposite subconscious desire. This subconscious desire is viewed by a human being as a resistance toward achieving conscious desire.

- **Role relationships** – roles the personality plays while participating in social life. Every personality plays several roles. The performance of each role is regulated by certain rules. These rules represent the limitations to which that personality is supposed to conform. These role relationships are determined by the laws, norms, and rules that regulate them. They are based on **debt and obligations.**

- **Role conflicts** – the consequence of the different understanding of the participants of the conflict of the rights and responsibilities of the roles performed by them.

- **Conflict** – the method of interaction of opposite sides of the personality while going through and acquiring the experience of survival.

- **Personal changes** – the transfer of negative experience to the conscious, the shadow part of one's personality.

- **Transformation of the personality** – the awareness of the opposite, dual sides of the personality, like two sides of one coin. Because of this transformation, personal pride, i.e. its notion of its exclusivity, disappears, while individuality, i.e. understanding of its difference from other people, remains.

- **Harmonization of personal oppositions** – acceptance of the condemned part of one's personality with gratitude and the balancing of opposite tendencies (mental, emotional, and physical) in oneself. Awareness of and the complete acceptance of the shadow sides of the personality.

- **Management of the personal duality** – a conscious choice to manifest one of two opposite sides of your personality.

- **Personal perception** – perception conditioned by one-sidedness.

EXPERIENCE

- **To have** – the state of consciousness that is identified with the experience received by it.

- **To be** – the state of consciousness that is NOT identified with the experience received by it.

- **The earthly experience of a human being** – takes place in the context of external situations and encompasses mental, emotional, and physical components.

- **Re-experience (review) of one's past painful experience** – entering prior painful experience in the state of awareness in order to accept and integrate its opposite aspects.

- **Integration of your personal experience** – accepting your own experience as a whole and with gratitude by coming to understand the opposite sides of your personal program that gave birth to it.

- **The experience of survival** – experience of the conflict of the opposite sides of the Lower "i" or personal dualities.
- **Experience of life** – experience of the partnership of the Supreme "I" and Lower "i".
- **Experience unaware** – the screenplay of life that is lived on the level of feelings and actions, explained by the conditioned mind without any understanding of the duality of one's own perception.
- **Experience aware** – awareness of the experienced life scenario as the interrelationship of the opposite sides of dualities of your personality. It leads to your de-identification with the experience you are living through.
- **Identification** – one sided, fragmented perception of yourself.
- **Identification of the personality** – perceiving yourself as a certain part of your personality.
- **Self-identification of the personality** – accepting yourself for the role you perform. Identification with certain notions about yourself.
- **De-identification** – perceiving manifestations of your personality with a full understanding that these manifestations are only your experience. They are not you.
- **Social roles** – roles the performance of which are connected to receiving a certain social experience.

- **A man and a woman** – a duality that is expressed physically. It includes passing multiple tests and acquiring a life experience.
- **The unknown** – experience that you have not yet lived through.
- **The known** – experience that you have already lived through, and that has been defined by the mind.
- **Meaning** – point of view or the way we see something.
- **Conscious model of behavior** – the model of behavior that is being realized consciously.
- **Sub-conscious model of behavior** – the model of behavior that is being realized subconsciously.
- **Conditioned love** – a good relationship with a human being, based on him being dutiful and compliant with rules and obligations.
- **Unaware creativity** – creativity that uses the energy of fear.

MECHANICALITY AND AWARENESS

- **Lesson of survival** – the experience of personality which it passes in complete identification with it.
- **The sleep of consciousness** – one-sided and fragmented perception of one's internal and external worlds.
- **A sleeping human being** – a human being who is submerged in a sleep of consciousness.
- **Mechanicality, sleep** – a state of consciousness identified with the experience that is being received. It is

characterized by a mechanical reaction that is based on the principle "stimulus – reaction".

- **Identification** – perceiving the received experience as yourself.
- **De-identification** – perceiving the received experience by the detached observer.
- **The old matrix of consciousness, Matrix of separating perception, matrix of survival** – matrix of consciousness created on the basis of duality in order to receive the experience of survival. It gives birth to the fight of personal oppositions and fear as the basic state of consciousness.
- **Spiritual development** – an aware acceptance in yourself of what you used to fight outside.
- **Inquiry to become self-aware** – inquiry to understand yourself through awareness.
- **Question** – characterizes the direction of perception.
- **Inquiry** – conscious tendency to understand something in yourself or to produce certain external or internal changes.
- **Problem** – conflicting interaction of the opposite sides of personality. The problem can be solved only when you clearly see the mechanism of their interactions. In that case, it disappears.
- **Problem** – result of simultaneous actions of two opposite tendencies, one of which is seen as the enemy.
- **Discernment** – an ability to clearly see and clearly feel both sides of the duality of your personality.

- **Principle of mirrors** – a feature of a human being that is reflected in other people as if in mirrors. It is used during self-investigation to learn the peculiarities of one's personal program.
- **Method of mirrors** – provides an opportunity to see and to become aware of the projections of the dual sides of your personality in the perception of another human being or in the appearing external situations.
- **Straight mirrors** – the reflection of the projection without deflection.
- **Crooked mirrors** – the reflection of the projection with deflection.
- **Transformation of a human being** – the process of becoming aware of one's own wholeness.
- **Wholeness of a human being** – the interaction of the three bodies of a human being and of the opposite parts of his personality based on their full awareness, acceptance, and partnership.
- **Awareness of yourself** – uncondemning and investigating observation of the manifestations of the Lower "i" by the Supreme "I".
- **Self-remembrance** – the process that leads one to experience, understand, and manifest a partnership between the Lower "i" and the Supreme "I".
- **Self-awareness, self-investigation** – investigation of your the Lower "i" with the help of your Supreme "I".
- **Paradoxical thinking** – thinking that is based on the aware perception of duality in yourself.

- **Paradoxical thinking** – thinking that views the opposite sides of duality as two sides of one coin.
- **Understanding of yourself** – the answer to the question: "What am I?" It has mental, emotional, and physical components.
- **Understanding of yourself** – the unity of thoughts, feelings, and actions of a human being. Full understanding of oneself is possible only when all three bodies of a human being are harmonized.
- **Personage** – a human being that plays certain roles in the show of survival.
- **Other people** – screens onto which personality projects its personal qualities.
- **Responsibility** – understanding that everything that happens to you is created by you.
- **Illusion** – something that does not really exist, but it appears to you that it does exist.
- **Truth** – one half that pretends to be whole.
- **Truth and lie** – two separated sides of one whole.
- **External world** – a mirror of the inner world.
- **Positive and negative** – technical terms that define opposite sides of duality, similar to the plus and minus of an electric battery.
- **Gratitude** – the state that appears as the result of becoming aware of the dual nature of your personality.
- **Happiness** – is not a result of the solution of problems but as a consequence of his understanding of who he really is.

- **Empathy** – the emotional state of an awakened or holistic human being who starts to see the suffering of sleeping human beings.
- **Understanding** – clear vision, awareness of things the way they are.
- **Knowledge** – system of ideas transmitted through notions expressed in words.
- **Energy of high vibrations** – the frequency of vibrations of consciousness sufficient to become aware of one's Lower "i".
- **Energy of low vibrations** – the frequency of vibrations of consciousness that is not sufficient to become aware of one's Lower "i".
- **Student** – the one who wants to learn to be aware and to love unconditionally.
- **Teacher** – the one who is aware and who loves unconditionally.
- **Teacher and student as one** – a human being who gets to know himself.

PERCEPTION OF A HUMAN BEING

- **Perception** – the way a human being sees himself in his inner and outer world.
- **Perception of a human being** – tuned in to receive a certain experience ordered by his Soul. There are two types of perception: **mechanical/identified,** and an **aware/holistic perception.**

- **Mechanical/identified perception** – one-sided, i.e. identified with one side of personal duality only. The consequence of the mechanical perception is an experience of the state of conflict of the inner oppositions.

- **Holistic/aware perception** – allows you to see the opposite sides of personality simultaneously, while understanding the mechanisms of their interactions.

- **Super task of a human being** – the transformation of personality and attunement of all three bodies that would allow a person to exit from the harshly fixated, one-sided perception to the holistic multidimensional perception of WE.

- **Frequency of perception** – indicator of the level of the tune up of your perception. High frequency of the tune up allows a human being to become aware of his personal program. Low frequency of the tune up deters him in identification with the experience received. In this case, he mechanically lives through his personal program.

- **Tuning of a perception** – change in the vision of the internal and external world of a human being through attunement.

- **Awareness, Self-awareness, Clear vision** – the observation of the mechanisms of functioning of the conditioned mind and of your personal program that work within the limitations of dual perception.

- **Multidimensionality** – characteristic of the consciousness that exited dual perception and transferred to the consciousness of WE.

- **Personal perception of reality** – what is being perceived by our Lower "i" as something self-obvious.

- **Horizontal perception** – dual perception of the personality.

- **Consciousness of the Lower "i" of a human being** – the ability to perceive your internal and external world physically, emotionally, and mentally that is conditioned by the imbalance of his three bodies and by the influence of the law of duality.

- **Internal world of a human being** – the world of thoughts, feelings, and sensations. It is perceived partially and fragmentally by the human being who happens to be in a "sleep of consciousness".

- **External world of a human being** – external world perceived by a human being with the help of the five senses. It is a reflection of the inner world of a human being.

- **Level of consciousness of a human being** – level of development of a human being's ability to holistically perceive his internal and external world.

-

CHAPTER 1

TO SEE IN YOURSELF WHAT IS

•◆•

A harsh and uneducated ruler once said to Nasreddin, "I am going to hang you unless you prove to me that you really possess that deep perception people attribute to you."

Nasreddin immediately declared that he could see golden birds flying in the sky and demons of the underworld. The sultan asked him, "How can you do it?"

Nasreddin answered, "You don't need anything, but fear."

Everything that surrounds you is you

— When we do something for other people, who do we do it for?

— *We probably do it for ourselves. If I do something, I want to receive gratitude in return. It means I actually do it for myself.*

— If you do everything for yourself, what do you demand from others?

— *I demand they remember it and confirm it by being grateful.*

1

— Yes, in reality you do it for yourself. Even if something is done not completely the way you wanted it to be done, not entirely up to your expectations, it is still you who did it. This is a very important point.

If you think that you do it for someone else, you will never be satisfied. When you understand that you do it for yourself, your expectations of gratitude for your actions become meaningless.

In reprimanding yourself for your own errors, you experience a feeling of guilt, which is corrosive and unpleasant. At a certain point, you start to feel that you need to get rid of this feeling, and you start to investigate the mechanisms of its appearance. The most important thing here is to take responsibility for what you do, because you create everything in your life yourself.

When you start to understand that everything you do, you do for yourself, you start to take full responsibility for everything you do. You will see that when you experience a certain reaction from people toward you and your actions, it is you who have created it. When people around you get upset, it is you who have created it. If people insult you, it means you have created it. People, like mirrors, reflect the states in which you happen to be, whether you are aware of these states or not. The external world mirrors your own internal states to you. When you start to understand this concept and to behave accordingly, you will be able to correct your states. First, you will start to see them. You will start to see every situation and every human being as a mirror reflecting your state. In the

recurrent situations and typical reactions that other people display toward you, you will start to see the internal states that are characteristic to you. In other words, you provoke the reactions of other people that later make you unhappy. This is a very important moment: you are wholly responsible for what you create in your life. You create everything. Everything that happens to you is your own creation.

— *Theoretically, everything you say is clear to me, but what can I do with this information?*

— Seeing things this way returns you to your inner state. You start to become aware of your inner state by observing people and situations around you. You start to observe your inner states. You start to become aware of them. You start to see the mechanisms of the appearance of the states you don't like. When you know these mechanisms, they stop influencing you. As a result, the external situations change. The external world is a criterion. It is a reflection of your inner state.

— *How can I correct my states? Let's say, I caught myself in a negative state, detached, and observed it. It goes away. Later, I can analyze what kind of dependency it was, what I expected from the situation, and whether the development of the dependency of this expectation is possible. I can see how it happened previously and what led me to that state.*

— What do we want?

—*We want to be comfortable and free. I don't want to experience negative states. I try to avoid them. I think it is normal for a human being not to want to experience pain. I can run away from it, but I can also do something about it. What can I do?*

— Whatever you run away from will chase after you. You can't run away from yourself. If you see the surrounding reality from a distorted view, as if it is one thing and your internal state is another, totally different thing, you will constantly try to escape from the external world, imagining it to be something unrelated to you.

When you understand that the external world and what happens to you is a reflection of your inner state, you come to understand that there is no escape. Then, there is only one thing left to do: not to run away from it, but to walk toward it, enter it, and transform it.

The first thing is to not run away. The typical reaction to something that you don't like is to try to escape. But what you don't like will continue to hunt you. There is no escape from it. You must understand that.

Most people constantly try to run away from themselves. When you escape one situation, another, even more complicated situation will appear. Every subsequent situation will get increasingly complicated, but you keep running.

You are afraid to lose what you have already lost

— What are you trying to run away from?

— *I am running away from uncomfortable states, sensations, and feelings. I am running away from the feeling of guilt, and sensations related to it.*

— *I run away from the fear of death.*

4

— When was the last time you died? Only illusions can die.

— *What about hope?*

— Hope is another illusion, such as illusions that someone loves you, someone respects you, someone would give you a job, etc. Hope can be viewed by you as something good. You may not want to get rid of it. It is hard when it dies. I, on the other hand, say that only illusion can die. What you choose to call it is a different question. Our mind is sly. It can use pretty words to name something in order for you not to want to get rid of it.

You changed your position in space. How many times does your pose die during one hour? It dies constantly. You change something, and the old thing dies. The state you are in is constantly changing: old is leaving, new is coming. A thought comes and goes, and then it dies. We, as a summation of thoughts, feelings, and sensations constantly change without noticing it. So, why are you afraid of death?

— *A man plans his future life presuming it will go a certain way. Later, he gets afraid that those plans may not come to fruition due to sickness and immobility.*

— What does it mean to become immobile?

— *Paralysis, for example. I am afraid to become a burden to my kids.*

— You are afraid of something. What happens to what you are afraid of? Does it disappear?

— *It gets reinforced.*

— The more you are afraid of something, the the stronger it becomes. You think if you are afraid of something, it will not

5

happen, but it is already happening. So by being afraid of something, you receive it. You need to understand this. An old proverb says that a brave man dies only once, while a coward dies a thousand deaths. It is possible to die in fear an infinite number of times.

— *I am afraid of responsibility. Everything stresses me out. There is an inner voice inside me that says that everything should be a certain way, but there is no desire and no power to do it exactly that way.*

— And where does all your strength go?

— *All my strength is used to push it away.*

— All your energy is spent on resistance, and you are feeling a lack of energy. Look at how interesting this is: you are afraid of responsibility, and all your energy is spent on fear. You are constantly afraid. In the end, you are afraid to take responsibility for this, for that, and for everything else.

What are you spending your energy on: on the fear of doing something, on trying not to do it, or on the work itself? Energy is equally spent in both situations, but in the first case scenario, you live in a state of fear that you will have to do something, and in this case, you will be forced to do it. In the second case, you simply do it. You are aware of your resistance, but you do not indulge in it. That is how awareness of the dual parts of the personality works.

Every one of us has energy. In using it properly, we can live in happiness, creativity, and love. That energy belongs to us. But you can see that something quite the opposite happens. People spend this energy living in fear, pain, and suffering.

Why does this happen? This energy is spent improperly because the habitual mechanisms direct it through channels of pain, guilt, and blame. If you could see these mechanisms, to understand how inappropriately the energy is directed, and to correct it, you would find yourself in the only state natural for you—the state of love and creativity. It is necessary to remove these distortions. My work is to direct awareness toward seeing the mechanisms that do not allow a human being to be who he really is, i.e. a loving and creative creature. So, what prevents you from being who you are?

— *I don't like feeling guilty.*

— What are you being blamed for most frequently?

— *My behavior frequently goes against someone's notions of how I should behave. I understand now that I should do only what I want to do, but not everyone around me understands that.*

— The external world reflects your internal state. You just said that you are obliged to do something you don't like doing, i.e. you are blaming yourself. What do you blame yourself for?

— *I see the reflection of my inner state externally. I see my fear that attracts it. I have my notions of how I should behave in certain situations. Sometimes I am not touched by someone's comments because I know that at that moment, I did what I wanted to do. But, in reality, I see that it offends me, mirroring occurs, and I immediately recall that first I felt guilty, and only later someone's reprimand followed. Sometimes I can see it, but not always. Sometimes I recall that that was what I said, and the reply I received was my own words. In these cases, I tell myself that people read the information about me, and returned it to me—there is nothing to sulk about. Irrespective of these infrequent insights, I continue to experience a deep feeling of guilt. I am not running away from it, but these sensations are heavy. I understand they also have their right to exist, and I allow them to pass through me. However, if I feel I was appraised as "bad", I still feel the heaviness of it.*

— If you consider yourself to be an investigator, you understand that you have entered this reality, with duality and separation existing within it, in order to investigate it. You came here because you wanted to learn every mechanism of separation.

An investigator conducts an investigation and writes a report. My books are my reports. They describe the results of the investigation I conduct. This is a very interesting way of life. It differs from living in a state of "How can I get more comfortable while other people constantly interfere with my goal?" I constantly remind you that you have entered the world of separation. When you want love, you will be given hatred. When you want justice, you will be fooled.

On the other hand, you can take the position of self-investigator. I simply investigate all these mechanisms. In this case, you have an additional and powerful stimulus that helps you meet your fears. Otherwise, you don't want to meet them.

The average man does not understand the subject we discuss here. He will say that this is gibberish he doesn't need. He can live comfortably without this nonsense. He does not understand that this is a dual world where everyone must deal with duality. He does not consider himself to be a self-investigator. Duality will constantly chase him: whatever he wants to remove from his life will stick to him, and whatever he wants to attract will run away from him. After living this way for many lives, he will suddenly start to think about the things we discuss, take a position of the self-investigator who is ready to take a risk, and start to experiment with difficult and dangerous things. He will develop a passion and will do anything to obtain a result.

I offer you the position of self-investigator because it provides an opportunity to go through duality and to exit to wholeness. I offer you not to run away from things and situations you don't like, but to meet them face to face, investigate them, and discuss the results you obtain amongst yourself and here.

For example, if you tried to avoid guilt all the time, you can become a specialist in mechanisms that give birth to guilt. Can you tell us about the mechanisms of the appearance of guilt?

— *I have a certain notion about how I should do something. If I do something that contradicts or not in compliance with this notion, I immediately blame myself. This mechanism was developed in childhood.*

"What if I were to tell you that you are an idiot and a whore?"

— Which particular accusations are hard for you to swallow? What would happen if I were to tell you that you are a whore?

— *I can take it easily now, as I understand that I should accept everything in me, and I am pretty sure I do have this sub-personality living in me. I sometimes have fantasies where I play the role of a whore.*

9

— But if you don't allow yourself to acknowledge these things, they will continue to haunt and scare you.

— *I started to notice what exactly I negate in myself. Currently, I am trying to observe this and to understand why it upsets me so much.*

— To see things as they are is very important. We think we are being unjustly accused, but when we meet what is inside us, we suddenly discover that we've had it all along. Everything is there.

Try to be an idiot, for example. It's nice to live the life of an idiot. It's hard to get an idiot upset. Everyone around you gets stressed out, trying to prove to each other which one of them is smarter, but you don't have to participate in this fight. You are calm and relaxed. Something will continue to hunt you until you agree with it and accept its presence in yourself. The mechanism is very simple.

— *The statement "I am here and now. I accept myself the way I am" frequently helps me to see myself in a current moment. Why do I feel uncomfortable? Does it mean that I, in not accepting something in myself, insist that I accept myself the way I am?*

— We came to this reality to acquire experience related to both sides of every duality of our personal program. Smart and stupid are two sides of one coin. You will never exit this duality unless you accept both sides as two equal sides of yourself. You must accept them not on the level of affirmation, but by feeling them internally and seeing them in yourself.

You need to spend some time in a state of a stupid idiot. Everyone here gets a certain "hang up": someone wants to be smart, another wants to be stupid. You must spend some time in both states. It is usually other people that point us in the direction of the side that we need to experience now. If you feel insulted by being called a stupid idiot, that is your pointer toward the state you need to experience.

What irritates you the most is a pointer. Whatever insults you is a pointer. You are being shown something. You do not understand what it is. When you start to understand, you will see that this is exactly what you need to experience now. When you finally experience this state, you will not be pointed to it anymore: you have learned the lesson.

A common mistake many spiritual seekers make is to declare themselves enlightened and to say that nothing irritates them anymore. We must allow ourselves to experience different feelings, including irritation. That will speed up our education. Otherwise, it can become chronic.

Allow yourself to feel everything. If you feel guilty, be aware of the mechanism of the feeling of guilt formation all the time. As a result, you will be able to get rid of it. You must allow yourself to experience guilt, fear, accusation, and sulking while being aware of the mechanisms of the appearance of these states.

— *When I start to analyze, I suppress these states.*

— We don't need analysis. We need an aware experience. Analysis is not worth much. You start seeing your inner dualities and the mechanisms of their conflicts as the result of the experience acquired by you.

When you have lived through a certain situation in a state of awareness, you can clearly see the mechanism of such a conflict.

When you look at what surrounds you in bright daylight, you don't need to describe it, you simply see everything clearly. We are dealing with the same thing here. Therefore, it is important to allow yourself to feel and to become aware of all your states, thoughts, and actions.

Clear vision will come as the result of the experience you become aware of. To experience something is to live through it, i.e. to feel it. **If you allow yourself to feel everything, you will quickly be able to see your personality.**

Analysis represents mental schemes born out of the dual mind. When you read something, you have a desire to tell others about what you have read as if you have experienced it yourself. However, this is just a mental construct. There is no experience behind it. It is your own experience that is important in our work, not the knowledge of mechanisms obtained somewhere else.

When you pass through both sides of a dual experience, you will see the mechanism of their interaction and will be able to describe it. You will not be mixed up anymore. Otherwise, it is easy to become confused. If you try to help someone out of a trap without having experienced it and becoming aware of it yourself, you will become quickly and easily confused.

Why is it so helpful to work with other people? It is helpful because you help them to get out of the traps of duality. If you can't get someone out of the trap, it means you have not exited it yourself. This is a good criterion.

If you declare yourself to be an authority, you will always avoid challenging situations, the situations you have difficult time getting out of. You will blame other people, saying that they are not aware or are stupid.

You cannot know everything. No one can know everything. It is better to start with the presumption of not knowing anything, especially when you deal with the unknown. In this way, you will easily enter and exit a trap of duality with another human being, if he wants to exit it. No confirmation is necessary in this case. You are sure that you know that. Otherwise, you will always need confirmation. You will wait to be told that you do everything right. You will expect respect and gratitude. But when you don't know anything, you can simply enter and exit a trap. That's it.

— *I want … such … a state … at home…*

— Take a look at how the throat center is being blocked when you want to say something very important. This blockage is commonly manifested in women. **You must allow yourself to cry. You can unblock it only by allowing yourself to speak about what is painful for you, and by manifesting yourself emotionally. You learned to control your tears. Now, you need to learn to cry. You need to master both sides of duality.**

— *I cannot allow myself to cry in front of people.*

— How long are you going to forbid yourself to cry? Powerful experiences that lead to seeing occur through vivid emotional manifestations. They are usually accompanied by tears. Those are not tears of pity. Those are tears of ecstasy. If you try to control your state at such a moment, it will hide and

13

become invisible to you. But it does not mean that it left you. Quite the opposite; it just gets stronger.

Betrayal is an illusion

— I would like to experience the states of happiness and creativity I experienced before. I think I suffer from the middle age crisis. I teach high school kids. Recently, I realized that I have nothing to say to my students aside from the assigned curriculum. I ascribed it to low qualification, and I started to work on it. But then I recognized that I am trying to hide from these kids because I don't have anything to say to them. I was always close to kids. I used to share their games. Currently, I cannot accept my inner masculine side. I have a difficult time with adolescent boys. I feel that I either don't understand them or do not allow myself to understand them. It seems to me they look at me and think: we know that you are one of us, but you have betrayed us, pretending to be a teacher. When I come home at night, I feel that all my energy was spent on this inner conflict.

— What is your relationship with boys?

— I suffered from tragic love at that age.

— That's where your difficulties with boys of that age are coming from. What happened to you back then finds its reflection now. All of that remains in you, and it is asking to be let out. You can give your adolescent fifteen or sixteen-year-old self what she wanted to receive so much back then.

We can return to our past and change it. That's how we can change our future. You need to return to that age when this happened, re-experience the situation, and allow yourself to have what you wanted to have back then. You need to live through it and truly experience it, not just mentally. You need to become yourself at that age and re-experience all your states anew and with a new understanding of them.

— *It is heavy.*

— It is exciting and freeing. You feel heavy all the time. I offer you to feel the full weight of this heaviness, not adding anything that does not belong to it, and to see exactly what is there. You always felt heavy. You got used to it and started to say that it is normal. In the meantime, an enormous amount of energy is being spent by you in order not to see your pain.

Your inner fifteen-year-old girl cries, but your adult woman does not allow herself to feel her state. You spend a lot of energy to suppress and to not see the situations that appeared in your childhood and adolescence.

Allow yourself to enter these states and to re-experience them. Such an experience will free a great deal of energy. Free your girl. She is currently stuck in hatred and pain. She does not understand why she was dealt with in a certain way. You need to return there and revive her, because right now she is not living. She is neither dead nor alive. She is frozen. Relive what happened to you then.

— *I am constantly reliving it in my sleep: betrayal after betrayal on every step of the age ladder.*

— You condemn yourself to the constant re-experiencing of that state. You experienced betrayal at sixteen, and you will continue to experience it for the rest of your life, unless you return, reevaluate, and see why and what exactly happened then.

Every situation is important from the standpoint of experience. For example, in order for you to understand what betrayal is, you need to experience it. That sixteen-year-old girl has her own notion of betrayal. Every young girl and every young boy has this notion, and, as a result, it remains in the adults they grow to be.

I say that there is no such thing as betrayal and cannot be, but you need to see this. A certain human being played a certain role to help you understand something. But you did not understand it, and, as a result, you continue to blame him.

You will experience an enormous gratitude toward him when you become aware of this situation, **as you have created it yourself in order to understand something.** Throughout our lives, we create the situations that are necessary to understand ourselves. But because we do not understand that, the feelings of guilt, hatred, and pain remain and accumulate within us. We need to return to these situations now and to collect these gifts of understanding and awareness of ourselves that we experienced back then. Let's take a look at the gift that is hidden in your situation.

— *I started to think of myself as bad. But I don't want to be left alone, so I need to behave and be good.*

— So, it appears that you are being loved for a reason. You are being loved for being good. An illusion was created that love can be earned by being good. Everyone here has his own understanding of what being good means. For you, for example, to be good means to be a good specialist. Do you really think you can be loved for being a good specialist? No. You can receive money and earn respect for it, but you cannot be loved for it.

— *I want my students to love me.*

— They want the same from you, not just an approval for well-performed homework or good behavior in the classroom. People want to be loved, but they don't know what it is, because love here is being dispensed for a reason.

There are just a few human beings here who can love for love sake. Those are people who found Unconditional Love. That's what we are aiming for. Each one of us is walking his own journey and learning his own lessons. But all of us are walking toward this love. However, unless we learn all our lessons and get to understand ourselves, we will not be able to acquire this main gift.

"Bad girl—good girl"

— *My father was a workaholic. He spent all his life at work. Mom was a drunkard. She blamed him for her affliction and for not spending time with her.*

— Your mother took one extreme. In any system — and family is a system — when someone takes one extreme side, the other is simply obligated to take the opposite side. Otherwise, the system will collapse. You can talk your head off, but your partner will insist on the opposite side, because you insist on yours.

The only way to harmonize this situation is to allow yourself to do what the other human being is doing. If one is irresponsible, the other will surely be very responsible. So, the irresponsible one should become responsible, and the responsible—irresponsible.

Someone must make the first step. You need to become aware of this. Otherwise, you will not be able to balance this system. Can you turn into an irresponsible girl and allow yourself everything under the sun?

— *I found a way out. I would go to the bar with my girlfriends. We would spend hours there talking and smoking. My husband is a very proper kind of guy. So, in my family system, my husband is good and proper, when I, a wife, am bad.*

— Those are technical terms. You were constantly fighting for the title of "good girl". Now you are fighting for the title of "good woman". Can you be a bad woman?

— *That's very difficult.*

— There is nothing simpler. You need to learn the other side. You got stuck in "good girl". What does it lead to? A "good girl" will be with a "bad boy". It cannot be otherwise. Otherwise, the system would collapse.

When a "good girl" will start to become bad, a "bad boy" will start to become good. You need to learn to balance between the opposite sides of personal dualities here.

This reality is constructed in such a way that you can only pass it by walking through the middle of the paradox or duality. This world is based on dualities. You cannot get away from it. While you are here, you are submerged in dualities. It appears that you are constantly attracting one pole of this duality.

You were inculcated with a notion that you must be a "good girl". You move closer and closer to that pole. You want to become a "perfect girl". But each one of us contains two sides of any duality, including this one. The more you actualize the "good girl" the stronger your potential "bad girl" gets. This "bad girl" will be manifested in thoughts, dreams, unconscious acts, etc. You constantly fight it, showing the world that you are good. That constant conflict stresses you out.

When you accept equally what you call "good girl" and "bad girl", you will get in the middle, and this duality will not affect you anymore. Otherwise, you will blame others. You will become intolerant and aggressive in this respect. For example, if you abhor prostitution, your daughter may wind up in the red light district. You will compel your child to plug that hole.

Those are the universal laws that no one can bypass. People don't want to see them, but no one will be able to avoid them. Those are the mechanisms that govern us here. We can only exit these mechanisms by getting in the middle of duality. To do that, you need to accept and experience both sides of yourself.

— *I need to experience it myself?*

— Yes. You don't have to spend the rest of your life being a prostitute, but you will if you will not become aware of this. I don't know how it will happen. I don't want to suggest anything. A training situation can suffice for someone. You can allow this to exist by saying, "Yes, this is in me, and I fully accept it". It should not be repeated as an affirmation. You need *to be* it. Then, the accusations you harbored toward other people will disappear. Who and do we accuse all the time and why? We

19

accuse people who manifest our opposite side—the side we suppress within ourselves.

— I had frequent dreams related to this theme. I was always surprised about what I was capable of doing in these dreams. I cannot allow myself such a behavior here, in this reality.

— Exactly. You do not allow yourself such behavior in this reality. So, where do these thoughts that you block go to? All these thoughts are experienced by you in the parallel realities. Not a single thought disappears, because we want to receive the entire experience. If we were present only in one reality, we would not be able to do that.

We are simultaneously present in many realities, where we receive different experiences, and these situations are being realized in other places. But in those realities, you force yourself to experience a life, for example, of a desperate prostitute.

On the other hand, if you were to combine and accept all of this here, you would help yourself greatly in one of these realities. You can become enlightened only by becoming aware of both sides of your personal program. If you understand that, you will not relate to anything with accusation.

Where does accusation and the feeling of guilt come from? They come from intolerance. You cannot accept something because you don't want to live through a certain experience. You negate it.

— We are governed by moral norms here.

— Of course you are. Everything here is built to prevent you from becoming aware of yourself. If you want to follow commonly acceptable norms, you will neither become aware nor enlightened. You must make a choice. It does not mean you must go down the drain and break everything around you. Do what you consider necessary based on your understanding of what we discuss and do here. If you choose an experience of, let's say, a prostitute, you understand why you are doing it. An average human being does not understand why he does what he does. He is being thrown from one side to another. When we choose to experience something, we understand what we are aiming for and why.

Another human being or a part of me?

— *What about the fact that we should pay for everything? My husband condemns me for what I do for awareness.*

— You husband is a part of you. In your case, he is condemning and punishing you, but nevertheless it's your part. It's irrelevant whether it is your husband or someone else do this to you. These are all your parts.

You need to sort things out with your inner parts, not with your husband. In the illusion of separation, our perception is strongly fixated on the external world in the illusion of separation. You may say that you have a husband who is not satisfied with you, but the essence of the matter is not in him but in your own part that is being embodied within your husband. When you see this part and start to transform it, your husband will either leave or change.

But if you don't want him to change, it means you don't want to change that certain part of you. Then, who will you direct your questions to? All your questions are directed to you. When you use such a perception, all your questions are directed to you.

The external perception is very stable. It is not easy to switch and to direct your attention inside yourself. We are constantly looking at other people, not realizing that they only reflect our own parts to us. We need to look at other people as our own parts and to be ready to change and transform these parts inside of us.

— *My older sister was treated with great respect by my family. I was never taken seriously. My parents wanted a boy, but I could not play one. I felt it all my life.*

— It appears to you that a man is important, while a girl or a woman is a second sort citizen. As a result, you experience this fear in front of a man who can punish you using law and morality. But all of this is inside you.

— *One day my father spoke to me about the meaning of life. I told him that he can always stand in the position of a small child requesting love and protection from the world and be angry at not getting it, or he can choose the position of the one who gives love. He was surprised. At the time, I thought I entered the golden middle. Then, this situation at school happened that I have discussed earlier. It was completely opposite to what I had said.*

— That's the duality you need to work on. What you felt internally is one thing, and what you expressed externally is another thing. When you are not aware of something in you, it strongly manifests itself externally. But you don't see it. Because you don't see it, you cannot manage it.

Recently you were saying that it is very important for you to receive a job qualification as a method of obtaining love. Being unaware of what Unconditional Love is, you conduct the idea of conditional love in your classroom. You desperately want Unconditional Love. However, you have a notion that love can be obtained only through high professional qualifications, and you do everything in order for your students to receive such qualifications.

But what are high professional qualifications? High professional qualifications are connected to low professional qualifications. As a result, we emphasize the importance of grades. For someone to stand higher, someone should stand lower. How would you know that someone is a good student and someone is not? You use grades. A good student can be seen only on the background of a bad student.

— *That's where I collide with the system. I tell them that I am ready to give everyone grade A just for coming in, but I cannot do that because I am squeezed by the system.*

— That's your second hang up: morality and the grading system. Morality is built on this system. At school, it manifests itself as a grading system. That's the same mechanism. Until you become aware of this, you will continue to be in conflict with it.

Internally, you want Unconditional Love the same way your students do. But the notion that love must be acquired through professional qualifications that is connected to a grade, which in turn is connected to morality, got fixed in you. That's it. Until you become aware of this, you will not be able to manifest love in a clear form. I understand that everything is entangled here,

23

and you cannot simply come to your school and say that everything is an illusion. First, you need to understand it yourself. Then, you will be able to see the best options you can use in the conditions you are in. Everyone happens to be where he supposed to be. Every one of us does what he must do where he must do it. You do it at your high school. That's a harsh system which is difficult to change. Everyone passes through school. That's the place where multiple conditions are downloaded into people, conditions from which they suffer. But, nevertheless, you can do your work there, and they will be grateful to you and you to them. You can do it even in such a system, but first you need to understand the system and how it works.

— *I should also understand myself.*

— Yes. In the end, you should understand yourself, because you are everything. Then, you will not have such a strong emphasis on grades. You are going to use the grading system because that's what accepted here, but you will understand the relativity of grades. Your main emphasis will be different. It will be Unconditional Love.

And then it is not going to be relevant who got an "A" and who got a "D". Kids will be grateful to you for both. Education is necessary, but when the only thing school can offer is just an intellectual education devoid of love, everything gets ugly.

A child seeks love, but he is given a math problem. Unless the child's main need, i.e. love, is satisfied, he will take everything the wrong way and succeed in it.

Kids don't study well in school not because they are stupid, but because they are so stressed out there they cannot think straight. All their abilities are being slowed down. If they were to be educated in love, everything would be different.

— *I just recalled what I did in school as a kid: I tried to find a key to every teacher so the information would flow directly from them to me. I did it instinctively.*

— That's how it always happens. There are no technologies here, but it is precisely through Unconditional Love that you can transmit everything to another human being, and he will happily accept it.

— *I don't have enough energy for everything.*

— You don't have enough energy because you do it without love. Love is an endless and limitless source of energy to which you need to connect. The more love you would give, the more it would come to you. This is a wise power that clearly sees what and who to give to. It is difficult to explain this in words. It must be felt.

— *Do you always feel it?*

— Yes. Otherwise, I would not do what I do. This is a question of life and death for me. My work is difficult. There are situations where I can be blamed for many things when people do not want to take responsibility. If it was not for love, I would not do this work.

Awareness is the highest level of development of the Intellectual Center, while Unconditional Love is the highest level of development of the Emotional Center. This union of the mind and the heart is very important for people.

I frequently encounter difficult situations. Love and intuition help me pass through them. I know exactly what to do, and I am calm. It does not mean that I am not experiencing different feelings getting into different traps. I do. I am a playing coach, and I enter multiple traps. I experience different feelings, but I am calm and observant. I love it. My manifestation might be different. I can scream at you. I can use harsh language. I can throw you out. I do many things that, in the opinion of many people, are not compatible with the behavior of a teacher. I behave the way I must behave, depending on the situation.

— *So, you are sincere in your manifestations.*

— I am totally sincere. I experience everything with you. I enter dualities that would have swallowed me if I was not in a state of love and awareness. It is not easy to enter the traps of other people. This work can only be done out of love and constant awareness.

— *Everything here is an experience I can observe. I cannot run away from these experiences, but they should not be positive or negative. When such a state is reached, enlightenment would be reached.*

— They will be positive and negative. As your heart opens, you start to allow everything that exists into it. Moreover, you allow the most difficult negative states to enter it. You can accept negative manifestations of other people only by accepting them in yourself. You allow yourself to see and you accept them inside yourself.

We have discussed already that we condemn others for what we do not allow ourselves to feel, think, or manifest. You can learn to hide your hatred and accusation to the vices of others, but that is fiction.

I have many faces. This is the reason I accept everything in other people. With the widening of consciousness, you start to encompass wider diapasons of people. When you encompass all of humanity with your consciousness, you will see everything that exists there: from the lowest scum to the humblest saint. You accept all of them inside yourself. Whatever you accept in yourself, you can accept in other people.

In the process of doing this, you must be completely sincere with yourself mentally, emotionally, and physically in order not to mistake fiction for true feelings. Your physical body will react. It never lies. I constantly orient and align myself with my body. My vision comes through my physical body. I experience limitless confidence and power in this state.

I don't need to be appraised by others in respect to the correctness or incorrectness of my actions. I have an inner compass that guides me, and it guides me correctly. You can only come to yourself on a wave of feeling. To do that, you need to open your emotional center.

— *I always considered myself to be someone who is full of love and understanding. I felt that I was capable of giving love to others. This notion was destroyed, and now I feel bankrupt.*

— That's great, because only an illusion can be destroyed. Reality can only be reached through a clear vision of the illusions. The more illusions you see, the closer you will approach what is not illusory. Therefore, every illusion that left you is a cause to celebrate. What you told us now appears to be tragic to you, but for me it is something to celebrate. I am happy for you because you are freeing yourself of what may be cherished and habitual for you, but what are just illusions.

Nothing happens here incorrectly. What do most people suffer from? They suffer from thinking about what they did right and what they did wrong. There is no such thing as wrong here. It does not matter what road you take; you will come to Unconditional Love.

Give a penny and take a million

— Everyone who has come here intends to see his illusions. This is an intention of your Supreme "I". But the false personality is attached to these illusions. It does not want to talk about them. The greatest gift you can receive here is to clearly see another illusion. It is painful, because you don't consider it to be an illusion yet.

You thought you loved someone, but it turns out that you don't. This is a great gift. Another weight was dropped and you soar up as an air balloon that throws heavy and unnecessary ballast down. The personality can cry and feel sorry about it, but I get excited, because it is impossible to lose what is real. One can only lose an illusion.

We hold on very hard to small things, when we are offered so much more. We don't want to part with a penny, when we are offered a million. But until we part with the penny, we will not be able to receive this million. Much more awaits us. I am happy about this, because I know that someone will pass through fear and pain and receive something priceless in return.

I know this because I have I passed through them myself. To do that, you need to be ready to receive and to accept your dual experience.

— *Will our planet be able to live through all of this, or are we going toward complete destruction?*

— Everything depends on us. There are many options available for Earth evolution. The question is which option you will choose. Some people consider that the end of the world must happen, and they will take part in the realization of this scenario.

I chose the option of Ascent, i.e. the option of transfer of the Earth to the next quality of consciousness—Unity. This is a colossal process in which human civilization will become aware of its unity and will transfer to a qualitatively different level of consciousness. Unity in love will start a great aspiration and break through into the unknown.

The fight between good and evil, light and darkness has been going on for a very long time. It has drawn in a great number of people and other creatures in the universe. Now is the time when everything can unite and create something beautiful. I see the future. I want to participate in it, and I do everything I can for it.

— *Jesus said, "We will not die, we will transform".*

— Yes. This is going to be a transformation of a great power and beauty.

— *When is it going to happen?*

— No one will tell you the exact date. No one will do anything for you. No one will give you any guarantees. You can pass close by this door. This is not a Russian revolution. This revolution occurs inside a human being, and those who will take part in it are those who will transform themselves.

Others may simply not understand it and not find out about it. Some still blame Jesus for saying that God's kingdom was close, but for two thousand years it did not come. But those who grasped what he was saying are already there. They have passed. They are the only people who know this. Others keep blaming him. For them, God's kingdom does not exist.

Christ spoke to those who could feel it inside. Everything happens inside. When we look around us, we see a grim picture. Darkness gets heavier before the dawn, but presently there are quite a few of us who are ready to become aware and to unite ourselves.

— I felt it watching your video. I sort of tuned into your conversation.

— Yes. That's what I transmit. By entering new vibrations of consciousness, you start to feel them and live by them. However, some people fall asleep later on, and for them it fades away. That's why your awareness and love should become stable. Stability is a sign of mastery. You should show consistent results; not just once, but ten times out of ten. To do that, you must perform constant inner work directed toward awareness and the harmonization of dualities of your personal program.

Your presence in this reality with all its dualities and problems tremendously increase the speed of your growth and experience. There is a huge potential here, which needs to be used.

When you stop blaming and pitying yourself, you will see unlimited opportunities. It is difficult here. There are many limitations here. But due to these difficulties and limitations, you can achieve great results and strengthen the power of your spirit.

Passing through these limitations offers fast growth. Based on this understanding, all your problems are excellent training grounds. When you start to look from this point of view, everything changes.

— *Sometime ago, a question arose in me: "Who am I?" I felt as if I had entered a certain game. I started to see that I am not a mother to my child. This is just a role that I need to play well. I can play any role, and now I want to know which role is really mine. I clearly saw many of my roles, but not all of them are me. I understood that I was capable of choosing any role, calling it mine, and performing it well. But which role do I choose? When I get tired of uncertainty, I sink into a state of meaningless existence. I don't run away from anything, but I don't gain anything either. What do I have except my roles, and what are the criteria that would tell us that we did not get out of there empty-handedly?*

— As we discovered, you can be anyone. You entered this reality, and you play certain roles. You entered it in order to acquire something.

— *Theoretically I know that, but I don't remember how I entered.*

— By playing a certain role, for example of a mother, you receive something that helps you understand yourself. This role is meaningless unless you understand what it gives you. Why did you become a mother?

— *That happened subconsciously, and the role has been played out already.*

— You are not finished with it. There is fuzziness in your understanding of the reason for which you have performed it. You can extract many gifts of awareness out of every role you have performed, but you must dig deep and find them. Otherwise, you are going to be akin to a student who says that he suddenly became aware that, in reality, he is not a student, and everything created by a teacher is garbage that he does not need. But this is not so. This is just a way to run away from homework.

To enter a lesson, you need to identify with it. Can you, for example, lose awareness while being aware? To receive a particular experience, you need to be unaware to a certain degree. I am not afraid of this. I can dive deep, knowing I can come back to the surface any time I want.

If you are aware, you can choose the experience you want to receive. That's where your freedom lies. The one who is not aware cannot get away from a lesson that he was assigned and the experience related to it. Whether he wants it or not, he will go through it.

When you are aware, you can enter any of the experiences available on this playground. I choose the experience I want to receive. I also choose the actors I want enter it with. For example, we receive a vast experience by being in relationship with our relatives. We acquire masculine roles in these relationships: father, son, husband, brother, and lover. We also play feminine roles in these relationships: mother, wife, daughter, sister, and lover. If a certain role has not been mastered by you yet, you will have to meet and work on it.

Those are the roles available in the repertoire of human experience. If you have experienced these roles, you can say that you have received the entire human experience. Women must accept masculine roles, and men feminine roles.

— *What do you mean?*

— What is the most difficult thing for you to accept in me?

— *I feel you are very close and dear to me. When I arrived, I immediately pegged a role on everyone here, and I understood that I am here to recall my childhood.*

— We could have met many times already, and we could have played different roles in relationship to each other in parallel lives. Many conflicts and problems that appear in this reality can be connected to the unsolved situations in those other roles we played between us. In particular, you will not be able to relate to me as a teacher if all your masculine roles have not been thoroughly worked through. You will get stuck in the qualities you have the greatest difficulty seeing in me.

— *I can sub-consciously determine which role a man can play with one glance.*

— That's exactly how it is done. Usually, it occurs without conscious awareness.

Why is a woman afraid of a man?

— Can fear of men appear because of this role assignment? If I, for example, assign a role of a lover to a certain man, morality can get turned on, and I will not allow myself to experience that.

— Fear is a reaction to the unknown. The only way to get rid of fear is to investigate what you are afraid of. What are you afraid of in your relationships with men?

— I can't stand jealousy.

— The greatest way to get rid of the feeling of jealousy is not to want anyone. As soon as you want someone, jealousy will manifest itself. So, it is better not to want anyone. In this case, you will not feel jealousy, but it remains hidden, and it will eventually manifest itself. For example, a woman does not feel that she realized herself as a woman, and as a result, she avoids situations that would require her to enter sexual relationships. She finds a husband who tortures her with jealousy. This explains her avoidance of other men. Avoiding these situations, she does not allow herself an opportunity to become aware of her shadow side.

— I don't know where to start.

— You need to act. If you don't start to manifest yourself in unusual ways, you will never learn anything about yourself. You need to go straight into the shadow territory in order to investigate it and to get rid of fear.

We cannot become whole until we acquire the entire experience we came here for. We must "graduate from the

34

school of three-dimensional reality and get a diploma". By avoiding a certain lesson, I simply delay my graduation day.

— *I want to find out what my life assignment is. That will give some meaning to my existence.*

— No one will tell you that. You will find meaning when you start your self-investigation. No one will tell you who you are and why you are here. You are the only one who can figure that out and assign meaning to it. We assign meaning to everything we do ourselves.

You can render any one of your roles meaningless, or, in reverse, assign great meaning to it. But the meaning you assign to it depends on you. The meaning you assign to the mother role will determine the experience you will receive by living through it.

— *I find meaning in raising my child and being close to our school.*

— Why do you use the word "close"? Using this word, you exclude yourself from this show.

— *I just observe what happens here, performing my role. For eighteen years, I did everything I had to: fed, cleaned, clothed…*

— Do you love your child?

— *Of course!*

— You keep talking in past sense.

— *My son left, and whatever we had is gone. He asks me for money from time to time. He asks me to run errands for him…*

— Please, pay attention to what you emphasize talking about your child. It's primarily material things.

— Nothing is going to happen in the future.

— There was nothing to begin with. You took a position of detachment with your child. This is the way you defend yourself from something you are afraid of. The opposite side of it is jealousy toward your husband. There is total involvement on your part there.

— Perhaps that happens because my son is internally older than me and never perceived me as mother. I have never been an authority for him. I was not upset about it, because in the family in which I grew up, that was an acceptable attitude towards mother. I accepted this from my son.

— This is habitual for you.

— Now I know that my mother is the dearest person to me. I understood how great she is when I gave birth myself.

— Do you love her?

— Of course. This love came to me when I was an adult. It took me thirty years to understand what mother is.

— Why do you love her?

— My father treated her with disdain all the time. I grew up ashamed of my mother. I was ashamed of her peasant background and being uneducated. When I gave birth to my first child, I suddenly realized that everything society respects a human being for is meaningless—there are no feelings in it. I suddenly saw that my mom was the only one who possessed these qualities.

— Your mother related to you as you relate to your son, making sure that you are materially provided for.

— That was natural for her, as it is natural for me now, but I used to justify my behavior somehow.

— *When my son was born, I experienced oneness with the universe. I had a feeling of enormous gratitude toward him. It was through him that I understood what love is. I felt that the entire world feels what I felt. That was the greatest experience of my life.*

— Take a look at these two different relationships with children.

— *My relationship with my three kids was different. It was not very important whether they were fed or not. I always wanted to be close to them, talk to them, to know how they understood and perceived the world. By being close to them, I could share their states. I think we frequently emphasize the material well-being of our kids without talking to them soul to soul.*

— Those are two sides of one coin. Every one of us must feel both sides of it. In this reality, love is dual, and it gets converted into hate. That's very important to understand. We have been given certain conditions of this love, and we need to find out what they are.

Who causes you to be jealous?

— What causes you to be jealous? What kind of a woman will you be jealous of more than others?

— *My husband still loves his first high school sweetheart. I know her. She deserves his love. I don't feel jealousy toward her, because I understand that she is one of those rare human beings that deserve to be loved. I am ready to share my husband's love for her.*

— Are the three of you going to go to bed together?

— *That's not what I meant.*

37

— I touched a painful spot. Are you ready to become aware?

— *I think I am.*

— You are constantly emphasizing *thinking*. You are an intellectual. That's where you are fixated. So, which woman will you be jealous of?

— *I feel jealous of stupid women. My first and my second husband left me for women I cannot consider to be my rivals. These were women of lower moral standards. They allowed themselves to flirt with other women's husbands. I cannot allow myself to do that.*

— You don't accept your flirtatious side.

— *My first husband was always surprised to see me getting jealous. He used to suggest that I take a lover. That was humiliating. The same thing happened with my second husband. I am fixated on the ideal relationship.*

— He will find a prostitute. He will need to find many prostitutes to balance your extreme.

— *That's what happened.*

— So, who pushes him toward these women?

— *It's me, of course.*

— I think for the one who wants to see, there is enough material here. You need to accept the idiot in you that can spread her legs as soon as she is asked. If you allow yourself to accept this idiot, activation of the other side of polarity will occur. You are experiencing high voltage right now while trying to absorb what I said, because your "idiot" part thinks she will not be able to understand it. Look and see her inside yourself, and you will have an opportunity to consciously manifest this part, the part opposite to your "smart" part. Blocking this "idiot" inside of you, you are also blocking your "smart" part.

You need to learn to see the mechanisms of interaction of the opposite sides of your personal dualities. When you start to see and understand them clearly, you will be able to govern them. Currently, they are controlling you.

You are constantly tense. To become an idiot is to relax. This tension prevents you from understanding what you want to understand. Therefore, you need to write what I say. You are the only one here who takes notes. It's great to be stupid. I am an idiot myself, but I am an aware idiot. I am relaxed, and as a result, I hear everything people say, and my other side—my smart side—gets activated. These twins—the smarty pants and the idiot—are always together.

I allow my idiot to manifest himself, and he gives me total relaxation. That's why I can easily absorb everything you say, process it, and come up with what I come up with.

You have strong tension in your intellectual and sexual spheres. They are connected. The sexual sphere is vetoed. Very strong moral convictions do not allow you to become aware of anything.

The guards of this reality introduce certain blocks to control people in order for them not to exit the borders of the allowed diapason of consciousness. Why do people dramatize everything to such a degree? They do so because these guards are on high alert. They make sure another enlightened one does not escape from here.

— My situation is the opposite. I am so tired of the pressure my husband applies to me; I sometimes want to ask him to get a lover on the side. Naturally, I am not for open sex marriage or free feelings.

— What is natural about it? Your inner woman is afraid, and as a result, she finds a man who will not allow her to do what she is afraid of doing. I would ask your inner woman what she afraid of.

— She is afraid to show that this is who I really am. I see those manifestations in school with my adolescent boys, who I perceive as potential men. I understand that being a teacher, I should not be in that position. That's why I am afraid to allow this energy out.

— What's even more interesting is that they feel it too. Until something is not thoroughly processed, it gets stronger and stronger. People pretend it does not exist, but it does. Until you see what is there, you will not be able to do anything about it.

— I understand that this is the strongest energy there is, and it pushes my student to become a stellar student. But I know that I should not use it the way it should be used.

— Why can't it be used? You can use it if you allow it to exist. Otherwise, you are afraid of it and you hide from it. In this case, it will be used for something else.

Every energy should be used as directed. But observe the substitution that occurs here, the situation gets totally mixed up: I want him as a man, but I insist he gets a good grade. That's it. We are totally mixed up.

He is also feeling this energy intuitively, but he cannot say anything because he is not aware of what is going on between the two of you. And it takes on perverted forms. We need to

40

untangle this ball. Then every center will work as it destined instead of substituting for the work of other centers. You are solving your assignment by using the wrong energy. You can't solve an intellectual problem using sexual energy.

— *When you feel sexual attraction toward someone, the question of age becomes secondary. There is a student in my class who reminds me of my first love. A few months ago, I told him that I love him. It seems to me that he also felt this connection that appeared between us. This turned out to be beneficial for him. We understand each other better now, and his performance in classroom improved. We understand each other much better now.*

— That happened because there was no fear there. You were sincere with him, and a human being replies to sincerity with sincerity. Where fear is present there is no sincerity: I feel, but I am afraid to feel it. Strong refractions appear in such cases.

— *Yes. I strongly deny my feminine side. My mother suffered from alcoholism, and she was surrounded by alcoholics. I understand now that this was her revenge on my father. Theirs was a romantic, unequal marriage. I developed an association with my mother. I cannot accept and I don't love myself as a woman.*

— We need to heal our inner boys and girls, because they did not disappear. They are inside of us and they want to receive what belongs to them, while we continue to suppress them, i.e. to play the scripts downloaded by our parents when we were kids. Now we become a child and an adult simultaneously. If we heal our own parts, we will become totally different beings.

— *I would like to run away from many of my fears. I am afraid of tomorrow. I am afraid for my kids. I have a very difficult relationship with my younger son. We are constantly at war. Our financial difficulties don't help.*

— What appears to be the most difficult issue in your relationship with your younger son?

"I cannot accept his lies…"

— I cannot accept his lies.

— **What else do we have here in this world aside from lies? There is nothing here except lies and half-truths. A man insists that he is telling the truth to you, but this is half-truth. This is the truth of one half of his personality. There is also the truth of another side of his personality, which is opposite to it.**

— But I was taught that "it is better to have a bitter truth, than a sweet lie".

— Give me at least one "bitter truth" that is better than "sweet lie".

— Whenever I did something inappropriate, I always acknowledged that.

— I think that your problems with your son are not related to this. What you call truth is your one-sided conviction. Tell me at least one truth regarding how to live.

— I don't know how to live. For the last six months, I have lived in fear. Fear is in every cell of my body. I sleep with my fists clenched.

— What are you afraid of? What is the scariest thing that can happen to your child?

— He can become an alcoholic.

— If it were meant for him to become an alcoholic, i.e. to receive this experience, he will receive it. Do you understand that every human being that comes here, whether it is your son or your daughter, is a being that comes here to acquire a certain experience? I am not looking at this from the position of morality. If someone is acquiring an experience of an alcoholic, a drug user, a prostitute, or a killer, that's the experience he or she needs. In the multitude of previous lives, each one of us received different experiences, including those. If you have not received something yet, you will receive it.

— Is there also self-pity there?

— That's primary. You are not afraid for your son. You are afraid for yourself. We are only afraid for ourselves. We cannot be afraid for anybody else. This is very important to understand.

— I completely forgot about myself. I only think of my children.

— Do you see the degree of your aloofness from yourself?

— I don't love myself. I want to learn to accept myself. It seems to me there is nothing to love in me. I am harsh. I am always in negative emotions.

— To experience negative emotions is neither bad nor good—it is just an experience. You can love someone for no reason. Love is just a quality of a human being, because he is love himself. I love you not because you are smart or stupid, but because my quality is to love.

— I recently admitted to my son that I am unhappy as a woman. I did not love his father. I did not love my second husband. I don't love myself. I constantly blame myself for this. People frequently ask me what my aim

is. I have only one aim: to be a good mother and to help my kids, even if only with an advice.

— If you don't love, you will not be able to give any useful advice. Let's figure out why you don't love yourself. Do you think you don't have what it takes to love yourself?

I keep telling you that you came here to receive this experience, and you are receiving it. I am not looking at it from a moralist point of view, because as essences we all come here to receive a certain experience.

There is an experience of a good mother and a bad mother. From the standpoint of the essence, you must have both. You have received yours. Do you understand me?

— *Not really.*

— For example, someone is acquiring an experience of a drunkard. Will you be able to understand him if you have not been a drinker yourself? No!

The society of Alcoholics Anonymous was created, and this was the correct thing to do, because people who work there get clean, and they learn how to relate to others based on their own experience. They have been there. They know it all. I want to emphasize that the most important thing here is your experience, which is neither bad nor good. You have it. You acquired it during your entire life.

— *I didn't acquire anything but fear.*

— This is also an experience. Look, everyone here lives in fear. We receive the experience of fear, separation, pain, and suffering here. If there was anything else here, we would not have gathered together to have this conversation.

Once you are finished with one experience, you can move on to the next. But, without having it, we cannot move to Ascent, Enlightenment, or anything else some of us talk about as our desired aim.

Your experience is very valuable for you, as you exist precisely for this experience. Perhaps you are ready to move to another one. Everything that you received was necessary. Nothing was wasted. If you can understand that, you will be able to accept yourself and your entire experience. That's a necessary step to move to the next experience.

— *Is that a step away from the complete negativity that turned me into a corpse?*

— Yes. Do you think I did not pass through it, and I don't know what hell is? I did. It is precisely the hell I went through that led me to discover what I discuss now. I am grateful to it and to all the people that participated in the acquisition of the experience I required.

— *I still don't understand. I cannot accept it. I am tired of negativity. I harbor a high level of aggression that I might spill onto my child any moment. He sometimes looks at me and asks me why I am so angry, why I don't notice him being in a good mood. I hate myself when this happens.*

— You constantly maintain yourself in a negative state. I just told you how to get out of it.

45

Start to love your negative experience

— I don't understand anything. According to you, I like my sufferings, and I cannot part with them.

— Yes. You got used to them.

— I sometimes catch myself laughing when I feel bad. I don't laugh when everyone laughs from happiness, only when I feel bad.

— You do the same thing all the time. You recreate the experience of pain and suffering.

— Yes, I move in circles.

— I just showed you how to get out of this cycle. You need to accept your experience and come to love yourself for acquiring it. Enough of this experience was accumulated already, and you don't need to acquire it any longer. Come to love yourself for your negative experience.

— I can understand what it means to love someone for something good, but for this …

— Take a look at how strongly you hold on to your negativity. I am talking about a remedy that is hundred percent effective, but you blame yourself and receive a perverted pleasure from it. You reject the cure I offer. The only conclusion I can make is that you want to continue to suffer. Please, do so.

Your "i" has split in two here: one wants to continue, another does not. I am talking to the part of you that does not want to accumulate the old experience any longer. For you to stop receiving it, you must accept the part of yourself that wants to continue to receive it and express your gratitude for it.

— I want to add that her son came to this reality here in order to get to know the mother like her. As soon as she understands that, she will get the whole picture. I just realized that my childhood experience was a great goodness, and perhaps it was thanks to that I am here now, trying to become aware of myself.

— Exactly. You would not be able to understand what I discuss without this experience. You would have to experience and accumulate it first. Positive and negative experiences are two sides of one coin. You will not get this coin without living through and experiencing both sides.

— She did not tell you everything. Based on our last conversation, I can conclude that she has a strong unacceptance of men, bordering on aversion and hatred. It is projected onto her children, especially onto the younger boy. She was never able to accept her husbands. Now, without a husband in the picture, she projects this feeling onto her younger boy.

— Great. We can see the main story line.

— I am in the same shoes. The more I live the more I feel I don't understand anything. Everything I just heard relates to me. I have never seen my father. He was killed during World War II. My husband is an alcoholic, probably because I am so good. I have two daughters and a son. I brought them up myself. That's my life.

— Do you understand now that this was necessary?

— Being here, I start to understand that. But it is not easy to accept it, and I don't love myself.

— You have to come to peace with yourself. You don't have any reason not to love yourself. At least love yourself for going through these hardships. You came for them. We all came to experience this reality of pain and suffering. That was a great deed from the point of view of our essence, as not every essence enters these dimensions. This is hell, and we entered it.

— *Most likely, that's why I am here. As they say, it's not us who chooses the way. The way chooses us.*

— But this way was marked by us over there.

— *We marked it over there, but we don't remember it here.*

— This is also a part of the way we marked. We are already approaching understanding. Once we receive and become aware of our experience, we can exit it. That could be the most important reason why we gathered here. But first, we need to see it. Only then we will be able to accept it.

We have identified with our experience so completely, that we started to consider ourselves to *be* this experience. But we are not this experience; we are outside of it. We are not our body. We are not our thoughts. We are not our feelings. We are the Soul and the Spirit. But at the same time, while we are here, we are our body, thoughts, and feelings. These polarities need to be harmonized.

— *It becomes clear now that a human being and his deeds are not the same.*

— A human being is both outside this reality and inside this reality at the same time. However, if you only identify yourself with your personality and its experience, you will not understand much. You can only come to understand yourself through observing your personality and by de-identifying with the experience acquired by it.

— *I frequently hear that life is beautiful and wonderful, but I came to conclusion that Earth is a place of suffering and grief. I tried to convince myself otherwise, but I could not.*

— It is only when we come to that point on the way, that we can start to feel that life is the greatest miracle. This is another duality. Until suffering is experienced and accepted fully, we will not achieve happiness.

CHAPTER 2

YOU KNOW EVERYTHING ALREADY

•◆•◆•◆•◆•◆•◆•◆•◆•◆•◆•◆•◆•◆•◆•◆•◆•◆•◆•◆•

Mullah Nasreddin had a violin, and he constantly played only one note on it. His neighbors and his family were very upset. They kept telling him, "What kind of music is this? If you are learning to play a violin, learn it the right way. You are constantly playing the same note. This is unbearable!" His wife told him, "Enough already! We are listening to this month after month. No musician plays that way! What are you doing?"

Nasreddin replied, "Others are trying to find their note. That's why they change notes: they are still on the way, they are searching for the note they need. I, on the other hand, already found mine. I achieved my goal"

Feeling and the awareness of feeling

— What is your main state?

— *I am observing the experience I came here to receive. There is an experience, and there is an observer who observes it. We have talked about this theoretically, but I finally experienced it yesterday.*

— The theoretical knowledge will become your experience. That's why I came here. You know a lot, and you are ready for it to become your experience. Knowledge can come and go, it can be forgotten, but when it becomes your experience, you will never forget it.

— *I thought I had to stop feeling everything and to become quiet. Suddenly, being here, I realized that I must feel everything.*

— Yes. Our process reinforces and strengthens your sensitivity. It becomes so strong that you start to feel things that the average man does not feel.

— *I was afraid to allow myself to manifest anger and hatred, but here I allowed myself to experience everything.*

— That's exactly what we need. Anger is energy. If you don't allow yourself to feel it, you turn into a living dead man. These feelings, when you allow yourself to express them, move you to a new level and become transformed.

A feeling combined with awareness provides an opportunity to broaden your consciousness. A feeling by itself is insufficient; you must combine it with awareness. If you don't combine awareness with feelings, you will be cold. You will not experience any joy.

Yes, you can say something to people, and that might be a right thing to say, but neither you nor they will get better from it. It would be like a clear winter day: everything is clearly visible, but it's cold. For this day to be bright and warm, you must have feelings.

— *Earlier today, when music was playing, I allowed myself to experience what happened between me and my parents when I was a child.*

I observed it. I received a completely different result from the one I had when I tried to do it mentally by myself a few months ago. It is scary to go there. I run in circles all the time, unable to enter it fully.

— The atmosphere we create here allows us to enter our shadow zones. Whatever zones you enter and whatever you meet there, your fellow students and I will help you to get out of them. You can safely enter your deepest corners. No one will get stuck there. I promise you that.

— How can one get stuck in what one is already sitting in?

— A part of you is locked in your inner basements. Using awareness, you will open these basements, get down there, and allow the parts that were locked there to get out. There are many of these parts down there.

We are on the journey to see the hidden rooms of our inner house, rooms we have not visited for a long time. We are opening the doors and allowing everything that is there to get out. This is amnesty. There are many prisoners there, and we are freeing them. As they get free, energy is released. In using this energy, we come to understand ourselves better and to connect our fragmented parts into one whole.

— My life has been justified. I was allowed to live. I did not allow myself anything before.

— In the process of accumulating experience, you started to consider yourself to be this experience. This experience was very painful, and it was leading to self-destruction. This affected you in such a way, that you forbade yourself to live.

— For my entire life, I was trying to self-destruct.

— Yes. You have received this experience. You know what it is now. You understand that you and your experience are not the same thing. You can clean toilets all day long, but you don't need to identify yourself with the dirt you clean. However, many people identify with a particular situation and consider themselves to be a part of the toilet. You just came there to clean it, but you forgot about that. I remind you. Now, after you have finished your work, you can get out of there. That's it.

— *That's exactly what I felt yesterday.*

— *I put on some bright make-up this morning and went outside. I decided to observe myself. For some reason, only men came my way. I realized that I never looked them straight in the eye, and I started to do so. I noticed that men paid attention to me. I imagined myself to be a prostitute who could easily sleep with a drunkard, and I understood that it was possible. An alcoholic is also a human being, like the rest of us. I realized that I punish my husband with my prohibiting behavior. It turned out it was my revenge. I entered a store and saw something I wanted to buy. Suddenly, a thought pop into my head: "I will have sex with my husband, and I will have him pay for this purchase". While experiencing all of this, I noticed pain in the lower part of my abdomen. I started to observe it, and I understood that my sexuality is really suppressed; my inner woman is asking to be freed. I used to allow myself to be sexy. I've had men before, but I did not look for lovers. They were all impotent. I was looking to have a nice conversation with them. There was no sexual energy there. I don't see it in my husband either, because I do not allow myself to manifest it.*

— You do not allow yourself, because you use it for manipulation. This is a payment for your manipulation: I am so good, and you are so bad, and because of this you are going to do this and this for me. But then you force yourself to be "good", i.e. to forbid yourself many things. This is a payment you pay, and it is heavy.

— *When the thought to charge him money for sex entered my head, I suddenly understood that sex is exchange of energies, and money is an exchange of energies. Everything is interconnected. Now I understand why I did many things in my life. I wrote a letter to my husband expressing my love for him. I really felt it. I got out of the house with a clean conscience. Previously, I would have felt guilty. Coming here, I felt as if I was given permission to do many things that were forbidden before.*

— *I experienced anxiety, excitement, and aggression toward you. For some reason, I laughed at myself. I always knew I loved my children, but I never expressed it aloud. Today, I told my younger son that I love him dearly. I never thought of what love was. I simply accepted my parents and my grandparents. They never told me they loved me, but I knew they did. The first thing I experienced this morning when I woke up was relaxation. This was the first time in months that I slept well. I woke up fully rested.*

— *In my dream, I was under the water observing a house that was on fire. It was amazingly bright under the water. I felt I was in my natural habitat. I felt very comfortable. There was no fear. I was surprised by my calmness, as my kids were in this house. I am a very protective mother. That burdens me sometimes. As a child, I always had everything, but my parents never expressed their love verbally. I consider myself to be a good mother. I embrace my children with love. I tell them how I love them all the time.*

— *Yesterday, listening to music, I understood that I have to learn to be my own mother. I need to give to my inner sulking child whatever she did not receive. I need to change the state she is in, as this state of sulk takes a lot of energy. I want to be able to give my love to others. I understood that everything is just starting today and that by God or by nature I was given a very strong energy charge of love and happiness. I always felt myself to be a tender, unprotected flower. I want to remain this flower, but I want to become stronger and share love and beauty with others.*

— Yesterday I saw separation in all its glory. I experienced Soul awakening, and then I fell asleep again. I was in a depressed mood. I felt as if I was in a circle of men; they were throwing me around. It was hard. I observed what was happening to me in this circle, and sensed myself as two. I understood that I was seeing a duality. It was very important for me to feel duality. Somewhere deep down there is a certainty that I can do anything I want to do, but then a thought appears that this is not for me.

— This is a thought of a small mind in a box. The heart knows all the depth and all the width. Do not identify with a box. Enter your heart that has everything and that you feel so well.

The high is based on the low

— Negativity closes my heart. I always wanted to feel goodness, and only goodness.

— Negative and positive are two sides of one coin. One hand washes the other. Tell me, which hand is washing which?

How can you know what light is if you don't know what darkness is? The notion of light itself comes out of the notion of darkness, and vice versa. They are linked together. Don't lean on one side, as you will not understand the whole.

— My desire to have a grandiose assignment has diminished.

— The grandiosity is not in the mind. It is in the heart.

— *I lived my whole life walking on my toes trying to reach for the stars.*

— You can live in this state all your life. At some point, you will have to relax and stand on your feet.

— *This state is subsiding, but I am used to it and want to be in it all the time, as without it I don't have enough energy. Everything I have achieved in life, I achieved only because I wanted to become worthy. Ten years after I got married, it started to subside. My desire to invent something grandiose remains, but nothing comes out of it.*

— I can't imagine anything more grandiose than what we are doing. If a heavy weight lifter continues to increase his effort all the time, he will break. He needs to get to the mat, lift the weight, and drop it down. He cannot stand all day with the weight up in the air. There are moments when you must exert yourself, and there are moments when you must relax. These are periods. These periods can change during a day, a month, and a year.

To take off, you need to get low. You are getting ready to take off now. The hardest work occurs right now. During the time when this work occurs, it appears that nothing is happening.

The wisdom of life is in allowing yourself to relax. This change between excitation and relaxation is very important. You must learn how to achieve your aim and how to be in a state of aimlessness. You can set up a certain aim and achieve it. Then, you need to allow yourself to spend some time in aimless wandering.

You need to use this opposite side to save up energy for the next jump. This is a beautiful period during which something new gets born. Otherwise, you are going to repeat the same thing again and again. This period provides you with an opportunity to receive something greater. You are standing on the doorstep of it.

— *But, the waiting period is getting longer and longer. One stands and stands on the doorstep wanting to enter.*

— Do not hurry. Everything will happen in due time. Learn to wait. This is very important, and you can only see it by being calm and silent. The ability to act is also very important. The waiting period can be so long that one may lose the ability to act.

One must learn to relax not only the body, but the thoughts and feelings as well. The conditioned mind does not allow our bodies to relax. The body is very wise. If you don't push it very hard, it will live an amazing life. Look at cats. They know how to relax and how to collect themselves in an instant.

— *I felt as if a second wind opened up in the area of my heart. I had a sensation that I am everything and that everything is me, but then I felt tired and sleepy.*

— **Those words sound like a prayer. Christians say, "Create the prayer within your heart". Be in your heart all the time. You don't need to pray using words if you have moved to the heart. Being in the heart means you have come home. Be at home. Enjoy being there.**

Information comes during the day, but it is absorbed during sleep. You need to have a good night sleep. Pay a lot of attention and love to your body. It is very important for our work, as the body is an apparatus that accepts information. It should always be in a good shape. It should be taken care of. It should be loved.

Our process relates to the opening of all energy centers. There are thirteen of them. Connection with the solar, intergalactic, and universe systems starts with the seventh chakra. Our life force is in the first chakra. It is called Kundalini.

When chakras start to open, Kundalini starts to move up through all the chakras. It can be followed by different and sometimes unusual sensations in your body and activation of the mental activity of the conditioned mind. It can get activated and create constant noise. It is to be expected with the upward movement of Kundalini. Just observe it as interference.

— I clearly saw that I attract pleasant things and try to repel everything unpleasant. I have never perceived this as a lesson passed, which ended in the acquisition of a certain experience. I feel that I don't want to experience unpleasant states. They are not good for me.

— By submerging into the darkness, you intensify the light. The deeper you submerge, the stronger the light. It's the passage through darkness that intensifies the light. The negative states you speak of are not a punishment but a huge opportunity. I can understand the light only as much as I understand the darkness. This continues through eternity. So, learn to enjoy difficulties.

— I always crave a steak after the seminar.

— Regulate what you eat. When you enter very high levels of consciousness, you can leave this reality for good. In order for this not to happen, you need to eat some meat to ground yourself.

— I agree. I participated in a group that studied certain esoteric spiritual practices. We were not allowed to eat meat there, but I craved it so much, I was breaking the rules. I noticed that those that did not eat meat spoke about love a lot, but were very angry. I read your books during that time, and I started to openly express my feelings. I was talking about the fact that we don't love people around us, as we see our shadow side in our neighbors, and those encounters are not always pleasant. I left that group. When I go deep inside myself, I start to harmonize my life and my relationships.

— People think they get rid of their aggression by eating meat free diet, but in reality they become more aggressive and try to force others not to eat meat, insisting on the vegetarian kitchen and their goodness, but aggression just flows out of them.

— The more serious I am about something, the funnier my "clown" gets. I don't want to relate to life seriously. During childhood, I was very natural. People around me did not like it. I had to fight them all the time. Turns out I was fighting myself.

— Life can be seen as a deck of cards. We drop these cards one after another, and at the end we are left with a joker. When you finally dump him, you become free in your choice of a life path.

— It is funny to see how seriously I used to take things that in reality are the illusions.

— It is precisely one's inability to laugh at oneself that allows him to maintain the illusion as reality. It is difficult to deal with very serious people, because they cannot detach. They are so serious that they get completely identified with their beliefs.

Laughter allows you to exit borders. A good joke is always a paradox. It brings laughter that allows you to exit the limits of the conflict of oppositions.

Multidimensional vision

— We have discussed already the fact that we happen to occupy many different realities at once. The linear time that exists here represents just one out of many varieties of existence. In reality, time is multidimensional. As a soul, we happen to be present simultaneously in countless shows and realities. Moreover, these shows intercept, and as a result, the picture of our existence is multidimensional. I invite you to see some important moments that happen to you in other realities and influence what happens to you here.

I will ask you to observe and tell us about yourself in other realities.

— *I saw you dressed in the medieval Russian warrior robe. You were standing in the middle of a group of similarly dressed soldiers. I saw myself killed in this battle. Then I saw an old palace. A young man was walking with me. His left hand was on my shoulder. A big bright candle was burning in his right hand. In my third vision, I was pregnant, and I gave birth to you. I found the progression of what I saw to be very interesting. First it was death. Then, I saw that something was burning and generating light. Birth followed that scene, and finally I married you. It started in medieval time, and ended today. The union of different forces and energies accompanied it. That was clearly seen during our wedding. We stood there holding hands.*

— We could have met many times in different roles. The roles and plots we played in other realities are reflected now in what happens to us here. When you start seeing that, you start to better understand what is happening now. By expressing what you see happening in other realities verbally, you introduce other realities into the current reality.

— I found my being killed four times very important. I felt that a part of me died yesterday. A young man with a candle is always with me. He is my savior, and he helps me to see my pathway. I experienced birth. A child that was born was not just you. I gave birth to something big, new, and unifying. We are always looking for our second half unaware that it can only be found inside us. This wedding united something in me.

— What you discuss is happening and will continue to happen. This is not something unrelated to you. These pictures show what will happen to you here in terms of your inner world. They tell you about the process of inner transformation. They are very important.

— I see dark ages. Something happened. I see a group of people with torches in their hands. They appear to be happy. I stand on top of a tall tower. It's windy. I feel happy. I feel reborn.

— I am on a boat, and you are waiting for me on a shore. I am a currier. I am carrying a very important letter, and I deliver it to you. I remember you. You are very tall. You are dressed in a white robe. Your hair is gray. You are calm. I have a feeling that my duty was performed well. There is no pride there. Then, I see an endless sea. You are Neptune, and I am swimming behind you. Both scenes are filled with great happiness.

— I was coming down, and I saw a great pillar of light. It turned out that this light was coming from people. They were coming in great numbers, and as a result, this light was getting brighter. At first, they were walking in total darkness, but then, as they were passing through the area filled with sharp stones they started to cut their feet. The light started to come out of their wounds. Together they were creating one common current of light. The major thing I experienced was that light appears through pain.

— I suddenly felt myself being love itself. I felt tears coming, but I could hold them. This feeling was grandiose. I saw light coming out of me. I felt one with the Earth and everything on it. I was Mother Earth. I felt enormous love inside, but I did not trust myself to express it.

My consciousness and my heart are open for you

— There are certain stages that we will have to pass through. Nothing in life happens without a reason. When you become aware of this, you gratefully release what happened to you, understanding how necessary all of it was. Everything that happens next is the result of what happened to you before.

— I experienced tremendous suffering. I looked at myself and I thought that on one hand it is pain, but on the other hand it was enlightenment. I thought about what my soul can give to others. Going through such pain, I probably can carry the light.

— You are already doing this. When I came to the group for the first time, I saw this warm light in you.

— I was constantly bothered by the meaninglessness of my existence. I felt this pain, but at the same time, I knew that it was given to me as a gift.

— This is an act of great courage. Every one of us here, in this dual world, has to perform and transform it through suffering. The hardest period during which you did something without being aware of your actions is ending. The time to become fully aware of what you did and do now has come. Nothing was in vain. Everything was necessary and very important. Behind it is your power and love.

— *Can you please tell us as other groups' work? Working on our own using your books and videos, we got very absorbed in sorting out different situations and scenarios. It seems to me that having the opportunity to figure out something else, we would feel differently. I remember how difficult it was to enter these old life situations for me. Listening to you now, I understand that everything is going to be different. We come to group not only to be sorted out piece by piece, but also to collect all our parts into one whole. This turning oneself from inside to outside is very difficult. I sometimes don't want to live. I am asking for your help. How do you do it? Perhaps we are doing something wrong. Perhaps, instead of helping a fellow human being, we are hurting him.*

— We do this work to meet ourselves, and as you can see, this work is not easy. You were different before, and the work that was required of you and done by you was different. You have changed, and as a result, our work has changed too.

Every group is different. Guided by awareness and love, I help you to feel the connection with other people who are in our process. That does not mean you are going to become them. Our bodies consist of two legs, two arms, and a head. Each one of these organs performs its own function, but together they belong to one organism. I don't create many arms. I create one unified organism. Groups enter this organism as different organs. Each group is unique and individual, and this is great. All of us together create a strong organism that has many opportunities. We have created our group by passing through multiple obstacles. We had to pass through them. Everything was right. Everything was done the way it should have been done, and the result of this work is our meeting today.

— *I have a feeling that people in groups get together as families. The roots lie somewhere deep in past lives.*

— We entered different realities together many times. My coming here was not coincidental. I come to places and work with people with whom I worked before and share a big experience accumulated in so called "past lives". Every one of us knows a lot and can do a lot. We just need to wake up from the sleep, drop the illusion, and start to recall who we are. Everyone here will start to recall.

— *How can I discern self-remembrance from fantasy?*

— Don't worry about it. Consider that those are fantasies, but try to understand that they are no less real that what happens here. We spent an entire day being in what you may consider to be a fantasy, and your mind is very dissatisfied with it.

In the physical reality, you will not get out of the small box or a closed circle of perception in which your conditioned mind keeps you. You need to start feeling everything. The meaning of creation is in meaningless, aimless love that does not require anything because it has everything. It does not depend on anyone or anything. It has everything that is necessary. It is everything.

Your mind constantly worries about meaning: shuffling different meanings like a deck of cards. Open your heart. Let your feelings out, and you will stop worrying about it. I can introduce meaning into anything if my mind is free and unlimited.

— *What good does it do me if I cannot do that?*

— You will be able to do that when you start to feel me. You prefer a very limited, cumbersome, and time consuming method of information transfer. I transferred a lot of information during today's meeting, but from the standpoint of some traditional psychologist, it may appear that nothing happened, people just sat there listening to music. In reality, quite a lot happened today.

I understand it very well, because I do everything with awareness. This can be done only in a state of delightful relaxation, but you prefer to acquire information the way you were taught to acquire it, writing fast after a teacher in order not to miss anything.

If you get into the heart for a moment, you will feel me, and through this feeling you will receive everything that you want. My heart and my conscience are always open, but you can only access them through love. By entering them with love, you will effortlessly find everything that you need. Just open the door, enter, and take what you need. Feel, love, and you will have whatever you want. Don't insist on the old ways. Enter the state of Unconditional Love from where everything that we discuss flows.

— *From the beginning of the seminar, I was in a very good state.*

— Don't hold to your states. Experience whatever state comes your way. This is very important, because as soon as you attempt to hold onto what you call good, you will immediately face the bad. You may get upset, enter a depression, and forget everything.

"When I read your books, I understand that I know everything…"

— I desperately want to remain in a state of understanding. When I read your books, I understand that I know everything, but somehow this knowledge does not stay with me for very long. When I get into difficult situations it leaves me.

— You have this hastiness that is being manifested now in your pressured speech. Just listen. I speak now, and you want to say something in reply. An impulse appears, and it is difficult for you not to express it. Try to get into a state that is similar to a neutral gear in a car. When you are in it, you can shift to any position, i.e. any state. This state of inner neutrality is observation. You can easily enter any state from out of it. When a man gets angry, he experiences multiple states: irritation, aggression, depression, etc. He prolongs these states and experiences this entire cycle. It is not necessary to complete this cycle if you know how to be in a "neutral" state. This is a state of the observer.

There are no good and no bad states for the observer. Whatever happens, the observer observes it. The conditioned mind will simply appraise. The observer will observe the mind that appraises.

— *You are right. I have this hastiness in me. I want everything at once. When a desire appears, I want to fulfil it as soon as possible. I am in a hurry all the time, even during lessons.*

— You are in a hurry to transmit as much information as possible. This is a characteristic quality of many people, including school teachers. They say, "We are going to make today's lesson interesting. You are going to learn a lot of information". Many seminars and trainings are conducted this way.

If we were to look at how it happens during our seminars and webinars, we would see that I do what I transmit. I understand that if you swallowed some food, you need to digest it. What's the point of putting food in your mouth if you cannot digest it? You need to take as much as you need and absorb it. Then you can take a next portion.

You need to know your limits. The mind accelerates, it needs more and more, it asks, "Let's go! It's great! It's so interesting!" But then you can get into a depression, because it gets overfilled and cannot digest anything anymore.

It is like a horse that has bolted. You need to learn how to slow down. You can't force this process. You must use the observer. For example, you will observe the tendency of your mind to talk a lot. At a certain point, by becoming aware of what's happening to you, you will stop doing it. These tendencies of mind are present in everyone. You need to observe them and know them. Then you will master them.

— I even invented an exercise for myself. I try to be silent for long periods of time.

— That's especially important when you want to speak up. You ask countless questions, but you don't hear the answers. You need to remain silent and simply observe the activity of your mind. You will start seeing when and how it slows its activity. The most useful thing for you is not to ask questions— but to just observe them. You will see that answers will come from inside, and only to the necessary questions.

You will not have many questions while in a state of observation. There will be only one, but the one you really need. Your mind will not overflow with superfluous information. You will enter a quiet, harmonious state.

There are two types of exhaustion: psychological and physical. Physical exhaustion can be removed by special relaxation techniques or during sleep. Psychological exhaustion can end up as depression. It is related to sinking toward one side of duality. In this particular case, it has to do with activity in the external world and should be equalized by passive contemplation or meditation.

I am not talking about complete cessation of usual activities. They must be balanced. You can take a walk in the woods. That's an excellent meditation. Breathe in fresh morning air and feel it. Look at the trees and feel them. Feel your every step and every movement.

This state of being here and now is very powerful. While being in this state, you can acquire power and understand what you need to understand. **You need to be in this reality; it is a**

starting point for exiting to other realities. Ordinary people are never here. It appears that they are here, but in reality, they are in their own realities, hallucinating with the help of the conditional mind. That's the basic activity of the conditional mind: to give birth to multiple hallucinations. For the mind to exit this state, it needs to enter here and now. Yet it resists that strongly.

— *I frequently don't have energy for this.*

— You don't need any energy for this. You need energy to throw yourself from the past to the future, or from the present to the past. The mind gets into the habit of doing everything in a hasty and forceful way. It appears that everything should be done that way. Your mind is afraid that if it quiets down, it will be laid off. But that's not true. It is not being laid off. It is given a vacation. It is invited to take a rest.

— *I am constantly occupied by thoughts.*

— Don't be afraid of this. Just observe your thoughts. You are getting anxious, and you transmit your state to others. This is a mechanical transfer of your anxiety to a fellow human being, who immediately starts to become anxious too. As a result, you create conflict.

— *If only I was able to do that …*

I transmit a feeling, but you try to analyze me

— You say it as if it was impossible. Observe how your mind rejects what I discuss now. It is used to acting constantly, and my words call either aggression or sleep from within it—it becomes defensive.

Just observe. You can come to understand everything when you are in a relaxed state. When you really understand something, no one will be able to take it away from you. If you don't understand, irrespective of how much you exert yourself, you will not be able to understand it.

The main communication does not occur with the help of the conditioned mind; it's an exchange of energies. It's a beautiful dance. When you stop concentrating on the conditioned mind and its paranoid analysis, you will be able to see the dance of your energies.

I transmit feelings and states, but you try to analyze me. What happens now will never repeat itself. If you are not in the here and now; it will disappear for you.

Is there something important that you would like to share with us?

— I had an unusual conversation with my husband yesterday. It was very open and sincere. I told him what was important for me. I told him about my feelings. I told him about something I wanted to buy, and he told me that he would buy it for me as a present. I suddenly understood that I had been blessed with many presents already. You brought new sensations to our group. Everything else is secondary. When I woke up this morning, I did not feel the usual chronic pain I experienced prior to this conversation with him. I did not analyze anything. Leaving home, I left a note for him with loving words. I have not done it for a long time. As I was closing the door, I realized that I did not want to be a prostitute for him.

— Prostitution is love that is sold. You can deal with different people. You can give your love to people without getting paid for it. People communicate on mental, emotional, and physical levels. That's why problems frequently arise. For someone with a prevailing physical center, close interaction implies physical interaction. He or she will have a difficult time achieving an understanding with someone who is predominantly intellectual.

Wholesome communication includes all the centers, including the spiritual body, and that's beautiful. For this to happen, all centers must unite. When that happens, you will meet a human being as equally wholesome as you. The union of two wholesome people is already God's kingdom on earth. The usual communication is fragmented. That's where suffering comes from.

— *Yesterday I discovered what real observation is. It is wonderful. I smoke a lot, but only yesterday I understood what it means to experience pleasure from a cigarette. I finally figured out the mechanism that forces me to smoke. It turned out that my mind works when I smoke. Sometimes I feel bad when I smoke too much, but something insists: smoke, smoke. This happens when the mind has not finished its work. I discovered this mechanism.*

— What happens when you start to observe your reactions? You lose emotionality. It's very unusual and uncomfortable, especially for women. It's not natural for them.

There is another option. You allow yourself to experience everything. You enter the experience, and awareness comes as the result of this experience. You don't force anything. You just enter the current of feelings, and as you experience them, you receive awareness. This is a very important moment.

Why do we need awareness? Awareness, observation, and detachment are necessary to see and de-identify with the conditioned mind, which is just a collection of habits and convictions. It needs to be done while you simultaneously feeling the situation, i.e. you need to allow yourself to feel. In this case, you exit the borders of what your conditioned mind dictates to you in feelings.

You allow yourself to feel everything and to receive interesting presents of awareness, without being stuck in observation. In this case, you don't get tired of observation. You don't get bored with it. You can become a robot by making a mechanical operation out of awareness. You cannot make feeling mechanical, because it changes constantly.

Awareness as a conception may become mechanical. That's what the mind tries to do. Feelings will constantly take you to the unknown. If you follow your feelings, whether you want it or not, you will start to become aware. It will not be forced on you. It will be the result of your acquisition of experience.

I activate the knowledge you already have. You don't need to take notes. You don't need to memorize anything. This should be done when something that you don't know is being transmitted, and you are afraid of forgetting it. I tell you things that you already know. We will open blocks of memory that were closed and experience what was locked up there.

I invite you into my consciousness

— I invite you into my consciousness. Every one of us has consciousness. It is the instrument of the spirit. We are big, creating beings in search of realization. Our consciousness can enter multiple realities, worlds, and dimensions, receive certain experiences there, and expand.

I am ready to share this experience with you in an unusual way. I invite your consciousness to come as a guest into my consciousness and to discover everything you want. You can enter with any intention. Imagine me standing on the border of my consciousness. I am standing there and offering you my hand, inviting you to enter. We are going to travel together to get the answers to the questions you have.

— *How can we help the Earth. I saw people in a state of war. They were falling into a huge pit. A big cross was rising from this pit, and they were all passing through it. Water was flowing from it and washing the Earth, which was blooming.*

— *I experienced a descent into a dark abyss, and through it I entered the light. You said we had to get to the heart, and this happened through the cross. It looked like a cross-shaped glade. I fell in it and passed into another world. We were flying to the sun and entering another world through it.*

— The sun is consciousness of a solar system. A solar system is a live being. Planets, stars, and the Earth are living beings. When you exit the borders of the solar system, you can access completely different worlds. I create situations in which you receive experiences. This is a much more efficient method than simply lecturing you. This is a voyage of consciousness.

73

The conditioned mind does not participate in this process. Therefore, you can receive much more here.

— *I asked to be shown the fourth dimension, and I immediately experienced a fight within the mind, the arguments between my multiple parts. As a result, I could see my separation clearly. I was unable to get there.*

— In order to get to the fourth dimension, you need to connect the fragments of your mind that were activated. You saw your nut house. You saw what you really have.

You wanted to get to the fourth dimension, and you saw why you currently cannot get there. You need to see your part that asserts that you cannot get there. As soon as you see it, it will lose its power.

The ability to observe the conditioned mind is what is necessary here. If you observe, you know that this is only one part. It starts to melt like snow under the sun, and eventually it disappears. While observing, you understand that this is just a part of you. This is not you in your totality. This will allow you to de-identify. We are learning to use the instruments of awareness, such as your experience and observation, correctly. It is impossible for something not to lead to a result here. As soon as you announced that nothing has happened, you have crossed out a part of very important experience.

— *My heart received what it wanted.*

— Of course. The question is who you consider yourself to be. If you identify yourself with a part of the conditioned mind that says you will never be able to succeed, this is habitual for you. But if you identify with the heart, you will feel that you have received a lot by seeing the work of your conditioned mind that does not allow you to fly. I constantly appeal to the part of you that feels and knows, because that is who you are.

— *I wanted to try to get into the state of here and now and to ask questions from this state. I saw myself inside a hoop. I was rotating with it, holding it with my arm and legs. As soon as I asked another question, I was back into the hoop. Answers were coming from afar as a rustling wind, almost inaudible.*

— To hear the correct answers to the incorrect questions, you need to be very sensitive. The question "how" is the question of the mind. The mind, unable to see its own limitations, constantly asks this question. But it is precisely these limitations that do not allow it to see what is outside its habitual borders of perception.

You don't have to ask how to get up from the chair to get up from the chair. You just need to get up. To be here and now is very natural. Multiple conditionings of your mind led you to forget your natural state, and you ask this inappropriate here question "how" again. It will not lead you to the correct answer.

If I start to answer this question, I will activate your mind and it will take you away from the state of "here and now". It is very important to ask the correct question. In the process of learning, you can ask what would be the correct question to ask now. If you ask a question and understand that your question is not the correct question, this is very important in and of itself. You are ready for another question, and you ask what it should be. You have a question about the question.

— *When I approached the border of your consciousness and asked something, I heard, "Why do you ask? You know everything yourself". My mind got turned on immediately. It said I cannot know anything, and the conflict started.*

— We play a funny game here. You try to convince me that you don't know anything, while I try to convince you of the opposite.

— *I wanted to investigate your consciousness. I felt that I was submerged in a fog. I saw an old man sitting in a chair. The closer I got to him, the stronger I felt an invisible wall that I understood would be difficult for me to pass while in the form I was. I realized that I needed to get to my knees and to lower my head. I did that, and I saw something that was standing on its knees. That was my personality. It was standing with its head lowered. I easily moved through what appeared to be an impenetrable wall, and I saw an old man, a child, and a youth in the chair at once. Then, I was flying. I was totally balanced. I asked whether this was harmony. The answer came, "That's how it always was".*

— You expressed what I talk about all the time very well. What is your attitude toward what you saw and participated in? Do you consider it to be less real than what you are used to being in?

— *I don't.*

— I am constantly trying to show you the huge, infinite universe and everything that exists. Every one of us is an equal right creator there.

You are God

— Every one of us is a powerful, creative, loving being that does not have any limitations except those we have bound ourselves with. When we came here, we created limitations and chose certain roles in order to receive a particular experience we need. But at the same time, every one of us remains who he was and who he is in reality—God.

I speak to you as God to God, as a Creator to a Creator. But that limiting part of your essence that came here to receive a certain experience cannot grasp this idea. This is the conditioned mind programed to receive a dual experience.

But the time has come to exit duality and to experience who you really are. To do that, I must bypass the conditioned mind. As you can see, it is impossible to fight it. This fight can continue day after day. It will lead us nowhere.

Our work is a shock to the conditioned mind. I am not talking about leaving this reality. You need to see this reality and who you really are simultaneously. Only in this circumstance will understanding come. When you come to understand that *That* is as real as *This*, the process of our joined movement will accelerate greatly.

— *This is a miracle.*

— Yes, it is. This is a miracle, and we are a miracle. We are born for miracles, and we witness miracles all the time. We just don't notice them.

— *We entered big golden gates that were full of light. Birds were singing, and I felt that we were entering heaven. At the same time, I felt we did not need to go there, that we came to see something else. Suddenly, we descended to a platform that looked like a big sun. There were many violet essences around us.*

— The picture changed and I saw myself as a wolf howling at the moon. I was an alpha wolf, and the entire pack was nearby. You were an eagle and were flying next to me. I was running very smoothly, jumping from one mountain to another. I accelerated, jumped, and started to fly. The eagle was next to me all the time. I slowed down and landed at the edge of the precipice where I metamorphosed into a woman. The eagle landed on my shoulder and suddenly turned into a swirling energy. It started to circle around me and turned into a cocoon with me inside. I felt the vibrations of that energy. Centuries passed while I relaxed in this cocoon, but suddenly it fell to pieces and I turned into a golden road. Packs of wolves were running on this road, and I provided light for them. Then I turned into a creature that had the shape of number eight. I saw that there was no up and no down. I was completely free in the universe knowing that I was this eternity. I was moving between the stars. Some stars were moving after me. I was the Milky Way connecting people through their hearts. I gave birth to billions of stars. It was very exciting. I was participating in all of this.

— Yes. Everyone here participates in it.

— I've known about this for a long time, but I only now have started to believe in it. I am still very excited. I still shake. Somewhere deep inside my soul I know everything, but I don't trust myself enough.

— This mistrust in yourself is habitual for you now. Everything else is a result of this state. You cannot trust a man if you don't trust your inner man. You cannot trust a woman if you don't trust your inner woman. You can't trust God if you don't trust yourself. We are what everything starts with and what everything ends with.

The duality "trust—distrust" will swing you from one side to another. The Trust I am talking about is not dual. It is based on your knowing this duality and experiencing it. If I trust myself, I trust the entire universe. I trust everything that is present here, because everything here is me. Both the external and the internal are me.

— *The mind and fear work anyway: you will not be able to do it; it is only a fleeting moment. He will leave and everything is going to be business as usual.*

— Observe this. These are the ways the mind uses to fixate you in this reality. It makes you believe it is king here, while it is just a servant in one of the billions of rooms within your house. You are the owner, but the mind tries to convince you that it is the mind who is the owner here. You are the owner of this endless and limitless house, while the mind just occupies one of its rooms. Being in this room only, it cannot be in any other room, and therefore its primacy is limited by its walls. It wants to convince you that there is nothing here except this room. In this case, it becomes a king. But this is an illusion.

— *But there are moments when the mind really is the king.*

— It will be the king as long as you consider it to be the king, or in other words, until you don't see it from the side.

— *A medical intuitive once saw an essence attached to me. He told me I was feeding it. I did not believe him. Now I understand how my mind was roasting me: work and smoke, work and smoke. My body was falling apart. I felt horrible. I asked for help and tried to quit smoking. I tried everything to push this essence away, but it overpowered me.*

— The mind created this essence. Moreover, the mind is this essence. This is a hallucination of the ego. It forces you to believe in its own reality.

— *And it makes me afraid of it.*

— Please, understand that you are the real owner of the mind. When it creates something, you are the owner of this creation. You can keep the essence created by it, but you can also erase it. This essence is not something external in relationship to you; it is what your servant created.

If it is a servant that serves you, you can order it to do everything you consider to be necessary. Otherwise what kind of an owner are you if your servant does everything it wants without your permission? You need to master your mind.

— *I sense my "i" to be bigger now. I think that the Sun and the Earth are also me while I am alive.*

The creator can be anyone he wants to be

— Correct. Imagine that the creator, which every one of us happens to be, wants to create a certain universe. For him it is a common thing. He creates it, and then he wants to become someone in the universe created by him. He wants to become a tree, for example, and to live in this image for thousands of years.

The one who created the universe with billions of creatures becomes a tree just because he or she is interested in being a tree. He created this playground, came here, and he can become and experience anything he wants here.

— *I don't understand. I am not sure I can accept that.*

— The small "i" cannot accept it. It goes out of its mind and goes crazy. But the small "i" and the big "i" are two sides of one coin. I just showed you that the big "I" can become small and that the small "i" is simultaneously a big "I". Try to experience this without resistance, and you will learn that this is how it is.

— *I don't know. I feel resistance to what you are saying today. How can God, who is higher than anything, suddenly turn into a tree?*

— This is an old fairytale. When you teach a small child, you don't teach him calculus right away. You start with fairytales. As the child grows, he listens to other fairytales. I am telling you fairytales for adults, but it looks like you still want to listen to children's fairytales. You can remain in kindergarten.

Many fairytales were told to people, and they believed those tales. Those were fairytales about God who they had to worship. He could have become angry if they did not do something the right way. This was a God created by a human being in his own image.

In essence, this is a model of familial relationships common to Earth. These relationships have come to a dead-end. Contemporary upbringing is dead, but no one knows what to do with it. The old fairytales don't work anymore. I am bringing you new fairytales. You can realize them if you want to. They are for the older group. But if you prefer to live with and by the old fairytales, you can do so.

If I, for example, want to rule people, I would come and say: "I am God". I will start to show miracles. People will drop to their knees. They will accept me as God and wait for my orders. I will play this game, but at a certain point I will get bored, because I am not interested in playing with slaves. They do everything, but they are automatons. Who do you want to play with: slaves or co-creators?

— *I am interested in playing with co-creators.*

— So, become a co-creator. Feel yourself as a creator, not a mechanism who thinks like a slave.

— *It is scary.*

— A slave is always afraid of his owner not being happy with him. He is always afraid of punishment.

— *My life consists of constant suffering.*

— You confirm yourself in your own suffering and impotence. You are a habit. I am talking to a habit, to a mechanism.

— *Gee, thanks. I thought I was a human being.*

— I know that you are a human being, and I talk to you as a human being. But I am being constantly shown a mechanism. To fly, you need to take off and fly. You are holding on to a jumping foundation. So, take off and fly away. You need the foundation to push off it, not to swing on it.

— **How can I jump?**

— **In order for something to happen, you need to intend for it to happen. That's it. You don't need higher** education. You don't need books. You only need an intention to do it.

You need to say, "I am ready to do it". And everything will happen. The question "how" is not appropriate here. Everything will happen the way it should happen. If you really want it—form an intention.

The lie will not pass here. It does not have the energy. You cannot create anything based on a lie. Only a clean intention will work. You lie to each other and you lie to yourself all the time here. That will not fly here. The most important question is whether you want something or not. You are in habit of lying, saying that you want to do this or that, while in reality, you want to keep things the way they are.

What is your true intention? You can see it now. If you really want to jump, I offer you this opportunity. Imagine yourself at the edge of a cliff and tell me what you are going to do.

— *My intention was to allow my true "I" to enter. At first, I was standing at the edge of a cliff. There were honeybee combs all around me and sunlight was coming through them illuminating everything around me. I was suddenly illuminated by this light. I came down the cliff and became you. Then, I turned into a bright light. Everyone here was illuminated by this light. Suddenly, I realized that "i" already have a true "I". I don't have to prove anything to anyone, and if I want something, let it be so. I don't need to ask anyone for anything. Everything will be done instantly the way I need it to be done.*

— We have unlimited opportunities. We can create anything we want.

— *We need to allow ourselves to feel it.*

— That's right. We already have it, and we happened to be it. This reality is very inert. We transform and embody our thoughts and feelings into the physical objects and situations. Everything that exists here is created by the thoughts and feelings of people. Our creation is limited by the physical constraint of a given system of coordinates and linear nature of time. Over there, our thoughts and feelings instantly turn into reality.

— *Something gets lost when we verbalize our thoughts and feelings.*

— You speak only to feel that here you happen to be who you are there. You announce yourself as God here. That's the basic thing. This is not a question of transferring information, because everyone knows everything. We just remind each other about it. We need to recall who we are and to help others to recall who they are.

Recall who you really are

— *I was standing on the edge of a cliff thinking that I can only jump up. I pushed off slightly, and I was airborne. That was a fantastic body dance. I flew with the clouds and energies.*

— You jump into your own creation. You don't have anything to fear. Feel yourself as God.

— *During childhood we lived with our feelings and sensations. Afterwards, we pushed our feelings down. During the last three days that you were here, my Soul felt good. I want this music of the heart to be constantly with me.*

— Whatever you want will happen. The question is whether you understand what you want or not. As you can see, most people choose to suffer, experience pain, jealousy, etc. We are the creators, and we get whatever we want. Your word is law. Your intention is always realized. So, you can't blame anyone.

When you become depressed or jealous again, or experience a similarly negative feeling, ask yourself, "Do I want this?" When you come to understand that you've had enough of it, you will be able to receive a different state immediately, without any psychotherapist's or guru's help. Perceive each other as creators, big godly beings.

— *Only now comes the understanding that I can allow myself any manifestation. I am happy because I allow myself to hear and see everything I have inside. My husband listened to me very closely yesterday.*

— *My husband is different.*

— If he is a computer programmer who sits in front of a computer day and night, that is one thing. But if you can see Christ's consciousness in him, that is a completely different thing.

— *He only perceives me as the mother of his kids and a sexual partner.*

— He perceives you as you want him to perceive you.

— *Are you saying he perceives me as I perceive myself?*

— Yes. All your questions should be directed to yourself.

— *His constantly reprimands me, "How long are you going to live based on your feelings? When will you return to Earth?"*

— Who claims what and from whom? All your questions are to yourself. We are approaching a very important moment—the masculine and feminine parts inside us.

Who is your inner man and who is your inner woman? The external men and women who surround you reflect your inner man and your inner woman. You need to start seeing that everything that surrounds you reflects the internal aspects of your inner men and women. God's Mother has many faces, but all these faces are one of God's Mother.

Every woman that lives on the face of the Earth represents one of many faces of God's Mother. Every man is one of many faces of Christ. Who do we see when we look at a woman: a housekeeper, a daughter, a lover, a wife, or God's Mother? And who do we see when we look at a man? That's the question.

What we actually want can be called God's kingdom on Earth, and it is connected to totally different relationships. These relationships are built not on separation and the physical distribution of roles, but on the understanding of the wholeness and individual peculiarities of every one of us.

Changes and the transformation of your personality lead to the appearance of new relationships. If you don't change your relationships, while talking about your own changes, you look like someone who sits on two chairs that move under him in different directions. In this case, you will experience separation between our meetings and life, between ideas and your actions. That will be manifested as disequilibrium, separation, and conflicts.

— I just felt that I am the owner of my inner world. I can instantly change my states on my own. Observing what happens to me, I can do it without any inner dependency. I want and I change.

— Yes. You can do it without any techniques or systems. You intend, and this happens. Your intent is the only thing you need. Your intention expressed in your word is law. Previously, you did not understand what you were creating, and, as a result, you were afraid of your own words. You tried to find a guru who would tell you what to do or to read a smart book.

— Sitting with my eyes closed, I realized I can paint anything I want. I have the power.

— Yes. Become a painter of your own life. Create not on the canvas, but directly within this reality. That's how a true creator creates.

— We just don't trust ourselves. We thought up a certain reality, and we wait for it to come.

— You are waiting for permission. You don't need to do that. However, you need to meet with the program of your personality and get to know it. Do not become identified with this program. You will not be able to eradicate it until you become fully aware of it.

What prevents you from opening up?

— If we came here to understand something about ourselves and others, then we need to open up, or at least start to investigate what is preventing us from attaining this understanding. Otherwise, our presence here is meaningless. What prevents you from opening up?

— *Have you written your book based on your interactions with people?*

— Yes, all my books are written based on my seminars. I don't invent anything. I am only interested in live interchange of thoughts, feelings, and energies. Communication is such an exchange.

— *We came to you with an open Soul.*

— In order to feel with a Soul, you have to start feeling deeply. This is the main problem for a human being. I can tell you that I rarely encounter a human being who can feel deeply. The emotional centers of most people are blocked.

— *Why do you make everyone feel guilty? If most people cannot feel, they are unhappy. And on top of it, you make them feel guilty.*

— Everyone sees and hears what he wants to see and hear. There are as many visions of what I discuss here as people here. Who does your opinion relate to when you offer it to us? Does it relate to you or to me? Who can we even talk about but ourselves? We forget about it, and we think that we talk about someone else. We don't want to see that everything we say is related to us. Meanwhile, we fight those who, as it appears to us, accuse us, fool us, or scare us. If you don't have fear, nothing will scare you. If you don't have guilt, no one will be able to accuse you of anything.

— *But everyone here has everything you have mentioned.*

— Many do. Can we get rid of it? That's one of the most important questions. Fear manifests itself in multiple forms, which later lead to conflicts, aggression, wars, and diseases.

This is probably a generic question everyone has: what is the reason for fear and how can one get rid of it? It is fear that gives birth to everything negative, difficult, and horrible in life here. Conflicts, misunderstanding, and loneliness are the result of fear.

There are many of us here, and I want everyone to leave with the gift of awareness. In order to do that, we need to find something that is important and exciting for everyone.

— *I think fear interests everyone here.*

— Please, pay attention to the way you formulated your sentence. You said that fear interests everyone. Based on this, I can conclude that you are interested in horror movies. **You form the state you happen to be in as you speak, the way you speak. Your thought determines your state.**

— *So, how can we get rid of thoughts?*

— Why do you need to get rid of thoughts? If you happen to get a bad chair, it does not mean you need to get rid of all the chairs. You just need to get a good one. Perhaps you need to learn to think right.

You cannot formulate what you want. You don't feel it. Something strange happens inside you. Perhaps the time has come to figure out what is going on there. But how can you do this if you don't speak up, if you are not sincere?

— *It is probably fear that does not allow me to open my mouth.*

— Then, you at least need to say that you are afraid. To feel love and fullness of life, you just need to remove what interferes with it. Originally, everyone has everything. In reality, I cannot tell you anything new, because you know everything. You just forgot it. The reason for this forgetfulness is in the personal mechanisms that do not allow you to feel that you happen to be in love and understanding the same way you happen to be in fear. Therefore, you don't need to talk about it. The only thing that is necessary is to remove what prevents you from seeing all of this.

— *Why do you think you are always right? Why don't you ask what others think? They might think otherwise.*

— If I were to ask others for their opinion, I would not be sitting here. I don't give a damn about others' opinions, in particular yours.

— *I understand.*

— And what do you feel now?

— *I think I am trying to explain something to you, but you don't give a damn about it. I feel bad.*

— Do you feel or do you think? Do you have anything except your opinions? I insulted your opinion. Do you have anything else in you, or are you only your opinions?

— *I have feelings.*

— What kind of feeling do you feel toward me now?

— *I think, "God give me patience".*

— You think, while I feel, and as a result, I do exactly what needs to be done.

— *And what do you feel?*

— I feel love toward you.

— *Love can be expressed differently. Your way of manifesting it is quite strange. You don't pity me at all.*

— Why should I pity you? I don't see pitiful people here. I see strong, beautiful people here. Why should I humiliate them with pity? I don't have pity, but I do have love.

— *One should have some pity.*

— What for? What did pity give you in life?

— *Nothing. I work in a hospital, and it appears to me I should manifest it toward people that come there.*

— How does a human being feel when you pity him? **What is pity?** The feeling of pity appears when you think that everything should be otherwise, while things are the way they are. So, you are not satisfied with what is. Will you pity someone who is satisfied with what is?

— *I am talking about a situation when one is in pain.*

— Okay. You are not satisfied that he is in pain. Do you know why he is in pain? He is in pain because he does not like what is. A disease appears as a result. **Disease is a consequence of unacceptance of life, oneself, or others the way they are. Pity is the essence of unacceptance.** So, take a closer look at pity.

— *When people are pitying you, you want to stay sick.*

— Yes. And that can bring you to your grave. What does pity give you? Can pity empower you? Does it make you stronger or more balanced? Look at how you hold on to pain and suffering. In reality, it is very difficult to part with these states.

People come saying they want love, happiness, and understanding, but when it comes to work, they hold on to their fear with a deadly grip. I am not a philosopher; I am a practical man. I do what is necessary for you to see the situation you happen to be in now.

I don't provide definitions. I don't need them. I work. If I am a surgeon and my patient is about to die, I am not going to say anything—I am going to operate. If you are a scholar, you are going to talk to this patient about his disease on his death bed. So, who should a surgeon be: a scholar or a practical man?

— *He should be a practical man, and I need one.*

— Then, what is wrong? You came to one. I practice spiritual surgery.

— *Your surgery maims.*

— If this is so, why are you still here? You had time to see and to figure out who I am. I offer everyone who is not satisfied with me or my methods an opportunity to leave now. Don't waste your time. Do it now.

The biggest con

— Does anyone want to share his or her feelings about what is happening now?

— *I am happy.*

— I was not happy, and I experienced fear. I was afraid something bad would happen. I sensed tension.

— You expected to have a good meeting, and you think if someone leaves, the meeting is bad. In order to have a soccer game, a soccer team should have twelve players, not thirty. If thirty people jump onto a field, it is not going to be a soccer game. For the necessary work to be done, we need those who need to be here—we need a team.

— I used to insult people without experiencing a feeling of guilt. I look at you, and I like how you do it.

— I will ask you to discern between cruelty and pitilessness. A human being who pities others, i.e. himself, moves toward another extreme—toward cruelty. When you start to observe, you will see that people who pity themselves manifest themselves as very cruel. Pity transforms into cruelty. I am talking about pitilessness not in terms of cruelty, but in terms of the absence of pity. This is an important distinction.

— I feel very good. I feel that the tension, connected to some people leaving, dropped.

— Tension or excitation is not something bad. "Bad" and "good" are appraisals of the mind. If you need to make a jump, and you are in a sluggish state, you will not be able to do it. A sportsman, an actor, or anyone who does something important, is always tense.

— It was probably fear, not tension.

— Fear also can be transformed.

— *I feel satisfied by your dialogues, and I think that people who gathered here are quite adventurous.*

— Self-investigation is the riskiest game one can play here. If you want to get into the riskiest gamble of this reality, choose self-investigation. Otherwise, you will not learn anything. You can stuff yourself with other people's thoughts and notions, but it will have nothing to do with self-investigation. One can only conduct self-investigation through oneself. I can create an opportunity for it, but you need to do it yourself. To do it, you need to wish to do it and to do it. Otherwise, you are not going to succeed.

— *I felt uncomfortable, and I want to free myself from this feeling by speaking up. When I arrived, I felt a strong resentment toward everyone who I thought did not belong to our group. I was scared. I wanted to become invisible. I was completely overwhelmed by fear. I have a feeling that with age my fear grows, while I want to be smaller and smaller. I want to learn how to feel love for everyone around me, and to get rid of this small, scared snail inside that prevents me from doing it. I don't evolve because of this fear. I am closed up, and I am self-destructing. This resentment of people appears because of the fear of not being understood. I would like to transform this feeling and to ask everyone for forgiveness.*

— What do you want them to forgive you for?

— *I want them to forgive me for sending these impulses.*

— Who is asking for forgiveness? It is the one who feels guilty who asks for forgiveness. Everything that happens in this world happens the way it should happen. If someone wants to insult, he will find the one who wants to be insulted. If one wants to oppress another, he will find a victim. People do not

94

find each other coincidentally. Nothing here happens coincidentally. Therefore, everyone who receives something receives what he wants. If someone is sulking or finds himself in the role of a victim, he was looking for an oppressor.

— *But I don't want to be an aggressor.*

— Whether you want it or not—you played that role. Now you can simply see what you did in that role. By de-identifying with this role, you will be able to see it from the side. Why did you experience guilt? If you understand that everyone here searches and then finds what he is looking for, then what does guilt have to do with it? Every one of you experienced what he wanted to experience.

— *I did not want to experience this state.*

— You did not want to see your state, but you wanted to do what you did, and you did it. Accept responsibility for what you do. Otherwise, you are going to experience guilt eternally. There were a couple of people here who wanted to take offense, and I played the role of an offender for them, being aware of what I do.

— *How is that possible?*

— "How" is a question of the mind. I am talking about your feelings now. Neither I nor anybody else will be able to explain anything to you regarding feelings if you don't feel yourself. Can you answer the question "How do you love me?" No. You love. That's it.

If your emotional center is shut off, you will never understand it. There are many books about making love, but they all miss the important part—love. They describe

95

techniques instead of love. People know nothing but techniques, and they are interested in techniques only. Your question is analogous to this.

— *If I were to feel it, I would find a way to explain it.*

— The main thing is not to get to know the answer to the question "how", but to allow yourself to feel. Your mind forbade your heart to feel, and, therefore, it asks the same questions again and again: "how, in what way, how much, etc."

It is difficult to reject an idea upon which your salary depends

— *In certain situations, feelings can stand in the way of work and career.*

— Yes. It is difficult to reject an idea upon which your salary depends. You need to choose what's important for you.

— *It is my salary, of course.*

— Then, you are going to feel bad here.

— *Those are two totally different things.*

— No. This is exactly the impossible thing that people try to do here. They try to sit on two chairs that move in opposite directions under them. That's why it is better to say right away, "Yes, this is what is important for me, and I am ready to pay for it with fear, pain, and jealousy in exchange for money—the surrogate of respect, etc."

I am not insisting on anything here, but I can be straight forward in my prediction of what is going to happen. You will not be able to combine all these things. You will only wind up with a serious inner conflict.

— *One can always combine a pleasant thing with a useful thing.*

— What we are dealing with here is different.

— *I am talking about my boss who may react inadequately to my feelings.*

— You have such a boss because of who you are now. Everyone has what he wants.

— *Do I appoint my bosses?*

— You attract your bosses, and they are attract you. If you believe that you should not feel, you will get a boss who will forbid you to feel. You will have an opportunity to delegate to him and say that he is the boss that pays you money; you depend on him, and, therefore, you should not feel. You will find justifications.

People learned to justify very well. I will be showing you how you do it. If you really want to allow yourself to feel, your life situations and your environment will start to change.

— *The material goods also have their weight in this world.*

— The spiritual and the material are two sides of one coin. You are trying to impose your point of view on me, as if I consider that the spiritual is more important than the material. Those are two sides of the same coin, but you choose one side—the material—and get stuck in it. You can protest and resist now, or you may not want to deal with it now. I will not argue with you.

97

— *I have my point of view, and I express it.*

— And how do you like living with your point of view?

— *I live well.*

— Then what are you doing here?

— *Perhaps I want to find who I am through you.*

— What if I were to say that in order for you to find who you are, you need to get in touch with what you don't like?

— *Okay, let's do it.*

— Do you think it is that easy? You were just resisting it. What are you afraid to lose more than anything?

— *I am afraid of losing my job.*

— Are you ready to lose your job in order to understand yourself?

— *No.*

— That means you are not ready to understand yourself.

— *Perhaps you are right.*

— Take a look at how easily you refuse. What are you so afraid of? What does your work give you? If you love to work, I am going to provide you with work for the rest of your life. What do you need: work or salary? Try to be more specific.

— *Work and salary are the same for me.*

— But those are two different things. Look at the mess you have in your head. You say that you want to work, but in reality, you need the money. Let's dig further. What do you need the money for?

— *I need the money to provide for myself and for my family. I need to feed my kids. I want to buy a big screen TV.*

— So, you don't need the money. You need food, and a big screen TV set.

— *I need a big car. I need a Jeep.*

— And why?

— *I need it for prestige.*

— Aha. You need prestige. Look. We started with work, but it turns out you need prestige. If we go further, we'll find out why you need a TV.

— *It's my ego that wants something.*

— I am not against your ego. I am just sorting out what we have, and those who are interested start to sort it out too. This is self-understanding. We can continue if you want to and get down to more interesting stuff.

— *He is not calm and self-assured enough.*

— Where would calmness and self-assuredness come from if he badly needs work, but he is not sure he is going to have it? He depends on his boss, who depends on another boss, who in turn depends on the country's economic situation, which in turn depends on the world economy, etc. You will never be calm, right?

— *Yes, one cannot be calm here.*

— Then let's not build an illusion in this regard. You pay for it with your anxiety, and it will be eternal. Do you understand that you are not going to be free of it unless you part with what you are so afraid of losing? You need to pay for everything here. This is the payment you pay to have what you want to have.

CHAPTER 3

BY CHANGING YOURSELF, YOU CHANGE THE CONSCIOUSNESS OF HUMANITY

•◆•●•◆•●•◆•●•◆•●•◆•●•◆•●•◆•●•◆•●•◆•●•◆•●•◆•●•◆•●•◆•●•

Dosin once asked his teacher, the third patriarch of Zen Buddhism, Sosan:

— Please, show me the way of liberation.

— Who enslaved you and when?

— No one enslaved me.

— If that's the case, — the teacher said, — why are you searching for liberation?

Fear—the road to love

— Take a look at how strongly you hold on to your work. In reality, you hold on to money, status, etc. But you pay a big price for it. When you start to see both the positive and the negative sides of your work, the scale will start to get balanced. This will allow you to step away from the situation. But you cannot do that if you are afraid or want something in connection with it. Those are the chains that bound you.

A human being is tied to many things. He is crucified here. How can he be in a good mood? How can he understand anything? A man cannot be in a good mood or understand anything while in such a state, but he refuses to see his chains and creates multiple illusions in order not to see them. Some people come to the seminar just to become upset and leave. They receive what they want to receive.

How far do you want to travel on the road of self-awareness? Which mirror will you see yourself in? Will you run away from it or accept what you see? You will see your entire self in the last mirror, as if on an X-ray. If you manage to pass through this experience, you will exit to a fourth dimension, whole and enlightened. You will have to encounter many mirrors before you get there.

Some people bolt and run away after they encounter their first mirror. Which mirror are you ready to meet? I create opportunities for people to pass through multiple mirrors in an accelerated pace, but this makes sense only for those who want to get to know themselves. My task is to show you your mirrors. Your task is to see yourself in these mirrors and to pass through them. Nothing is guaranteed here. Everything depends on you.

Your ability to pass through these mirrors will depend on the strength of your inquiry, on your longing born out of an understanding that you can no longer live the way you have been living. If you are comfortably living in a nice house and come here to receive new information, you don't have an inquiry. If you are stressed out, experience difficulties, but are not succumbing to depression, then come here to figure things out— you have an inquiry.

I am interested because I am the same way myself. I will work with you for as long as necessary. We will travel together. When one member of a team of mountain climbers falls, other climbers pull him up. You must be selective here. You cannot go on those trips with just anyone. My seminars are not nice lectures you can listen to and go home afterwards. People who are interested in this work will work together for a long time in different cities. This work may lead to powerful results. Everything depends on our intention and our team.

— *Fear is a feeling, and love is a feeling. We experience both. Why is it more difficult for us to feel love? What prevents us from feeling love?*

— In order to feel love, you need to pass through many fears. The most common reaction to fear is to run away. That will not work here. You need to enter your fears.

If you feel jealousy, enter it and experience it completely. It will be transformed. When you thoroughly live through a certain feeling and exhaust it, it transforms. A feeling is energy. It does not disappear. It transforms and turns into something else.

You need to see what is in you. You have many fears. You need to face them and say, "Yes. I see what is in me the way it really is, and my power is in my seeing it. I am ready to meet my fears, experience, and transform them." As you pass through your fears, you become stronger and stronger. As you pass through your fears, you take their power. But it is useless to philosophize about it, it must be experienced.

— *This is very difficult.*

— Who told you it is going to be easy? Is it difficult to get an Olympic medal?

— *Yes.*

— Our work is much more difficult than winning a medal. Everything will happen when you are ready. You are going to set an assignment for yourself, and you are going to solve it yourself. If you set it up, you will solve it. That's for sure. Then, you are going to set up another assignment. You will solve it also. If there is an assignment, it means it is in your power to solve it. This is not going to be easy, but you will be able to do that.

Determine your first step. Every journey starts with the first step. What is at stake? Something that is larger than survival is at stake here. You need to be possessed to be on this road. You need to feel the powers inside you. How strong is the group of your parts that wants love, awareness, and new life? Perhaps it is very weak. Tell me please, what is the positioning of powers within you? What percentage of your parts wants these changes?

— *In my case, it is fifty to fifty.*

— *In my case, it is less than that.*

— Observe the parts that resist now and become aware of them. Listen to their arguments. That will allow you to shift the balance towards the powers that want change.

— *I trust people easily. It seems to me; I am completely for it.*

— What does an excessive trust lead to?

— *Does it lead to conflicts?*

— It leads to excessive distrust. How does your distrustful side manifest itself?

— *I avoid getting into situations in which I might be manipulated. I limit my circle of communication.*

— So, take a look. On the surface, you are trustful. But we start to dig, and it turns out that you are equally distrustful.

If you were in the aware state throughout today's meeting, you should have tracked down those opposing and resisting thoughts and feelings that appeared in you in relationship to me. Can you verbalize the arguments your mind came up with? You cannot do anything about it if you don't see it. This is self-investigation.

How can you manage your inner world if you don't know who and what is there? Your inner world is a big and complicated organization. Can you be the president of an organization if you don't know your employees? When a president decides to proceed with reorganization, he needs to become familiar with the opinions of the people who work for him. Otherwise, he can encounter resistance that may destroy everything.

— *I am afraid that you will give me an assignment that I will not be able to perform.*

— You are demonstrating your part that wants to sit in a corner, far away from what is happening here. This part is afraid of doing anything on its own. Look at the results of your self-investigation. You cannot dig it out of the books. You can obtain something here only by digging deep inside yourself. We are reviewing the golden grains of self-knowledge here. We are not interested in the abstract ideas.

— *I, on the other hand, am very impatient. I want to do something to see myself in different manifestations.*

— We are talking about the parts that resist.

— *I feel stuck. In observing you, I kept thinking whether or not you feel what you say.*

I am your screen. Project onto it.

— Please, be frank and tell us about the thoughts related to my callousness that appeared in your head. You must be direct and honest here. I clearly see all the mechanisms and understand that I serve as a screen to which everything you have inside will be projected, especially things of which you are not aware. I am now trying to bring it up on the screen of your consciousness.

It will be easier for you to talk about me, because you experience it toward me, forgetting about the fact that it is yours. To become aware of the thoughts and feelings that appear in you is the highest level; in this state, you don't need to verbalize anything. A thought appeared, and you immediately became aware of it. But you must come to this, and it can only be done by speaking through and projecting what is in you onto someone else, in our case— onto me. During this process, I will return your thoughts

and feelings to you. You verbalize them in relationship to me, while I remind you that they are yours. Once you understand this, transformation will occur.

This is the principle of the mirrors the use of which you can develop awareness. If you are interested in me, you will not make any useful conclusions about yourself. What we do here is not about me. It's about you. I am not here to show you how smart and enlightened I am. I am here to help you figure out who you are. Tell me anything you want. Openly speak about your grudges and dissatisfactions with me. Bring up every thought and feeling that you experience during our meetings. That's the only way to receive a profit of awareness.

— *I am irritated by your hysterical laughter.*

— Does it mean I am a hysterical man?

— *No, that means I am a hysterical man.*

— Continue to develop my image.

— *I saw that you do it on purpose. You want to educate us.*

— Describe what you did not like.

— *You are pitiless. You sit there thinking that you can do anything you want to us. We are guinea pigs for you.*

— You have a difficult time talking because of the resistance. Where is it coming from? If you continue to look back at me and other people, deciding what is good and what is bad, there is not going to be any self-investigation.

My behavior serves a particular purpose. I can do anything I want, depending on the situation. I am not bound by techniques. I am not bound by methods. I always feel what I need to do next. I rely on my feelings. We have everything inside us. What we don't see inside us controls us. If I know that I can get hysterical, that is one thing. If I don't know that I can get hysterical, I will throw tantrums and roll my eyes; I will not even hear what people say about my hysteric behavior, because I don't see it.

Let's say you are afraid of something. Does *this something* leave you when you are afraid of it?

— *Yes, if I know what I am afraid of, it leaves me.*

— Okay. What are you afraid of?

— *I am afraid to lose my family.*

— What happens as the result of your fear?

— *Those thoughts of mine are eating at me.*

— You are constantly losing what you are afraid of losing. As soon as you start to entertain a thought that you are afraid to lose your man, you have lost him. This reality is created by thoughts. A thought appears, and the realization follows. As soon as you become afraid of losing someone, you have created the situation you are afraid of.

— *Do I create it in my thoughts?*

— You create it in your thoughts and in reality.

— *In the future?*

— In the present. As soon as you thought of losing your man, you have lost him. A coward dies a thousand times, because as soon as the thought "I am afraid of death" appears in him, he dies. Since a coward is afraid all the time, he dies all

108

the time. It is very important for all of you to understand this. That's how life and fate are created. That's how this reality is built.

— *When one starts to understand that this is the way this reality operates, one starts to resist it. But there is nothing we can do about it.*

— The more you resist something, the more you strengthen it. You have all tried to fight your fears. What have you achieved? We would not be talking about this right now if that approach worked. It does not work. Moreover, it works in the opposite way.

The more you resist or fight against something so-called negative, the stronger it becomes. If you understand what I am talking about, then you understand a lot. But to understand this.

What is the difference between a lecture and practical work? I can tell you about galaxies. I can tell you how they have been created. What is the use of that? The important thing is what you feel, what you experience. I talk only about things I have experienced. This is the way it is, because I lived through it. What you have not lived through yourself is just a piece of information that will be forgotten tomorrow.

To experience something, you must allow yourself to experience it. To allow yourself to experience something that you don't want to experience, you need to have a very strong intention of doing it, and to understand why you do it.

— *I was afraid you would ask me to do something. The unknown frightens me.*

— You are scared to act. You are not afraid of the unknown. You are afraid to do something you need to do. You need to jump. It is your turn to jump. Theoretically, everyone here is ready to jump, but you are afraid. This is the fear of action.

— *I am irritated by you talking about the fear of unknown. You escalate this fear.*

— Are you afraid of the unknown? How can you be afraid of something you don't know? The mind provides you with the formula, "I am afraid of the unknown," but there is nothing to be afraid of, since you don't know what is there. Fear appears in the mechanical parts which must change yet don't want to change.

The source of fear is in the resistance of the mechanical parts that don't want to change. Look how sly this is. A human being says that he is afraid, and he doesn't even attempt to figure out what is behind his fear. I am going to try to access those parts of you now.

— *I saw my fear. I was afraid to approach a man during the last assignment. I am not in the habit of approaching strangers. So, I just sat here.*

— Yes. It is habitual for you to sit. Your fear is an expression of the resistance of the part that is in the habit of sitting. Look how easy that is. What are you afraid of here? A part of you creates an illusion that you would be scared if you were to approach someone. How does the part we just uncovered feel?

— *I don't know. I need to think.*

— No. You don't need to think. You need to become aware. As soon as you become aware of something, your feelings for example, it transforms. If you are not aware of it, it becomes fixed and stands as a lump in your throat. Permanence is an illusion that falls apart when you start to become aware, i.e. when you start to see what happens inside of you. Have any one of you tracked down the changes in his feelings toward me today?

— *When I saw some of the participants living today, I felt indifferent.*

— What do you usually experience in situations like that?

— *I usually try to understand and to prevent people from leaving.*

— I asked about feelings.

— *Regret? I would normally blame myself for callousness.*

— Is blame a mental construct or a feeling?

— *I did not feel anything. I only had some thoughts.*

— What did you feel when people were leaving the room?

— *Regret.*

— *Anger.*

— *Pity.*

— *Unhappiness.*

— *I experienced regret and disdain that they did not pass the test.*

— Look, every feeling you have mentioned is negative. Have you experienced any other feeling?

— *I experienced satisfaction. Our group is small, and we are close to each other.*

— A human being can experience a number of feelings in one situation, but you tend to experience negative feelings.

— *It is a habit.*

— Yes. Look at how you narrow the experience of your life. This is the mechanical existence I discuss all the time. It narrows life down. It deprives it of fullness. It is two dimensional.

What is the difference between a three-dimensional object and its two-dimensional projection? Most people prefer to live in the two-dimensional projection. They choose something, and they say that this life is the Truth. They deny the rest.

They choose one slice and they say, "This is me." But this is not them. This is just one projection of many. We live our lives thinking that it cannot be lived any other way. To find these other ways, you need to release the old, small, and flat projection of yourself. But it resists.

So, how can you release this small projection? You can do something unusual and track down the reactions of resistance that appear in you. When you see these reactions, nothing will interfere with your other planes shining. You will see an amazing emerald. For this to happen, you need to see your resistance. It will leave, and you will have everything.

— *As soon as you asked me to look inside myself, I immediately felt the resistance. My mind refuses to think about anything.*

— The mind blocks your attempts to redirect your attention inside. Your old habits are very powerful. They can even turn off your senses: vision, hearing, etc. These old habits can lead to chronic diseases. They can turn off the normal physiologic functioning of your organs. They take over your inner world completely.

What about me irritates you?

— What about me irritates you?

— *Nothing.*

— Okay. What about me do you like?

— *I like your openness and your knowledge.*

— What about me do you think irritates him? What about me does not he like?

— *Whatever he listed as positive irritates him.*

— **What we like about people is what we also dislike about them. We love people for the same reasons we hate them. I am interested in the basic question: how is this reality made? Self-investigation provides us with the understanding of the laws of the organization of this reality. I can predict any reaction, because I know what works here and how it works.**

— *I like your confidence. I like that you don't get upset and don't hold grudges. You have your own way, and you follow it.*

— You like my confidence, but this is not the usual confidence that is based on defending one's point of view. I don't have a fixed point of view, and you don't understand where my confidence is coming from. For you, the man who is confident in himself is a strong man, and you want to find the source of his power. Power is energy. Am I right? What about

113

feeling? Feeling is also energy. What about confidence? Is it a thought or a feeling?

— *It is probably a feeling.*

— So, the source of power is in feeling, not in a point of view, which happens to be a mental construct. So, where is the source of power?

— *It is in feelings. It is a certain mood: I am strong; I am sure of myself.*

— You are trying to get to the source by using the wrong key. Mood and affirmations also represent mental constructs. It turns out that power is in confidence, and confidence is feeling. What do we do with feelings?

— *We have to be open. We should not suppress them.*

— So, the secret is in the feelings. But we do not know this sphere at all. We have some ideas what thoughts are, but what feelings are is not clear at all. A human being has at least three spheres: mental, emotional, and physical. These three spheres represent different powers. Which one do you like?

— *I like all three.*

— To meet an equal representation of these three spheres in one human being is quite rare, because a human being is divided. The goal of self-investigation is to connect these three bodies—mental, emotional, and physical—in ourselves. This is not easy to do, but if you accomplish this, you will connect with your spiritual body.

A human being prefers to do what he is used to doing. If he is in the habit of thinking, he is constantly strengthening his mental body—other two remain weak. If he is in the habit of living based upon his feelings, he trains his emotional body only. We, on the other hand, need all three of these spheres. Can you share with us which center you emphasize, and which center you ignore?

— *I am an intellectual type.*

— *I think it is my emotional center that is well-developed.*

— And what are women going to say?

— *Emotional.*

— You forgot about the physical body which has its own needs. Do you allow your physical body to satisfy itself?

Judgment—action of the conditioned mind

— **We are bringing to the surface the old notions that determine the life we are bored to death with. In order to do that, we need to dramatize them. Only then will they declare themselves. If you just sit here, you will leave this place in exactly the same state in which you arrived. We need situations that would allow your personal programs to manifest themselves. That will allow you to see them.**

If you want to receive something here, we need honesty and action. Our old programs are similar. By observing the manifestations of others, you will be able to understand your own manifestations.

What are we running away from? What are we afraid of? We run away and we are afraid of the very things, that in reality, we want more than anything. We bring up multiple explanations regarding why we should not do what we want to do. This stereotype creates our life. It is not something episodic. It occurs all the time. Our life is built on it. That's why we run away from something we want more than anything.

— *What if they don't understand us right?*

— Will someone judge you if you hug any one of these men now?

— *No, not here. Nobody will judge me here.*

— You will be accused, judged, and condemned by the conditioned minds of people who are present here, because this mechanism can only judge. It cannot do anything else. You will be told that this is an unacceptable societal behavior. Who wants to tell us how such behavior is usually judged?

— *I usually judge for something I am afraid others would judge me for.*

— It is not people who judge other human beings, a human being judges himself. People don't see anything but themselves, and because they happen to be in hell, they don't see anything but the hell they are in. This is a very interesting situation.

You think everyone thinks about you, but this in not so. Everyone is preoccupied with his own problems. When someone sees a problem in you, it is his own problem, not yours. Therefore, he speaks about himself, not about you.

— *This is jail! Everything is in me. I am forced to experience these emotions.*

— This is a very interesting jail: everything is inside you, and there are no jailers. As soon as you think you can receive pleasure, someone appears and asks, "Are you a whore?" Everyone here blames himself in his own specific way by using his own derogatory terms. And that's it. You are back in hell.

Everyone is sitting in his own garbage bin, but if someone wants to get out, others scream, "Don't make waves!"

How is the prohibition on intimate relationships built in your case? Can you approach someone, hug him, and say, "I love you?"

— *The prohibition is manifested as fear: how will they perceive my actions?*

— *You are creating an artificial situation.*

— Look, this is a defense. You just need to do it. You cannot investigate something if you forbid yourself to do it. You will sit here, boiling in your own juice. The fear of intimacy appears because of the mix up with sex. This is just a mechanism. Unless we sort it out, we will be stuck in it. Intimate relationships provide us with pleasure, but they can also lead to remorse and heavy responsibilities.

— *My prohibition on sex manifests itself as fear of responsibility.*

— **You came and you hugged another human being. What kind of responsibility is there? Why should you experience sexual feelings while doing this? You can experience sexual attraction or not. The initial impulse comes from the heart. You can decide whether you want to turn on the sexual center or not later on.**

117

— I hugged one, another, and the third one, and a feeling of fullness appeared. It's enough.

— A human being lives in a city, surrounded by exhaust fumes. One day he goes to the country side, takes a deep breath of fresh air, and says, "I had enough. I need to go back."

— I am afraid to approach anyone here, because of my fear of rejection.

— You can free yourself from something only if you see it. You can see only if you act, if you do what you usually forbid yourself from doing.

To start living, you need to die. Most people neither live nor die. To be reborn, you need to die.

Heroes, killed by the enemy in many Russian fairy tales, are brought back to life with the help of two different kinds of water. First, they are sprinkled with dead water, to make them dead. Then, they are sprinkled with the life water. That brings them back to life. All the mechanisms that block your ability to live must die. Otherwise you will neither live nor die. This is the worst state of affairs, but a human being can get used to anything. What is one man's horror is another man's norm. He will tell you he has lived like that his entire life, and he feels great. He is sick, but he got used to it, and for him it is normal. If you don't understand what it means to die, you will not come to understand what it means to live.

Pain is the consequence of your resistance to changes

— Take a look at what happens when your personal mechanism is held up to light. Observe your reactions. I showed you the mechanism that creates hell inside a human being. Can you see how you defend your own hell? You don't run to the doors of the jail to get out. No, you reinforce the doors of your jail. That's how those mechanisms work in every one of you.

The minds of most people are filled with similar mechanisms. Their fate and life consist of these dual games. When a dentist pulls out your tooth, you feel pain. However, a few hours later you start to feel better. Do you want to continue to experience this pain, or do you want to get rid of it? If you continue this run and hide game, you will continue to be in pain. Face this pain, become aware of it, and walk out of it.

We were taught to avoid pain and negative thoughts. If we continue to do that, we will not be able to understand anything, because pain carries very important information. Pain appears and continues because we are not using the information it contains. We need to enter our pain.

Why are you in pain? Any pain—physical, emotional, or mental—is always the result of resistance to change. Life consists of constant change. But the ego does not want to experience change; it resists. It creates the illusion of constancy and stability. The ego creates the illusion that you are constant and that everything around you is unchangeable. But that is not true. Life constantly changes.

Pain and suffering appear as the result of our resistance to change, i.e. our resistance to life. We need to get in touch with our pain, to enter it encounter the negative, horrible thoughts and feelings we harbor inside, and allow them to open themselves up. If you resist that, you experience pain.

Resistance leads to pain. You can talk endlessly to a man, and he will not understand anything until he decides to get rid of this pain himself. I know there is a lot of pain in each one of you.

As you can see, it is not easy to acknowledge the presence of painful experiences. You must take this first step. The next step is to become aware of them. If it is difficult for you to accept mother in a woman, then you have difficulties with motherhood. The same can be said about accepting father in a man. Pain and hatred toward any one of them is connected to the lack of understanding. To investigate what is buried in pain, you first must accept pain as a fact of life.

A wife's inability to accept her husband or a husband's inability to accept his wife indicates a problem with those roles, connected either to the responsibility for the kids or other familial responsibilities. Problems between lovers point toward sexual problems. Daughter or son represents care for children, upbringing, wisdom, etc. Brother, sister—relationships with equals. Brother with brother—relationship between men. Brother with sister—relationship between a man and a woman. Sister with sister—relationships between women. So, look at what you have. This is not an abstract painting. This is your life.

If you say that everything is great with you, nothing will happen. When you admit your pain, you will start doing something. **You must start to talk about it.** The most difficult things hide within your close familial relationships. We come here to receive a certain experience connected to these relationships. Until we learn all these roles, we will not be able to exit this reality.

You can occupy yourself with abstract spiritual development, you might study philosophers, but nothing will change, because your lesson is buried within your life, which consists of intimate relationships with people who are close to you. They are your teachers. Your relationships with them contain your most important lessons.

— *It is very difficult to release what is holding me inside.*

— It is difficult to release a lesson that has not been learned and passed yet. You are holding on to something you have not yet understood. Everything was built very wisely on this playground called Earth, and you can get out of here as wise and loving although it appears that there is nothing but pain, suffering, and hatred here. That's the way the lesson goes.

Completed assignments will lead you to love and wisdom. Do not identify yourself with the experience received. Just discuss it the way a schoolboy discusses his assignment and the way he solved it. Once you identify with your experience, it appears as though you are exposing your soul here for others to spit at. It appears that you are not doing it right, while others have already mastered their lessons.

— *Yes, that's what I am afraid of all the time.*

— You are silent because you became completely identified with your lessons. But those are just lessons, just the experience. For example, there is a tremendous identification with the role of a man and a woman. The worst insult for a man is to hear that he is not a man, and for a woman that she is not a woman. But those are just roles. Those are the lessons we need to solve on our way to love and wisdom.

Let's not identify with these roles, and it will be easier to speak about your experience from the point of view of the investigator. We came here to investigate the experience of the dual life we have received. The investigator, who is identified with what he investigates, can't do his work. After you have done something, you need to step aside and look at what you did.

So, step away from the situation you have experienced. Take a look at it, and tell us about it. You will see what you need to do next, and what should not be done. By de-identifying, you will see the experience you received. It will be neither good nor bad, but it was the one you needed.

— *Currently, I am not married. I can't imagine any other woman in place of the woman I have been with. I have figured out why we broke up. I know why it happened the way it did. But as I investigate this situation again, I understand that the problem remains—it is in me.*

— What is the difficulty of the role "husband— wife"?

— *One can feel good with a woman in many respects, but a woman always limits a man's freedom.*

Can you allow your woman to be free?

— Can a man give freedom to a woman? Quite frequently, women say that men don't give them freedom. Men say the same thing about women. In reality, neither one of them give freedom to the other. If you free your woman, she will free you. No one can force you to do it, but you can do it yourself. Tell me the truth; do you give your wife freedom?

— *I spoke to my wife about this. We concluded that she cannot step over certain boundaries, while I can.*

— Then, why did you attract such a woman? It appears that she wound up next to you coincidentally, but as we already know, there are no coincidences here.

— *She is opposite to me in every way.*

— It is exactly the opposites that attract each other and get together. That's where all our problems are coming from. That's how lessons are assigned in this dual world. It means, this extreme is characteristic of you also, but in her case, it is actualized, while in your case it is a potential.

Dualities, the manifestations of which we see in the outside world, are in the inner world of a human being. A man actualizes one side of it, while the opposite side gets manifested in another human being. This second side is also present in him, but he does not see it in himself.

This is comparable to an iceberg that has a visible part and an invisible part. In attracting a partner, whose visible part is opposite to your visible part, you receive the conditions of your assignment. You need this in order to see both sides of the duality and to exit it.

What kind of duality is manifested in your relationships? When the lesson has been solved and passed, you will be able to describe the whole mechanism of such a dual trap, or your lesson, with a great precession. In essence, this entire world is an illusion and a trap. The mind is constructed in a dual way. It constantly falls into the traps of dualities. This is the problem everyone talks about here. You cannot exit a trap until you simultaneously see both sides of a duality and accept them in yourself. As soon as you accept them, you find yourself in the middle and you pass through it. The pass is in the middle of duality. That's where the solution of any dual lesson happens to be.

A magnet has a positive side and a negative side. They create a strong voltage between them. You are being thrown between one pole and another. By stabilizing yourself in the middle, you become neutrally charged. A neutral particle can pass without being attracted to these poles. That's what you need to achieve inside yourself. You need to become neutral in relationship to duality.

Any one of your problems represents one or a few dualities that are pulling you to different sides. This is a lesson. **First, you need to define a duality or a trap you fell into.** As a rule, another human being expresses the opposite side of a particular, currently activated duality. To harmonize your relationship with him, to accept and to become grateful to him is to achieve neutrality inside yourself.

Your greatest teachers are people with whom you have had the most difficult and painful relationships. When the lessons you have studied together are passed, you will experience enormous gratitude to them for going through these lessons with you.

— *I have experienced multiple conflicts with my husband, but I don't feel grateful to him. I feel he could have been different.*

— It means that you still want something from him, i.e. your lesson continues. In a state of neutrality, all your expectations disappear. You accept things the way they are. You see that other people simply perform the roles you need them to perform. Your husband, son, daughter, and other people simply play these roles. While passing through a lesson, you experience great dramatization and identification with them. When a lesson has been passed, you see what kind of a show it was.

— *I am in a similar situation. It seems to me that I do everything I can on my side to harmonize the situation, but ...*

— Okay. What is your major problem? Which role are you investigating now?

— *I spoke about mother, and then, digging further, I transferred to wife.*

— Your wife does not meet your expectations. Your problems with her are due to her not meeting your expectations. You think she should do things a certain way, but she does them differently.

— *She manifests intolerance and impatience. She does not want to listen. She is unable to perceive my point of view. It seems to me, I don't have these qualities.*

— She reflects your qualities to you. Look at yourself when you happen to be intolerant and when you don't accept another man's point of view. How does your intolerance manifest itself in relationship to women? It manifests itself already in your intolerance to your wife's intolerance. Other people are mirrors that reflect our hidden qualities to us. But we don't want to understand that. We see only negative qualities in others. We don't see them in ourselves. And we continue to fight against ourselves in the image of another human being. Such conflict is very difficult and painful. You believe that you are fighting others, while in reality you fight yourself.

When you hate someone, you hate yourself. When you insult someone, you insult yourself. When you kill someone, you kill yourself. Once you understand this mechanism, you need to rethink and rebuild your thinking process, which is currently based on the illusion of separation. This illusion makes you think that the negative qualities you see in others are theirs, not yours.

You need to return to yourself everything you say to other people, and review it from the point of view of yourself. I am here to stimulate you to understand that you always speak about yourself. See it and become aware of it. Some people have a very strong reaction to this statement. They scream and run away, because they cannot comprehend that.

They want to think the old way: "I am okay, I am normal, it is the world around me that is bad and people are nasty. Horrible things happened to me because of these people." They don't understand that this world is a reflection of themselves.

Who is the director of your life? Why do these things happen to you? Nine men out of ten will tell you that this is due to life circumstances that don't depend on them.

— *Is it enough to see it once, that all of it is your own doing?*

— No, once is not enough. You need to start and to do this work point by point. And there are many points here. The thinking process that is habitual here, separating and projecting, maintains a completely different perception of what is happening. You, on the other hand, must create a thinking process of an aware human being in yourself, who understands and takes responsibility for what he does. If you are insulted and hold a grudge against someone, you take offence of yourself.

Each one of us has an inner man and an inner woman. We can investigate our inner man and woman only through our relationships with the external men and women. If you don't accept men, it is your unacceptance of your inner masculine part. The same can be said about your feminine part. This needs to be investigated using the correct thinking process, not by falling into the habitual separating and projecting thinking pattern. The inertia of the old thinking process is very powerful and should not be underestimated.

All of humanity will be able to ascend. The time of loners who could become enlightened on their own has ended. **The fate of civilization depends on the decision humanity will make: civilization may disappear, or it may be reborn on a completely different level of consciousness.** This is not going to be an achievement of lone wolves. It will be a joint process.

The power of even a small number of people who will persevere on this road will be very strong. The energy of new vibrations will be everywhere, and even without understanding what is going on, people will feel it. A certain critical mass is necessary for humanity to transfer to the new level of consciousness.

This is what Ascent is about. This is my main work here. Will we remain in hell or get to the spheres of enormous possibilities—the choice is ours. Will we choose the habitual, wishing to be more spiritual while soaking in hell, or jump and push through?

This work is not easy. It requires all of you, but, in my opinion, nothing else is important here. Everything else is just a means for this. I do not negate anything. Everything is important, but only from the point of view of this work.

Everything is important in this world, and everyone gets attracted to exactly where he needs to be attracted to in order to receive certain, necessary for him, experience. And this is great. But do we use this experience for the investigation and Ascent, or do we live through it mechanically, trying to grab more for ourselves and to get more comfortable in our sleep?

— I thought my relationship with my father was water under the bridge because he died. Given every chance, I judged his behavior, and I made a negative example out of him. I understand now that I did not have a good father—daughter relationship. I was told very early that I must become

independent. Mom tried sporadically to express her concern for me, but I felt left out very early.

— Who is a father? A father is a man who takes care of his child. A husband does not take care of his wife the way father takes care of his child.

— I try to compensate it in my relationship with my son, in order for him not to feel what I felt. Neither one of my two husbands gave me the attention I needed. I always felt that I had to support myself. Neither one of them could perform his role.

— They could not perform it, because it was not planned in your experience at that period of your life.

— I understand now that it could not have happened, because I did not experience it with my father.

— Great. Would you want to feel it?

— Of course. I came to conclusion that one's relationship with God is one's relationship with one's father.

— And with one's mother. Why is it so important for us to be our parent's children in everything? It is important in order to join father and mother in ourselves. They left us with the inheritance of all their unsolved problems. We must solve them now. We need to accept and understand our mother and father. We will only be able to understand our personal programs through them.

When someone in a family line starts to do this, the energy of liberation passes through the entire ancestral line. To accept your parents, you need to see many things. You have chosen your parents yourself in order to receive the experience you needed. They provided this experience for you. Everyone here received exactly what he needed to receive.

Unless you understand this, you will be stuck in eternal accusation and unacceptance. You will stop experiencing these feelings if you come to understand that you have created your script yourself, entered it, and received what you needed. You need to accept what you received, because it was you who wanted to receive this experience. So, accept it and thank your father and mother for providing this experience for you.

— *I felt more like a mother than a father in relationship to my son.*

— Yes. You had to perform that role. We need to sort out why you block manifestation of a father in your life. This script was not chosen coincidentally. Which side of the experience have you investigated, and which side you have not investigated yet?

It is usually the negative side that is predominantly explored here. Because of this, a strong tilt to one side of a duality occurs. Investigate the positive side of this question. But to do that, you need to accept and understand the negative side, as the positive side is its continuation.

I am trying to develop a paradoxical thinking pattern of the self-investigator in you. If you accept this, you will begin to investigate your life. You will become your own teacher. The Supreme "I" is this experimenter and teacher, and you need to be connected to your Supreme "I", i.e. to yourself. If there is a connection with the Supreme "I", you will come to understand why you came here and what your lessons are to be.

Why did I hit this woman?

— Everyone reacted to a woman and her husband who left earlier today.

— *She expressed her opinion that men are the weaker sex, and her husband supported her.*

— Yes, but she also met a man today who slapped her face. I hit her. What was that all about?

— *You manifested her hatred toward men to her. She came here with her husband. She did not want to be here. He wanted to be here for a long time, but she would not allow him. He was afraid of her.*

— He is afraid of everything. She keeps him in fear, and she lives in the same fear herself. By killing the men who are next to her, she kills her inner man. She is on a revenge trip.

The slap on the face I gave her dramatized many things in all of you, but you have not allowed yourselves to express them yet.

Strong distortion occurs when a woman behaves like a man. She was screaming that there were no men left. Where would they come from if she does everything to kill her inner man and every man around her? This is a well-planned annihilation of one's masculine part. If you respect your inner man, someone who respects you as a woman will be next to you. Otherwise, this is not going to happen.

An enormous amount of hatred has been accumulated within every one of us toward men and women. You will not be able to get rid of this hatred until it is expressed. Understanding will not come if hatred, grudges, and guilt are blocked. Nothing can happen while these blocks are present. You will not understand anything until you express it all.

Being in hatred and guilt, you kill those who are close to you, perhaps gently smiling in the process of doing it. Until you free yourself from these negative emotions, this killing will continue. In killing others, you kill yourself.

— *When you slapped that woman, I felt pain, because I went through it and understood that the role of a victim is equal to the role of the executioner. I allowed myself to respond emotionally, and I felt better.*

— Everything I do to someone, I first of all do to myself. When I hit someone, I hit myself. You can do those things only through yourself. In this case, you will not go overboard. I never cause unnecessary pain, because everything returns to me instantly. When I do something, I feel that human being as I feel myself. If pain comes, I feel it and I transform it. I did not hit a woman. I hit a matrix of survival that makes her neither dead nor alive.

Humanity is one unified consciousness. There are roles that we all play in this show: man, woman, brother, sister, wife, husband, etc. But as humanity, we are one unified consciousness. When you reach the level of consciousness of humanity, you experience pain from every conflict. You feel it as your own. This is empathy, not pity.

A man who pities someone does not see anything except himself and his own pity. A man who empathizes sees everything and the interconnectedness between everything. As a result, he does what needs to be done, when and to whom it needs to be done. He manifests a high level of empathy. He manifests clear vision. Empathy is a vision of the heart.

I know very well that I will be able to deliver to you what I need to deliver to you only once you are ready to accept it. This will happen when you pass through all the key roles. If a woman is stuck and unable to accept a role of a husband, she will see and hate him in me.

When you see that what you call "love" is simply a business deal, you will be able to open up to the true love that does not have the opposite side—hatred. Unconditional love is not dual; it does not depend on anything and does not need anything. It is spreads around you like air. You don't see or feel it because your vision is blocked. You need to remove this block and see that what you have always searched for was always with you. It never left you, and it will never leave you.

— *You talk about the Transformation of the Earth. I want to help this process. Perhaps, I can change myself.*

— Humanity and Earth represent one unified essence. We move in the cosmos on the spiral of evolution together. The Earth is a being that gave us an opportunity to live on its surface, the same way erythrocytes live in our organism.

Everything is interconnected. We are part of the living cosmos. If something happens somewhere, it reflects on everything. Physical perception creates an illusion that we can hide somewhere, but when your vision becomes broader, you start to feel the interconnectedness of everything.

The program of destruction is connected to the ego. The ego is concerned only with itself, and it perceives everything in fragments. I am not judging this. This is an experience. This is only an experience. With the help of the ego you were receiving the experience of separation, suffering, and pain. But a qualitatively different experience is available to you now.

The reality is multivalent not only for a human being, but for a city, country, nation, and a human civilization. Everything depends on how you perceive reality. If someone believes in the Judgment Day and Hell, he will get there, and there is no one to blame for this but him, because he chose this option himself.

I chose an Ascent, i.e. transfer to the next quality of consciousness. Once other people choose this option, the critical mass will be achieved, and we will be able to start this process.

The Earth is a zone of free will. What does this mean? It means things will happen the way you want them to happen. Everything is allowed here. Each one of us consists of many psychic parts. Each part wants a different thing. The same thing happens in politics and in any organization. Awareness allows you to see what happens inside of you.

Every one of these parts performs certain actions directed toward getting something it wants. There are interesting nuances here. Everyone has his own phase of movement. Someone accumulates experience while living in separation and pain, and someday, perhaps in another life, he will be ready to become aware of it. But, first, this experience must be accumulated.

A human being goes through life in certain steps. One starts with childhood and ends with old age. The same can be said about the Soul. It develops and matures. There are fragments of young souls here. They are interested primarily in material possessions. Old souls may become interested in what we are discussing. Wise souls are ready to get out of here. For them, this is the last incarnation in which they try to transmit what they know.

People are very different in this respect. You and only you can decide whether you need what I say or if you still need to continue to accumulate the experience of separation. Perhaps you still need to accumulate the experience of not understanding. When you live through many lives in not understanding, the moment of understanding may come that you have had enough and need to start to sort this experience out.

For those who want to remain in the old condition, the information I carry is dangerous. I am not hiding it. If you take what I offer, you will not be able to remain who you are. Do you need it?

— *I saw yesterday that life is beating us, while we resist. When one's belly is stuffed with life of such quality, one can make oneself do something. One can change. We came here to see what state we are in. Life forces us to see it. I feel that we must enter a spaceship and fly somewhere. It is scary, but at the same time I understand that this is real and I can do something for this to happen.*

— Of course. We have not gathered here coincidentally. An intention gathered us together. This intention must be realized. This intention slowly opens itself up based on what's going on here. There is only Love and Aim or Intention in cosmos. That's how every universe is created. That's how God creates—with Love and Intention.

We have the same essence, and we create the same way. We pass through many difficult lessons in separation here in order to unite, to become aware of ourselves as creators, to feel love, and to learn to create through intention. This is the meaning behind all three-dimensional lessons of the earthly plane—the training ground for the preparation of creators.

When a certain being reaches a higher level of creativity, it cannot be allowed to carry the virus of separation, hatred, and destruction with it. That's why the zone we currently inhabit is isolated. It is created for training. Until you pass every lesson of this zone, you will not be able to step out of it.

Some pass through this zone fast, while others are slow. Everything evolves in cycles, and the moment when many cycles intersect has now arrived. This is the time of greatest opportunity for Ascent. This process involves the entire Universe. The wave of this process can take us very high.

— *I have recalled many things, and I understood that the notions of what I considered to be right frequently interfered with my life.*

— Great. Look at how this happens. A certain memory block opens, and you immediately see everything connected to this theme. Every one of us has everything within him. I do not say anything you don't know. My task is to have you recall it, and this is happening. Awareness and love are the keys to every door of your inner house.

Healing occurs without a fight

— **We are going to return to our past and heal it now. Those are real opportunities. Our consciousness can return to our past, see a certain situation differently, and release the energy that got stuck there.**

Our body is energy. It so happened that this energy got stuck there. It fell into a trap, and now it causes pain. To heal ourselves, we need to enter these painful zones. Those can be chronic diseases, weak spots that you constantly hurt by getting into accidents, etc.

Every problem concentrates in a certain part of your body. Are you ready to have your attention enter a part of your body and meet what is there? Are you ready to see, feel, and accept it completely? Are you ready to relate to it with love? If the answer is yes, then a situation will open itself up, allow you to see it in a different light, and release the energy that got stuck there. In the end, everything has to do with fear.

— *This is the strongest and the heaviest feeling here.*

— There is fear and there is love. Everything negative comes out of fear and accepts different forms of it.

— *Do we need to do something about these parts?*

— They have to be accepted by you. Don't do what you are in the habit of doing. Don't fight them. Make peace with your sensations and allow your consciousness to be in the parts that experience pain. They will start to show themselves and open their secrets.

Many parts of you got stuck in the traps. You try to run away from pain and fear, but that is impossible. Start meeting your parts. Open the doors and free them. I don't want to predict how this will happen in your case, but the most important thing is peace, acceptance, and total readiness to see what they are about to tell you.

— *I saw images from my childhood. You were there. You told me that I was playing in front of the audience. I was doing it to feel pity and admiration. Then, I saw my mom and the way she defended herself from my frequently drunk dad. She pretended to feel bad, so he would not touch her.*

— *I saw a VHS tape that my organism kept rewinding, reviewing old forgotten diseases.*

— The memory of every painful moment is written in the consciousness of the cells of your body. You accelerate your own healing when you speak about these things.

— *I have a problem with my lungs. I asked why they hurt. The answer came that I don't breathe. I asked, "How can that be if I am alive?" "The answer came that I don't live, I survive. I asked why that was the case. The answer came that I suppress my desires because my previous desires were usually not fulfilled. This has to do with the roots of the fears which are buried deep in my childhood.*

— *My nose frequently gets blocked. Turned out it is a sexual problem. For the first time in my life, I felt warmth in my pelvis yesterday. I asked, "Where is this coming from?" I saw my past life, and I understood why it is so difficult for me to watch movies with scenes of rape. It became clear to me that people around me who I fear or do not accept are people that raped me in one of my prior lives. I felt this sharply. I felt chest pain. My runny nose represents the tears I forbid myself to shed.*

— Great. I want to remind you to remember that we are all actors here who help each other to pass through certain experiences we mapped out for ourselves to pass. This can be a very difficult experience.

— *I tried to send out love, and I experienced palpitations. A strong energy passed through me. I felt it with every cell of my body. I felt like a small nuclear plant that exploded. I allowed myself to experience it all the way, and my heart started to pulsate. I asked what had happened to me, and I received the answer that I was stabbed in the heart before. Perhaps my current life is connected so strongly to my previous life that I came here the same day that I died in my past life. I felt my controlled hatred and my unacceptance of things. I almost cried. I talked it through, and this heartache left.*

— Take a look at how quickly and almost painlessly the repercussions of the heaviest traumas can resolve themselves. But you must go to the end, and you must be honest. This was just an experience. Don't become identified with it. Otherwise, you will feel uncomfortable, and you will not talk about it. You received the entire experience that was available here, and you can understand each other very well.

Healing occurs through all three bodies: physical, emotional, and mental. We started with the physical body. The emotional recall can occur now. It will allow you to see old pictures and feel different states. Start with the physical body, and then go to feelings. They will bring up some memories. On the other hand, the memories may appear in the form of thought forms followed by feelings. This recall should use all three bodies in order for healing to occur. If you don't try to slow it down, everything will happen fast and without pain.

The secret of healing is simple. You need to allow yourself to experience what you forbade yourself to experience, because you considered this experience to be unacceptable and horrible. You need to understand that everything you lived through was necessary to receive and accumulate a certain experience. That understanding will allow you to make peace with yourself now. Start to experience everything you have not experienced. Pain may appear in the areas where you have not gotten to the bottom of your experience, where it was not exhausted. You need to honestly share your investigation with others. That's it. You don't need anything else. This is necessary to completely heal yourself, i.e. to become whole.

— *I don't perceive this life as real. I perceive it as a show. I am totally de-identified with it. When I am in such a state, my ears burn. My pain disappears when I get to the world that is unreal from our point of view, where I can fly and walk on water.*

— One thing does not interfere with another. The conditioned mind always wants to get to the so-called Truth, i.e. the only truth: if this is the reality, then that cannot be a reality, and vice versa. This is not the case. This reality exists, and that reality exists. And many other realities exist.

— *I am tired of my fears. It seems to me they get stronger all the time. I feel I am pregnant with fear. I thought I would not be able to get rid of them right away. I must start with the physical plane, bring the situation to the level of absurdity, feel the weight of fear in my body, and deliver myself of it. Then, I can move to the emotional and mental planes.*

— You can continue to do what you did here when you go home. The most important thing is your intention to get rid of fear and to start to love. As soon as such an intention is formed, everything will start to happen as it should.

If you don't know where you are going, it is irrelevant how you walk

— You can't say to a stranger what you can say to someone who is close to you. That, in a way, limits his freedom. It's a manipulation.

— Do what you consider to be necessary for your soul? That's the most important thing. Everything else is a limitation that you put up yourself. Start to remove them one by one. If there are people next to you who do not understand you, find those who will understand you. You will find those that would not understand and share what you do but who will not interfere with what you are doing. There will be those who will try to interfere. Your own decision may change the situation. If you allow something or someone to limit you, it means you limit yourself. The primary thing here is your relationship with yourself. Everything else reflects it.

— I want to express my emotions. I usually do not allow myself to do that. In reality, those are just the borders I set for myself.

— When the mind operates, aliveness disappears. I turn into a robot: no smiles, no actions. I look awful.

141

— Our strength as human beings is in our feelings. Feelings allow us to reach the spheres that we cannot enter any other way. We can reach the amazing places on the wave of feelings, but we obstruct them. We are pouring gas out of the tanks of our cars. We sit in powerful cars that do not move because there is no gas in their tanks. Feelings are like gasoline. Your car is standing still because you are constantly pouring gas out of its tank.

— *As soon as I want to ask a question, I get the answer. I stopped torturing myself with the question, "Why do I come here, and what am I going to ask?"*

— Why go to a store if your fridge is filled with produce?

— *I don't know.*

— You confused yourself.

— *Perhaps I cannot explain what I want?*

— If you see a situation clearly, you can describe it well.

— *So, I don't see it.*

— You are being thrown from one side to another: "I know everything—I don't know anything", "I see everything—I don't see anything ". Do you see this swing?

— *The basic assignment is to ask yourself the major question.*

— Your life and your fate represent a direction that is determined by your inquiry. If you want to get to Moscow, you need to determine your route and go there. If you want to get to Berlin, you need to take the road that leads there. If you don't know where you want to go, you are stuck.

— *If you want to change your life, you need to trust your heart, even if it is not smart. Am I right? I ask a question, and I understand that I allow myself to feel although I become even more stupid.*

— You need to understand that smart and stupid are definitions of the mind.

— *Suffering is contained in these definitions.*

— Suffering appears when you separate these notions. You want to be smart, but I tell you that you are stupid. This is suffering for you. Nothing will upset you when you exit the borders of dual notions; your suffering will stop. You will see things the way they are. You will move beyond duality, and you will see what really happens. You will enter and exit it exactly when and where you want. If you like the game "smart—stupid", great, play this game, but you can exit it at any time.

— *I can do that already. I feel very light, because I can easily exit this duality.*

— Great. Continue to feel this state and watch out for the moment when you will try to drag yourself into the trap of another duality. You need to stay vigilant and observant all the time.

— *Will it ever end?*

— What should end?

— *Duality.*

— Try to slide on the wave of duality; it is fun.

— *It seems to me that when one understands everything, one stops worrying. The state of anxiety that is difficult to describe is present when something is not clear.*

143

— It is good that you worry. It means you are alive. A man who goes to a beach to take a quick dive in the ocean may not be happy to see big waves, but a surfer wants to see them. Become a surfer and start to navigate the dual wave of your experiences; start to receive pleasure by sliding on the edge. There is no pleasure greater than that.

A surfer who is learning the art of surfing frequently falls. He gets up and starts again until he masters it and starts to experience kaif* of sliding on a big wave. The bigger the wave is, the bigger his kaif.

You are your own teacher. In reality, you know everything. You just need to be in contact with your Supreme "I". Ask any question you want and receive the answer. If there is no answer, it means you have not asked a question. Theoretically, everyone knows this, but who does it? It is as though you knew about the existence of a cell phone but did not use it. What is the use of it then?

Every one of you has a connection with your Supreme "I". It gets interrupted for one reason only—you fall into unawareness again. In the state of awareness your connection is constant. It is much easier to maintain this connection during the seminar. Talk to yourself. Ask yourself questions and receive the answers. Do it. You need to practice.

— *I asked a question, received a funny answer, and started to laugh.*

— That's great. The way to yourself cannot be travelled with a dreary face. With all the tragic nature of this reality, I have not seen anything funnier. Laugh about the tragic situations of your life. When a human being laughs with his Soul, he is close to himself.

Every new human being brings you a present of awareness

— I want new people to show up in our group.

— This is very important. Our school groups are open groups. They can stay alive only if there is an exchange with the outside world, when new people appear. You cannot use unconditional love for your personal aims. This temptation always appears, but nothing good can come out of it, because the essence of this energy is to be distributed everywhere. Moreover, the life of a group depends on how open it is.

We do not separate people into good and bad, ours and not ours. Therefore, we have no reason to close our groups to anyone. New people always bring something important to the group. Some of them will stay and become a part of a group. Those who come afterwards will become a part of their assignment.

Every new human being carries a gift, i.e. an opportunity for a group to become aware of something. Someone will perform his role automatically, not understanding what he does, but in the end he will do exactly what everyone needs. We don't need to convince or recruit people. We just need to do what we do— live, feel, and become aware. Anyone who wants to join us can do so. We are always happy to see new people. They represent a part of us that carries something new. We integrate it.

Whether or not a newcomer is ready to understand what we discuss and will remain in a group, he is very important and valuable to us. I am grateful to anyone who comes. Irrespective of how mechanically he performs his role, a group will always have an opportunity to extract something valuable out of the situation if they pay full attention to everyone who comes, to every event that occurs here. The small is in the big, and the big is in the small. Everything here is interconnected and important.

Separation appears when you don't participate. When you participate, you start to understand that everything that happens to you is the result of what you do. You start to feel responsible for everything you do. If you don't like something, you can change it; other students will help. Everyone is in the same boat, and if it does not go where it is supposed to go, we need to figure out why. This is a joint effort.

This approach leads to powerful results. Our way is not easy. You are going to meet your own parts here in an accelerated fashion. Our way accepts everything. It does not reject anything. We are going to see our parts in everything and everyone. There are no ours, theirs, or others on this way. If you want to walk together, this way is for you.

— *Today was the happiest day of my life. I have not been irritated once. I think I came here to experience this state.*

— Yes. You will meet the greatest and the most horrible parts of yourself here. One of you will see his worst parts first. Another will start with seeing his beautiful parts. To achieve wholeness, where the horrible and the beautiful will become one, you need to see everything. You need to walk your part to get there. You will see that it is possible for you to live this way.

Don't try to suppress your emotional states, irrespective of what they are—that will get you in a trap. You need to walk this way to the end. In this case, awareness and love will become permanent. You have the light that will never be extinguished. You know where to go. The worst thing is to not know where you are going. When you know where you are going, you will have the stamina for everything.

— A woman approached me at work. She was interested in what we do here and expressed her desire to come to our meeting. We had a very interesting conversation. She has problems at work. She started to describe them to me. I thought I would have to listen to her again, but I suddenly got into the state I experienced after our last meditation. As she spoke, I felt a strong movement of energy in my body. I started to cry. Something amazing happened to her too. She came to me an hour later and said, "I feel great." She changed. Her problems resolved. She was jumping as a young girl talking easily. Something very pleasant occurred between us.

Miracles are part of our daily work

— Miracles are part of our daily work. Miracles are normal. When you receive the vibration of unconditional love, you carry it with you. There is nothing impossible for this vibration. Nothing can stand in its way. It creates miracles. This is completely normal for love and awareness. Feel yourself as the one who creates miracles.

People will come to you. They might not understand why they do that. They may start to talk to you about something totally unrelated, but in reality, they want to receive the unconditional love you carry. They will feel that you have it. That's why they will come. They may ask you what time it is or compliment you on your shirt, but this will be just an excuse to start a conversation with you. What they are really after is unconditional love. If you have it, people will come to you. Everyone wants to be close to it.

Someone will want to destroy it, because for them unconditional love is like a red flag to a bull. Be ready for this. You will activate everything negative in those people, everything they don't want to see and accept. They will blame you for everything.

— *Perhaps this is good.*

— Everything is good. In this process, everything is goodness. Whatever happens to you is good. What is tragic, dramatic, and horrible from the ordinary point of view is good for you. Everything is good here.

— *When Lyudmila was talking, I felt that everyone here was a part of me, and I felt myself in everyone. Those people are my parts. Judgment and appraisal disappeared. If I do not accept certain parts in myself, I don't accept a human being. But if I saw something and accepted it in myself, this human being becomes dear to me.*

— Exactly. Start to relate to others as you want them to relate to you. If other people are your parts, then by healing a certain part of you, a certain human being, you heal yourself and in the process become increasingly whole. Then, moral values, which appeared as the result of separated vision, hatred, and competition, are not needed anymore. They perform the function of a muzzle for an angry dog. If you remove them now, people will bite each other to death.

Currently, moral values perform a containing function. They are based on fear. We don't need them anymore. If you feel that another human being is a part of you, then, being in a sound mind, you will not hurt him or you will do it only to heal him and yourself. A doctor performs an operation to heal his patient. We are dealing with the same concept here.

— *Fear disappears when we start to use this approach.*

— Yes, because you start to feel that you are a part of the world. And if you love yourself, everyone around you loves you. Where would fear come from then? It does not exist, and life becomes a great adventure full of love, not fear. Look at how beautiful it is to know love and all the multiplicity of its forms. The creation itself as a form of God's love is enormously diverse.

— *Every day that I spend here with you, I received a present of awareness. This understanding came not out of what I have read somewhere, but what have manifested through all of us here. I found a part of me in everyone. I am grateful to everyone here, and I am ready to share what I received. I think we will continue to work and help each other.*

— Thank you.

— *I cannot part with the feelings and sensations I experienced yesterday. I cannot define them. I experienced and deeply felt the state of a woman who delivers a child. I don't want to do anything now. My movement became slow and smooth. I can't say that this is difficult, but this is not easy either. Observing the work of the mind, I saw its panic. This panic appeared because what was happening here did not fit any of the mind's definitions.*

— Initially, all of us are spiritual. We cannot lose it. But we can acquire false notions about who we are. This is the game of notions. If you understand what kind of a game it is, perhaps you are ready to end it.

"I saw pity in me, and next to it I saw cruelty and sadism"

— *I saw pity in me, and next to it, I saw cruelty and sadism. I saw how I, considering myself to be nice and responsive, sadistically treated my own body. I scoffed at others the same way I scoffed at myself. My cruelty approaches sadism.*

— It is not you; it's the mechanism of the ego. It is very important not to mix yourself up with the mechanisms.

— *I saw that. All my life I was afraid of being weak, thinking that the happiest people are those who live all their life together, as husband and wife, for example, supporting each other.*

— Only someone who cannot stand on his own requires a support.

— *My feeling of pity brought me to a place where I am all by myself. There is nobody around me. I don't have parents, husband, or kids. I am good and nice, but I am all alone.*

— Don't forget that you were acquiring an experience. You requested it yourself, and are writing a report now. Don't forget that life is an investigation.

— *I also understood that my soul is very powerful and courageous. It went for this experiment on its own accord.*

— *When I let certain things go, I receive energy. When I don't spend my energy on jealousy, envy, and hatred, I can use it for something else.*

— And what do you do with hatred and envy? This is also energy. The Russian Revolution did not happen based on unconditional love. It happened out of the enormously destructive hatred toward the elite. All of you know what it led to.

— *I have a problem with self-appraisal.*

— What is it?

— *I am constantly appraising myself based on the opinions of others.*

— Whose opinion is most important to you?

— *My own feelings are most important.*

— Whose opinion here is important to you?

— *If I am afraid of anyone's judgment here, it is probably yours.*

— What are you afraid of? Are you afraid of saying something wrong, or of me expressing doubts in you being enlightened to the degree you might have considered yourself to be?

— *I think it is fear of speaking. I can talk to some people freely, but not to you.*

— Why? Who do you have difficult time talking to here and who is easy to talk to? What is the difference between these human beings and me?

— It is easy for me to talk to people when I know that my knowledge of the subject being discussed is superior to theirs. When someone shows up who speaks about the subject I know nothing about, I get anxious.

— So, you are afraid of the gap in your knowledge.

— I am afraid people will find out that I don't know something.

— I never know what is going to happen next, and I never plan anything. The only thing I know to be true is that what I knew before does not work anymore and something new will come, something that is unknown to me. I happen to be in a state of not knowingness. I live in it.

Can you live in such state? As you can see, I know less than you. You are anxious about my knowledge, but I tell you, I don't know more than you, and I live in this state. I learn something new the minute it happens.

— I understand what you say. This fear of mine is subconscious and known to me since childhood. Because of the necessity, I had to learn Lithuanian language, but I cannot speak it when people are around me. I freeze. When I am alone, I speak well, but in the classroom, I cannot answer a simple question.

— This is anxiety of the ego. It is characteristic for many people.

— I have tried to sort out my false personality. I have tried to determine its main features.

— You can do it now. What are the circumstances that you find most difficult for you to be in? What are you afraid of most in the group?

— I am afraid to talk.

152

— Are you afraid to talk because your image will change? Are you afraid to lose your image?

— *Yes.*

— So, what kind of an image are you so afraid to part with? You have created this image yourself and you compare yourself with it all the time.

— *I feel I am in a pile of shit.*

— Where is it from?

— *Certain unpleasant things happened to me.*

— Have you thought that somebody else would be happy if those things were to happen to him?

— *I have not thought of that. That's true.*

— Everything depends on your appraisal of the situation. Someone, who expects a thousand-dollar gift, may get upset with a hundred-dollar gift. Another man will be very happy getting a hundred-dollar present. This world is created by our notions and expectations that are connected to them.

You can only control this world if you control your notions. This is possible only in a state of awareness. Everything we discuss here and everything that happens here is a result of notions that are born and remain in the mind.

I have described the mechanism that gave birth to your problems. You have created this mechanism yourself. I showed you different options that can be used to change this mechanism or to get rid of it. You can only do it if you see that the problem has been created by your own notions. They can be different, "People treat me nice," "I am a moral human being," or "I am bad." All we have here are just our notions, and if you are not aware of them, they drag you into their game. When you become aware of them, you can joggle them.

Victory of each one of us is our victory

— *I feel very excited. I feel that the group gave me everything it could. I am in a telepathic communication with everyone. I felt your strong support, and now I can walk without crutches.*

— We are one team. That's why victory of each one of us is our victory.

— *I feel I am a warrior of love and creativity.*

— A warrior of light has a sword that separates in order to see things the way they are and to unite them.

— *When I was falling, I was reciting a prayer:*

From the point of light located in the mind of God,

Let this light appear in the mind of a human being.

Let this light descend to Earth.

From the point of Love located in the heart of God,

Let this love appear in the heart of a human being.

From the point of space, where the Aim of God is known,

Let this Aim, that aware teachers serve, come to fruition.

— It is very important to perceive each other not as a man or a woman, but as a Unified Christ Consciousness, to see Christ Consciousness in a human being, to address each other as a multidimensional consciousness. When you start to look into the eyes of another human being attentively, you will see every mask he put on, and passing through them, at the end, you will come to the realization that we are Unified Consciousness.

— *Yesterday, looking at my face in the mirror, I felt contact with the Looking-Glass world, and saw the third eye between my eyebrows.*

— Continue to do that and you will see many things. You might see your incarnations in other realities. You might see a new Earth with two Suns. There is only one Sun here. The world here is dual. There is shadow here. This is the world of shadows. Over there, there are two Suns, and there is no shadow there. It is your shadow that creates the illusion of your own perception of yourself. It is not the darkness, but the shadow that you constantly fight.

— *Last night I experienced sudden drop in energy. I could not even walk. I sat down on the curb by the fence, and asked myself what happened. I thought it was related to what happened here yesterday.*

— *Correct. This happened to you after the completion of the last assignment, when exiting the doors, we were supposed to say, "I free myself of everything that prevents me from living." Everyone said those words leaving seminar yesterday. You freed yourself from what was interfering with your life.*

— I want all of you to pay attention to the fact that this has happened by the fence. This is symbolic. The fence is something that stands in our way. You approach it, and doubts appear: will I pass or not? The fence disappears as soon as you clearly see and become aware of your limitations.

155

— I have a feeling that coming to Moscow or any other city, I would immediately recognize people who belong to our group. I would not see them as strangers. I had a vision yesterday. We were passing a torch to one another. **I understood that not allowing ourselves to live based on feelings for a long time; we forgot how to do it.** *This was a life of a fighter covered in armor. What I received here is difficult to express in words. I am grateful to all of you. It would be difficult to walk this road on my own. Intellectually I understand everything, but as soon as a situation appears, my understanding leaves me. Work in a group is a step that everyone must make.*

— What should happen will happen. This is the scenario that we wrote together.

— I received an opportunity to understand who I am and what I am without comparing myself to anyone. All my life, I thought I could not do anything, could not understand anything. I used to destroy myself with those notions. The realization that I am a part of something whole came now. While meditating, I imagined a crystal ball with rays of light coming out of it toward all of us. We feed it, and it feeds us. We are this crystal.

— I saw the connection: the red river comes to us from Russia, and the blue river goes from us to Russia. Then I saw a crystal. It is very fragile. Our work is to maintain the power of this crystal. I received a lot during this seminar. I saw the dual nature of many of my parts. I know what to work with now.

— Conflicts appear during group work: you like some people, and you don't like others. Those polarities are both outside and inside of you. Observe your interaction with these people. People, who bring up the strongest emotions in you, whether pleasant or unpleasant, are very important. It is with their help that you will be able to see the duality you need to become aware of in yourself. Start to speak honestly and you will be able to see them. Then, it will be clear for you that we are one.

A group has everything you need to understand yourself. Newcomers will bring everything we need. Be very attentive to everyone who comes. They come to see something and provide us with an opportunity to see something in ourselves.

Spiritual kinship

— Prior to coming here I was in Tyumen. I experienced something very interesting there. I saw that everything that happens here is a result of prolonged war between fire and water. Fire and water are two mutually exclusive elements. They cannot form a partnership. We came to an understanding that this partnership could occur through air. Air is related to both fire and water. Fire represents enforcement, clearing, and transformation of emotions.

I will review what we did there and what we have received for the Tyumen group and for our process. The opening of the heart of Russia occurred there. Our pain was transformed through the duality "love—hate". We could exit the borders of Russia. A crystal was formed by a group: an emerald with the edges of a hexagon. It serves as a devise to conduct the energy of Unconditional Love westward.

— *I felt united with everyone in the group, and I felt a desire to unite all those who wish to become aware of themselves as a Soul. I had experienced these states previously. They have been confirmed now. I feel*

157

very confident in myself. I experience this power daily. As far as my personal aim, I want to return home as a Soul enriched by the experience acquired in this world of dualities.

— While working in the group, I understood what real friendship is.

— I saw a pyramid. Its edges were roads, and they were interconnecting. The group created this structure.

— This is a mountain every one of us ascends using his own trail.

— I saw white fog. When I got closer, I could see that it consisted of white lines. Each one of these lines was a pyramid. Then I saw the same picture in a mirror reflection. They were intertwining in different directions. There was a sphere in the middle, and it played with all of this.

— That's how the universe is made. Symbols can help you to see what happens during our process. Look and talk about it. New energy will pass during your conversation.

We have a telepathic connection with everyone who is involved in this process. You can get an answer to every question telepathically.

— Is there a code for this connection?

— You will have to find it yourself. It will be different for each one of you. Feel the energy of every participant of our group.

— I felt yours and Uri's energy as the energy of my son.

— When I awoke this morning, I felt that everyone here was my brother and sister. My daughter was my sister. I have never experienced this before. I wish everyone could feel it.

— This is a spiritual kinship. In reality, We Are One. Through this unity, we can enter any reality. You have the knowledge. You just need to recall it. The knowledge will come to you as you start to recall yourself.

CHAPTER 4

A THREE-WAY DIALOGUE

•◆•

During one of the meetings, the question of moral degradation was brought up.

— "If things continue to go in this direction, the world is going to turn upside down!" one of the students screamed.

As soon as he said that, Nasreddin noted:

— Who knows. Perhaps down is going to be better than up!

Sincerity is the beginning of transformation

— *I experienced something very unusual. Perhaps I finally got to the heart. The excitement left me. This state lasted for about an hour.*

— Shall we touch it?

— *Yes.*

— I see every seminar as a step up in our process that occurs at a certain geographic place. You invited me to your city. Every city I come to invites me through a certain human being who starts to gather a group of people around him. Such a human

160

being encounters multiple problems based on his states and personal program. But his problems also reflect the peculiarities of the place of his residence.

— *Yesterday, my head was occupied with the thought, "I declined an opportunity to see something as a whole." I am going to say everything that is important to me. I have never discussed it before. I want to see the whole picture. I want to understand what is going on.*

— If you sort it out, you will help many people who have gathered here. The energy of understanding spreads out. As a result, understanding will come faster, and it will be less painful for others. The first explorer experiences major difficulties, because he walks into the unknown. Afterwards, others can follow in his footsteps. He knows how to lead them. But someone must be the first. From the point of view of our work, we are dealing with the exit of the many, not just one.

— *Otherwise, we are going to walk in circles. Many things are being covered up by gibberish. I relate to the group as I would to a child. It means a lot to me. I don't want to have any tensions. I helped Uri to get the group together. I supported him, and I want the group to persevere.*

— The power of two self-investigators is greater than the power of one self-investigator, but the two of you will experience more hardships. If you pass together, you will acquire a lot.

— *I have a strong desire to sort things out, and I have big hopes for this seminar. I want to see and understand what I need to do.*

— *There are parts of me that want to understand and to start working, but I don't know what to start with.*

— Start wherever you can. We will come to what is important and necessary anyway.

— *I will start with my childhood. I grew up in a troubled family. My dad drank and was in and out of jail. My mom raised me and my sister on her own, and when I was very young, I saw what small kids are not supposed to see. We lived in a one-bedroom apartment, and my parents had sex in front of us. I used to watch them getting excited. I was attracted to sex very early.*

— You don't need to explain anything now. Just describe some episodes of your life. They will combine in one picture later on.

Fear and sexuality

— *That's exactly what I want. I was seven years old and my sister was three. Mom would go to work, and leave me to take care of her. I used to run out of the room to scare her. I would stand behind the door waiting for her to get hysterical. Then, I would return and calm her down, "Don't cry. Everything is fine." She would calm down, and I would leave again. That's what I did.*

— Did you do it in order to get emotionally excited?

— *Yes. I had to bring her to a certain state in order to get excited. As a child, I also stole things I did not need. It was the excitement that attracted me. I remember men who visited my mother. I would wake up and observe. I was disgusted and interested at the same time. Those were contradictory states. I was afraid of my dad coming home drunk. He might become violent then. He never laid a finger on me, but I was afraid of him when he was angry. On the days he would get his paycheck, he would come home late and*

162

smell of alcohol. I was always anxious on those days. I still feel this anxiety in me. I would get myself and my sister fully dressed and get ready to run. I would spend an entire night being anxious. I could not do anything with this fear. Even now, when I recall this fear, I get shaky. I run and it goes away. Then it returns again.

— A strong inner tension can be released through physical movement.

— *Yes. I instinctively start to run in order for this state to pass.*

When I was in a fifth grade, I masturbated while observing a girl who was scrubbing a floor. I was attracted by her pose. I remember the thought that passed through my head, "I am so smart. No one knows that except me." This was kaif. But then, I started to feel that this was not the right way to behave. That was also connected to very strong emotional states.

Another memory is of me in a bathhouse. I saw an old man with one arm. I thought, "He lost his arm fighting Nazis for you and your family, and look what you do." I cried. I experience the same feeling of guilt now. I am on the verge of tears. Pleasure attracts me, but I suffer at the same time.

Everything stopped when I got married, but fear came that I would not be able to have kids after I have masturbated so many times. I remember not allowing myself to have sex with my wife more than once a night. I was saving myself.

— And what would happen if you were not to have children?

— *I would feel like a defective human being. What kind of a man am I if I can't conceive a child? It would mean that I am not a man.*

I was very imaginative. I was attracted to a certain type of women. I used to search for them while walking the streets. I was initially attracted by a woman's breasts. Only then would I direct my attention to her face and legs.

— And what is a breast?

— *I don't know. Perhaps it has to do with mother's breast. It is something warm and filled with milk.*

— If we were to continue the association, it is maternal milk, maternal care.

— *Maybe it is love.*

When I look at a woman, I see breasts...

— A child gets his face into a breast and feels very good. He is protected, fed, and has everything he needs. It is important to understand what it means to you.

— *I am only attracted by breasts. When I look at a woman, I see breasts. Last night I caught myself sitting in front of the TV flipping channels and looking for women. At night, I watch porn while being afraid that my wife or daughter might get up and catch me doing that.*

— Recently I saw a movie called *"Crush"*. A man gets into a bad car accident and develops sexual excitement in connection with it. People who experienced similar crushes get attracted to him, and they form a group that constantly searches for and creates car accidents in order to get sexually excited.

I think sexual energy is the energy of life. It contains the impulse of creativity. How do people use it? Usually it gets fixated in childhood on a certain very dramatic, emotionally charged situation. For example, it gets fixated on the situation you have described.

This energy gets channeled; it narrows down and starts to create similar situations.

In your case, the situations that excite you sexually are connected to guilt: I should not be watching these movies, but I do. The mind starts to use this sexual energy to maintain a fixation on the feeling of guilt. The mind creates the feeling of guilt and it maintains it. The mind appropriates sexual energy and uses it to recreate certain situations in which it forces you to experience guilt and condemnation. This is the mechanism by which the mind maintains a state of fear in you.

What can we do to liberate ourselves? We can declassify this mechanism of the mind and free sexual energy. Presently, the conditioned mind controls it in order to split into two polar states: guilt and condemnation.

In your case, your perception is influenced by physical vision, and, therefore, physical forms such as breasts are important to you. However, this can be a different a stimulus, such as a wounded body that was presented in the movie I mentioned.

We can remove these fixations by using awareness. That's what we do here. In the usual psychiatric hospitals, doctors do not work with awareness. They do not exit the borders of the ego. They try to "re-tinker" the contacts in the mind. But by ripping up one connection, they simply attach another. All their attempts to bring the mind to a so-called "normal state" are illusions. The only way you can free yourself is to become aware of the way things really are. If you can see the mechanisms by which your conditioned mind fixates your sexual energy, you can free it. Then you will be able to create your life by having a choice. Otherwise, there is no choice; you just repeat the traumatic situations imprinted in you while not even seeing what you do.

— *I had a constant desire to tell someone about this habit of mine. I felt I could not handle it on my own. I can't tell you how many things I did to try to get rid of it. I used to bring my body to a state of total exhaustion, so it would not want anything.*

— Did you blame yourself and feel guilty?

— *Yes.*

— That's how you recreate similar situations in your life. Your notions are maintained when you spend your energy on them, including the energy you use to fight them. For example, you want something that you consider is inappropriate and forbidden to you. You fight this desire, and as a result, you want it even more. The power of desires like this accumulates like a snow ball.

This inner war weakens you. Fear escalates. In trying to get rid of this fear, you start to blame yourself even more. That leads to an even higher escalation of inner conflict.

Personal program is a mechanism.
It works only for itself.

— Are you ready to see the working mechanisms of your personal program? This is not easy. The mind is sly; it will protect them. Even when you discuss these mechanisms, they can reinforce themselves. The conditioned mind uses everything to maintain and reinforce itself. It can do all of this to receive energy. People listen to you, and energy comes from them. Where does it go? It goes to these mechanisms. The impression is being created that you discuss them here to become aware of them, but, in reality, the mechanisms can use this energy to reinforce themselves.

— *I desperately want to see one of these mechanisms, but there is something in me that resists it.*

— I would ask you to look deep inside and to tell us what is it in you that resists.

— *As soon as I spoke about my desire, I observed the resistance. The fear appeared again that you would ask me to do something, and I would have to do it. You may say, "If you are ready to part with this, do this and that now."*

— You are not your story. You are afraid of action. When it is time to act, fear appears in you. You told us that not everyone is brave enough to talk about himself, and it appeared that you were completely honest. You continued to talk. You tried to assure me that you would sort it out, but you did not even hear my commentaries. The mechanism is working on its own. It uses this situation to reinforce itself. I can create a situation now which will deprive it of energy. I am ready to do it. Look inside. What do my words activate in you?

— *Fear.*

— You will experience reinforcement of the mechanism now. It will start to show its tentacles.

— *I think that if something is to happen to me, you will bring me back.*

— Are you ready to free yourself from this mechanism completely? It should be uninstalled completely. The mechanism should be separated completely, piece by piece.

— *I am ready. Let's do it.*

Awareness of guilt and fear

— Okay. Perhaps, Larisa would like to add something. You are in it together. This is very important, as the liberation cannot happen to you alone. It can only happen to both of you.

— *I was brought up in a totally different family. There were three of us, three sisters. Our parents loved us dearly. They may not have loved each other very much, because at that time people used to get married based on necessity. Both were orphans who did not have a place to live. That's what brought them together. My mother was very strict. We were good students. Yuri was my first love. There was one more boy I liked, but I chose Yuri. My parents were against our marriage. They were afraid of his broken family, even though they had known him since childhood as a very quiet and nice boy.*

When we got married, we moved out. We were very fond of our children.
Everything was quiet. We had a normal life. We traveled a lot, preferring
active vacations. In 1994, Yuri opened his own business. He worked a lot,
but he was not successful. He was tired and irritable all the time. He started
to travel to Russia on business. During one of his trips, he met our neighbor
there. We can call her his femme fatale. All the men that ever got close to
her died very fast: some in automobile accidents, others from alcohol or drugs.
To make a long story short, they had an affair. I felt it immediately. I saw
dreams about it which I shared with him. I saw that it was difficult for
him. He felt guilty. We both suffered silently. I felt pity for him, and he felt
pity for me. One day he decided to go to Russia again. I did not even think
he was going there to meet this woman. I did not try to keep him from going.
He returned very fast, and told me that this work was not for him. I also
worked a lot. We had to sell many things to survive. He got a job. That
was a miracle. It appeared that we were healing. I frequently noticed his
excitement in the presence of other women, but I never perceived it as
something bad or forbidden. I was pleased that other women found my
husband handsome, but I did not even allow myself to think about him
having sex with someone else. That would have been a harsh ordeal for me
to bear. I did not want to experience it again. I always trusted him, and I
did not want to lose my pride. Something happened when we started to
attend group meetings. Something happened between him and Helen. I did
not get upset. I just told him, "Yuri! If this continues to develop here, it will
be difficult for everyone. The entire group may break apart." I did not notice
anything. I did not see anything. People used to tell me about what was
going on, but I did not want to believe them. But now I see an open flirt
here, especially from Helen's side. She declared herself as soon as she got
here, and Yuri got on her hook. I felt uneasy when he started to create
obstacles to my coming here. He started to schedule group meeting on the

days I had to go to work. He was looking for any opportunity for me not to be here.

— Can you see the mechanism of his behavior that was just discussed working here?

— I understood that he felt guilty and then reacted to this guilt.

— Relax. When people talk about such things, they get very emotional. That prevents them from understanding anything. You speak. And because the topic of your talk is painful, you speak nonstop. But to discuss a situation is not enough. You need to become aware of what you are saying. So, I am going to stop you from time to time in order to calm you down. Then you will be able to see the mechanism. When you see it, you will get rid of it.

This is not Yuri, but the mechanism that works in his mind. It is imperative to understand that we are talking about the mechanism now, not about the entire human being. **A computer program is not a computer. It can be changed or removed. That's what we do here.**

What is the mechanism of your situation? It is dual. There should be a side that excites and attracts, and an opposite side that does not want this to happen; it gives birth to the feeling of guilt and self-blame. The counter action of the opposite forces is created. One woman wants this to happen, another does not want this to happen. The situation escalates. Excitement grows. That's how this mechanism works.

It requires you to find a woman who will want to participate in this game. The same mechanism, which needs your presence to create the situation of resistance and guilt, works in her too.

Yuri loves you, but he also forces you to get hysterical. That leads to a very strong feeling of guilt. Please, thoroughly feel how this mechanism works now.

— Do *I need this stress to get excited?*

— Yes.

— *So, I was looking for these states.*

How the conditioned mind uses sexuality?

— Yes, because you felt alive in these situations. Sexual energy is the energy of life that creates the sensation of fullness of life. The mind, appropriating this energy and spending it on the work of its mechanisms, enslaves it. That's where all the sufferings are coming from. Perhaps Yuri would like add something now.

— *Yes, I tried to figure it out on my own, but I was unable to arrive at the conclusion that I was looking for excitement. I see it now. I thought that Larisa was in my way, preventing me from getting pleasure. That's why I was looking for ways to prevent her from coming to the seminars.*

— Sexual energy is the energy of Unconditional Love, but our mind makes it conditioned, separating it to two parts: **condemnation and guilt.** In this way, this energy starts to serve these states and ensures the work of these mechanisms. This is how the principle of divide and conquer is being realized.

If we become aware of and remove the dividing mechanisms of the mind, we will receive the undivided energy of the Unified Source. This is a direct way to yourself. But our personal program and the conditioned mind resists that in order not to lose power. How do they do it? They do it by superimposing the feeling of guilt and self-blame on sexual pleasure. Sexual prohibitions are the most important factors that preserve and maintain the state of sleep of our consciousness and make us forget ourselves.

— *I thought I should not experience pleasure.*

— Sexuality without prohibitions is a direct way to self-remembrance.

— *On one side, I create a stressful situation in order to receive excitement, but on the other side, I apply prohibition on the pleasure I want to receive.*

— Exactly. If we were to deprive a human being of pleasure, he would think of suicide, and at the end he can kill himself, by getting in an accident, getting sick, drinking himself to death, etc. When the degree of guilt approaches a high level, a human being starts to kill himself and others. He is in hell already. Pleasure is a last thread, and if it is forbidden, everything falls apart. But even pleasure is being overridden by the mind. It prohibits it.

You want to receive pleasure, but you cannot experience it to the fullest, because you are immediately overridden by guilt—you can neither inhale nor exhale. You can go from one woman to another, but you will always repeat the same scenario; your next woman will also provide you with a present of guilt.

It is not coincidental that the woman that got between the two of you turned out to be *la femme fatale*. She is on the road of revenge. Maupassant wrote a novel about a woman who was raped and infected with syphilis during the Prussian—French war. She wanted to commit suicide, but changed her mind. She started to sleep with the Prussian officers, infecting them with the disease. She did not have anything to lose. Her only desire was to avenge herself.

The program of self-destruction can attract such a woman. This is a mechanism. It works in men and women. You must see this program. Otherwise, you will be falling into these traps all the time. You may believe that you will be able to get something with the next woman, you're your situation will turn from bad to worse, because every next woman just exacerbates your guilt. In the end, you will become cruel and start to kill others.

— *I see his suffering. It upsets me, but I don't know how to help him. When I was mad, I used to tell him, "Here is our bedroom. Do what you want. Bring who you want here." When I was calm, I used to say that I understand and don't see anything wrong with it.*

— Stop. There is a very important moment here. You tell Yuri, "Do what you want." But he is not going to do it. **I see the mechanism here.** He is not doing it, and in that way removes the responsibility from himself. He does not want to take responsibility for his actions. You give him permission to do everything he wants, and if he is to use it, he would have to be fully responsible for everything he does. In that case, he would come face to face with self-blame, because he would not have you to blame him.

— *Does it mean he has to take responsibility for what is going on?*

— Yes. Let's say, you allow him to do something he wants in your own house.

— I can move to my parents and support myself.

You can free yourself of guilt only by accepting full responsibility

— The mechanism will not allow him to do what he wants to do. Why? It will not allow that because in such case, he will have to accept full responsibility for his actions. He will not have a side in front of which to feel guilty, and the mechanism will have to look for such a woman again. Then, he will have to bring two women home and to start the same game with both of them. One of them will get jealous, and he will feel guilty. This mechanism needs to experience guilt. If there is no guilt, and no one to feel guilty in front of, the situation exhausts itself. But for this to happen, he needs to accept full responsibility and to see this mechanism inside himself, not to project it onto other players.

This mechanism is based on masculine pride. Am I a man or not? You constantly ask yourself whether you are a man or not, trying to prove to yourself that you are a man. This mechanism forces you to do that using children and women. You want to be with a woman in order to understand that you are a man. You lack the inner understanding of your own manhood. If you had this understanding, you would not need any proof.

Many men and women start an affair to prove their qualification. Even the most beautiful women are not assured of their femininity. And even the most masculine men, as they may appear from one side, are not sure that they are manly enough. As a result, they must constantly prove their masculinity to themselves.

The inner feeling of confidence comes out of full responsibility for one's own thoughts, feelings, and actions. If that is the case, you don't need anyone to blame for your thoughts, feelings, and actions.

— *She wants to give me permission herself.*

— What do you need it for? You are constantly asking for permission. Why do you need to ask her for permission? Why do you need to feel as a little boy if you want to be with someone?

By taking responsibility for what he does, a man simultaneously accepts responsibility for all the consequences of his behavior. Let's say he wants to be with a certain woman and he is well aware of all the possible consequences of his behavior. Perhaps in learning about this, his wife would not want to be with him anymore and would leave him. He will make his choice and his wife will make her choice. This is full responsibility.

What happens in your situation? You want to keep both chairs. But in this case, you don't feel like a man—you need to ask for permission. Later, another woman will cause you to be in the same situation, and again you will ask your wife for permission. This is a vicious circle. If you want to do something, do it; make a decision and accept responsibility for every possible outcome.

Yesterday I told one woman here that she is neither dead nor alive. I was well aware of the consequences of my statement. I knew she would want to get up and leave. I was ready for it. I do things that might be perceived by some people as wrong, and I accept full responsibility for my words and actions. I understand that people may perceive them in a certain way, and I know why I do it. I don't need anyone's permission. I decide what I need to do myself. That's precisely when one starts to feel powerful. The power is not even in sexuality. Sexuality is the consequence. The power is in responsibility. I accept a certain decision, and I am fully responsible for the consequences of my decision.

— *He left without me getting hysterical. When he returned, I figured out everything, and I told him, "Yuri, I know that you have been with another woman." He got very uneasy. But I did not need his explanations. We have spent so many years together and loved each other that I felt everything immediately. He could not say anything to me. I said it for him. But now I think I should have him bring it up and talk about it. Perhaps he will suffer less.*

— He came here in order to be punished. We are dealing with the feeling of guilt again. It is the mechanism again that wants to be punished for what it did. If you are punished, you will feel some relief. "Sin and ask for forgiveness," — Rasputin used to say. But you cannot ask for forgiveness if you don't sin. So, you need to commit a sin, and then ask for forgiveness.

This idea is well-shown in Russian literature. Some people think they come closer to God when they ask for forgiveness. But to ask for forgiveness, you must sin. That's how you fall into the trap of duality.

If I want to do something, I do it. And it is not necessary to experience the guilt that carries the associated desire to be punished with it.

Nobody knows about it

— *Yuri had always experienced a lack of attention from his relatives and parents. He seldom spoke with his dad. He felt flawed because of it. When he grew up, he visited his dad's grave. He was drawn to it. From time to time he visits his mother. He has no contacts with his sister, but I know he wants to see her.*

I never talk to my mother about my life. Nobody knows anything about us except the group. I always hid my personal life from strangers. I did not even want to discuss it with the group. We live in a small town. Everyone knows everyone there, and it would be hard for me to hear something bad about Yuri.

— I can share a story from my own life. One always wants to hide something. I and my ex-wife had similar problems. About twenty years ago, someone came from America to conduct a tantric seminar. That was new back then. Everyone had to disrobe during the seminar. The organizers of the seminar decided to promote it and asked all the participants to come to the TV studio. I put my best suite on, thinking we are going to have a discussion, but they invited us to disrobe in front of the camera. It was recorded.

I told them, "You either record my face or my ass." They agreed, but two days later my wife came home saying that she was stopped five times on the street and told about me being naked on TV. We lived in a small town back then where everyone knew each other well. This gave me a very strong impulse to open my mechanisms. That's how the cork of the bottle of my subconscious side was pushed out. But we were already unable to live together at the time. I talk about it now, because something similar happens here.

— *I don't think we are there yet. I just want to help Yuri to come to inner peace.*

— You talk about helping Yuri, but in reality this has to do with both of you. This situation deals with your inner man and your inner woman. You are talking about your inner man now, and he speaks about his inner woman. Therefore, if you want to figure out what's going on inside you, you need to use this situation correctly.

Everything he said about his mechanism is related to you. You are not the last gear in this mechanism. It is very important to understand that. I am not reviewing you now. I am reviewing your personal mechanism that happens to be seriously enmeshed. His gears turn, but your gears turn with his gears. It is very important to see how both of you are stuck in the mechanism he just described.

— *Yes, both of us are stuck in it.*

— How do you maintain his mechanism?

— *He experiences guilt. I reinforce it. I don't express my discontent. I suffer silently.*

Pity transforms into guilt

— You express pity toward him, saying, "He needs love and care because he did not receive it as a child." But instead of love, you give him pity, that later transforms into guilt. If he is looking for guilt, you must provide him with condemnation. And you do that. This is your mechanism.

— *Does pity flip into condemnation?*

— Yes. You say, "I pity you, I love you." He thinks you do everything for him, while he—son of a bitch—is cheating on you. And then he experiences even heavier guilt. That's how pity flips to guilt. In your case, pity is being realized, but underneath this pity there is a constant condemnation. He feels this condemnation underneath your pity very well. Pity and condemnation walk hand in hand.

— *I see that. How do I get rid of it now?*

— You can only get rid of it by seeing the entire mechanism, from the beginning to the end. There is no other answer to the question, "How?" To ask this question while expecting another answer is to continue to do the same thing. You need to see every gear of this intricate mechanism, and there are many gears there. We saw the largest one, but there are many of them there, and they are all interconnected. You need to see each one of them.

— *I imagine she can have sex only with me, and she confirms this by saying she cannot have sex with other men.*

— This is the work of the mechanism again. From the usual point of view, it is great when your partner loves you so much that he or she does not want to be with anybody else. But let's look at what a man experiences in such a situation. He thinks, "If she is with me only, I should not be with anybody else. I should do everything to make her feel good. But can I do that?"

She superimposes prohibition on you that translates into a feeling of guilt and self-blame. Neither the physical nor the sexual centers possess those false moral values accepted by society.

A human being is energy. You can feel the energy of another human being, whether it is a woman or a man. Your energy starts to resonate with the energy of other people. Moral values say that this is unacceptable or acceptable within certain boundaries.

Moral values create limitations that give birth to blame and guilt. But the physical body acts based on the states it experiences, which are not connected to moral values. It starts to vibrate. The mind interprets it as, "I like this man. I experience a sexual attraction to him." But the voice of the moral values says, "I should not look at anybody but my husband. I should not like anybody else." However, the body does not give a damn about moral values, and conflict appears between the body and the conditioned mind that leads to a blockage of energy, strong inner tension, and negativity. This negativity should exit somehow, and it exits as condemnation.

A sleeping human being is not aware of what we are discussing now. The mind prevents him from becoming aware of it. As a result, the subconscious aggression directed toward another human being appears. It can manifest itself in different ways. You cannot say things directly, because the conditioned mind prevents you from seeing the whole picture. So, you start to pick on him. You may say that he is not dressed the way he should or does not behave himself properly.

— *I am interested in other men. Yuri is wrong when he says that I am not.*

— That may also be true.

— *Sometimes, I feel attracted to other men, but I don't want this attraction to lead to sex. Sexually, I feel happy with Yuri, and I don't want to be with anybody else. I probably would have allowed myself to go to bed with someone else, but it is not only about sex. It's enough for me just to hug someone during a dance.*

Family blackmail

— We are reviewing the specific mechanism now. It should have two opposite sides, one of which is "to have sex." For the system to be balanced, there should be another side: "not to have sex." Look at what you get based on the moral values that are commonly accepted here: you are moral, he is amoral. You have a reason to be proud. You win. In announcing that you like someone, but will never go to bed with him, you reinforce another extreme in your husband. That's how this mechanism works.

As you insist on a certain extreme behavior, your partner should develop the opposite behavior. Otherwise, the system will break apart. The gears will spread apart and the mechanism will stop working. But, as we can see, the mechanism wants to work, and it constantly maintains your gears in place.

— *I used to forbid myself from having sex with other women. A woman for me was just a physical body in bed. There was nothing spiritual about it. I hope we have figured one gear out. I frequently used my rights, speculating on the fact that she cannot use hers. As soon as I did not like something, I would say, "I want a divorce." This worked, and she immediately did what I wanted her to do. I knew that she suffered.*

— Your suffering is payment for you betting only on him. If he leaves, you lose everything.

— *That's another gear.*

— One has to pay for everything.

— *From my side, it was constant blackmail.*

— You provided a reason for your partner to blackmail you. If you don't react to it, no one can blackmail you with it. Let's say, someone comes to a woman, and tells her he has photographs that would compromise her, and he wants to send them to her husband. If she is afraid of it, she can be compromised. If she is not afraid of it, he will leave with nothing.

— *Something obscure turned out to be very simple and obvious.*

— Yes. It happened because the awareness came.

— *Sometime later, I stopped everything myself. I had a feeling that something could happen to her, she could get sick. I did not stop because I suddenly became nice. One night she felt really bad, and I had to call 911. I understood that if I were to continue on the same course, I would lose her.*

— And you will have to look for another player.

— *Yes.*

— Let's return to the work of the mechanism. A sadist will find a way to make his victim suffer. He does not want his victim to die, since in that case he would not have anyone to torture. He will take a good care of his victim. He will bring her to the condition when he can start to torture her again.

— *Perhaps that's how it works. I just became aware of why I did it. It appeared to me that I was trying to save my wife out of good intentions, but in reality, my motives were different.*

— We are sorting out the mechanisms of the fight of the opposites.

— *Even by refusing certain actions, one cannot solve anything.*

— Actions should come out of seeing things clearly. We are sorting out your mechanisms in order to see them holistically. If you clearly see the way things are, all your action will be correct, because they would come out of a holistic perception.

It's meaningless for me to tell you what is correct and what is not. Let's say, I offer you actions that come out of the correct vision, but you don't complete them. You will not understand what to do or you will do it in such a way that they will lead to the opposite result. That will happen because the perception of your dual mind will dictate to you its own actions, geared to enforce the work of the mechanism of conflict.

— *We need to see what happens and how it happens. How does my guilt create this stress? I want to experience guilt in order to receive excitement. That will lead to pleasure, which I would not be able to experience fully because of the feeling of guilt. As soon as I want something, I immediately feel guilty.*

183

— This happens simultaneously. As soon as pleasure starts to arise, guilt comes and lowers it.

— *Knowing the weak spots of Larisa, I can get what I want from her.*

She is afraid of what you want.
You are afraid of what she wants.

— She is afraid of what you want. You are afraid of what she wants. That's the mechanism of your interaction.

— *The system works well. Is that what you mean?*

— Yes.

— *I am fed up with it. I get to states I cannot control, and I think that the only way for me to survive is to divorce him. That will free both of us. I don't care about the house. I don't care about the money. The only thing that my soul needs is our country house, where I can occupy myself with gardening. Nothing else holds me. We are not going to have a war, dividing everything to the last cent. I only wish to have some peace. The kids have grown and are on their own. But will divorce solve our problems? Won't we get to another hell that is scarier than this one?*

— It is impossible to get rid of the mechanism of conflict this way. You can only change it by becoming aware of how it works. Otherwise, it will rebuild and re-manifest itself. You can leave today and find someone else to be with, but you will eventually end up in the same situation. If the mechanism is not understood, it will recreate itself.

— *My eyes have been opened to many things today. I understand this mechanism now. Thank you.*

— Good. I think we have accomplished a lot today.

— I was euphoric over the last three days. The most uncomfortable moments dissolved fast and became neutral. When I explored these situations before, I felt very uncomfortable. I don't feel that way now. I feel no regret about what had happened back then either.

— It seems that it is difficult to untie these knots, but we can do it easily. My intention is to untie them as painlessly as possible, because I know this pain. I went through it myself.

— You helped us to connect all the fragments.

— When you are identified with a situation, you cannot see the whole mechanism. You need to get out of the situation. That's when the mechanism becomes visible. When you exit a dual trap, you will be able to help others to get out of it. But first you need to escape yourself. By experiencing a trap in your own skin, you need to find an exit and get out. Then, you can help others to get out of it. That's why group work is so important. You need to help others to exit.

— Thank you.

You can exit the trap only when the entire experience has been received

— The problem I have has been dragging me down since childhood. I could not sort it out by myself or find help anywhere.

— You had to receive this experience. When and how can you exit a situation? It happens when the entire experience has been received. It could not have happened previously, because you were in the process of receiving the experience. The experience has been accumulated, and a situation appears now, when it can be integrated. I want to remind you that you were the one who planned and wanted to receive this experience. The most painful and traumatic things in life represent the major lessons and the most valuable gifts. It is the most difficult things that bring us the greatest gifts.

— *My major experience is connected to my entering my fear.*

— This is the most important thing. You were truly ready to see this mechanism. You were afraid of what I was going to do to you. But I didn't need to do anything. You gave your inner permission, and you did everything yourself.

— *I felt your support when you kept repeating, "This is not you. This is a mechanism." This worked. I could separate myself from the mechanism instantly.*

— If you identify with appendicitis, you will not allow it to be cut out, because it would appear to you that you would die without it.

— *It is important to know how to do this kind of surgery. I am scared now.*

— Sometimes I exacerbate fear in order for you to see it better. When a physician palpates a painful spot, he sees where the problem is located based on his patient's reaction.

— *I have made my decision. I feel scared now. I don't think I can hide it.*

— This fear points to the mechanism that gave birth to it. By using this fear as a pointer, you can see and open the mechanism.

— *For the first time, I was able to open myself up. I suffered and searched for people. I had to open myself up to someone. But it was impossible. Going over the situation on my own again and again did not change anything.*

— You need to have a clean screen in front of you. If you tell your story to someone who has not passed through the same experience and solved it himself, he will only be able to return it to you. The situation will only get obstructed more and more.

— *I noticed this during our group meetings. You are right, we did not pass and we tried to extrapolate and understand something based on the theoretical notions.*

— You are facing your own incomprehension. It gets reinforced, and you face complete incomprehension. But this is also meaningful, as it prepares the soil for sowing. Your conversations dramatized the situation and allowed you to approach today's conversation.

— *The entire seminar was prepared this way.*

— Yes. That's exactly how it was prepared.

— *I could not tolerate this suffering any longer. I had to do something.*

— I would define your state today as readiness number one. There is a different kind of readiness. When I first came to Saint Petersburg, its soil was not ready for sowing: you stick a shovel here—a stone, stick it there—another stone. It is much easier to work here now, because you have prepared the soil.

What is a cross?

— If we approach the personal mechanisms of the fight from the engineer point of view, we can come up with a universal system. We can see that people have different modifications of the same system. Everything can be seen clearly in this system.

For example, a good mechanic knows what an automobile is. Irrespective of the make of your car, he will sort out what is wrong with it, because he is an expert on how cars function. If you see the general scheme of a mechanism, you can clearly see how it works in a specific context.

What do I do? I take a "soil sample", i.e. I activate certain mechanisms or problems in those of you who come to the seminar, and I turn the music on. The mechanisms are activated, and they start to manifest themselves. If it is done only on the mental level, they put up a strong resistance. When the music is on, however, the heart becomes activated, and you start to see the mechanisms of your problems.

This is done to bypass the conditioned mind, and it works very well. The intellectual preparation is necessary to activate the problems. Everything else goes through music, i.e. feelings. That's why I have such a good music library. I provide different music for different situations. These mechanisms work on different energies. The music has similar energetic qualities. In time, I turn on the melody which best corresponds to a given problem or assignment.

— I have visions of *my own crucifixion. What is behind it: a feeling of guilt or of sacrifice? Sometimes I burn on this cross.*

— This is the crucifixion by three-dimensional reality. What is a cross? It contains vertical and horizontal bars. The vertical bar denotes the spheres of being, for example, one-dimensional reality, two-dimensional reality, three-dimensional reality, four-dimensional reality, etc. The horizontal part determines what level of being you currently occupy.

What is the expansion of consciousness? If we were to use a cross analogy, it is an upward movement on the vertical bar of a cross. What do Satanists do? They use the same cross which is turned upside down, i.e. they lower their vibrations.

In the case of a Christian cross, the horizontal bar is higher than the middle of the vertical bar. What does the horizontal bar symbolize? It symbolizes the duality of a given reality, i.e. the presence of opposite tendencies. What does a crucified human being signify? He signifies crucifixion in oppositions. On one side, he happens to be in all the spheres of being on a vertical line. On the other side, he is crucified in the oppositions of this physical reality here. He can only exit through the center, i.e. the heart.

A human being with his arms extended horizontally creates a cross. We can use an elevator analogy, the entrance to which is in the heart. You should enter your temple—the heart. This will allow you to use this elevator. You can descend. You must do that sometimes, while meeting a human being who happens to be in the lower vibrations. To bring him up, you must get to his floor first, and then ascend with him. That's how we can look at the cross.

Burning on a cross signifies the burning of the past in the flame of awareness. Some people say, "Our God is all burning and all devouring." That's how it is. Everything old burns fast in this fire, and you ascend to the higher levels of vibration. This process is like the process of an oil refinery: lower fractions go down, while higher fractions go up.

— *This cross with me burning on it appeared again in the beginning of the seminar. I saw it for the first time in 1994. I started having visions then. I have never hallucinated before. I forgot all about it, but now I remember because I saw it again.*

— All the images that come to you are the signs you need to learn to decipher. That's how you need to approach them. Usually, people treat them in a harsh predetermined way, which imposes on it only one of many possible views.

For example, people made a martyr out of Christ, even though he had enormous opportunities of awareness and came to show people what it means to be a Human Being. However, everything was flipped. The main idea people believed was, "Jesus endured, and we must endure." Who could have come up with this? Actually, it corresponded to the people's consciousness at the time. Many people are at that same level of consciousness now.

— *When I read the Bible, I tried to think what it said as best as I could at the time, and I understood it to be a science of love.*

— That's precisely what it is.

— *I left the church because I was not satisfied.*

— The church teachings are based on feelings of guilt, suffering, and sin. Until the church changes these feelings, nothing will change. It has difficulty doing that at present time.

CHAPTER 5

THE PATH OF A CREATOR

•◆•◆•◆•◆•◆•◆•◆•◆•◆•◆•◆•◆•◆•◆•◆•◆•◆•◆•

After many adventures, a man who wanted to become Nasreddin's student finally came to his door. Nasreddin was sitting outside. His hands were close to his mouth, and he was blowing air on them. Knowing that every act of a Sufi is filled with meaning, the novice asked Nasreddin why he blows air on his hands. "To warm myself up, of course," answered Nasreddin.

Sometime later, Nasreddin poured two bowls of soup, and blew air on his soup. "Why did you blow air on your soup, master?" asked the student. "To cool my soup, of course," answered the teacher.

After this statement, the student left Nasreddin, because he could not trust a man who used the same means to achieve different results.

Love. Is it a problem?

— *I have to sort out what is going on with me in order not to transfer my problems onto my daughter.*

— What can you transfer aside from your problems?

— *Only love, nothing else.*

— Is that it?

— *I don't think there is anything but love.*

— Do your problems have anything to do with love?

— *I think they do.*

— Does it mean that the more problems you transfer, the more love you transfer?

— *I feel I can't give her something. I have certain notions about how to love, and they create obstacles.*

— Are you saying that your notions about how to love create problems?

— *Yes.*

— Okay. So, is love a problem?

— *It should not be a problem. It should be a natural state of a human being.*

— Then where do the problems come from?

— *They come from my childhood, from my family. I saw many things that interfered with my life.*

— How did they interfere?

— These notions about how things should be create higher expectations from others, conflicts, and break-ups. I realized that I had to start with myself. That's what important for me now.

— But you have experienced all of this. This was a part of your life. It was necessary for some reason.

— Of course, this was my experience.

— What kind of experience was it?

— Perhaps, experience in solving the problems. That's how it is for me. But I have had enough of that experience. I think I need to stop, but I am not sure how to do that.

— If you continue with this experience, it means you are still interested in it.

— Yes. Life goes on. Lately, I have had a feeling that life keeps making fun of me.

— I recall my last seminar and the feeling of fear that prevented me from looking inside myself. I could not investigate anything then. But now I am certain I can take and investigate anything I want.

— I am in a state of emptiness. I don't understand anything.

— Would it be better if you were to understand everything?

— I want to understand at least something.

— Right now, you understand very well that you don't understand anything. And who said that we must strive toward anything?

— That's how I understood it before.

— Okay. If you want to strive toward something, do so. If you don't, then don't do it.

— I don't want anything.

— This is your state. You have chosen it yourself. But why are you so sad? You have what you want. If you choose something else, it will start to happen. This is neither good nor bad, and no one says that it should be that way or any other way. It should be the way you choose it to be. We are in a free will zone. The question is: do you choose something else?

— I want something else, but nothing happens.

— Nothing happens, because you don't want it to happen.

— I don't know what I want. I am submerged in what I am in.

— Everyone here is submerged in what he is submerged in. We need to see what we are in. Everyone has what he has chosen to have.

— I did not choose anything. It just happened …

— Nothing happens without a reason. If you have something or if you are in something, you have chosen it, even though you may not see or understand why. There are two options of choice: the unaware, mechanical choice and the aware choice.

— In my case, it happens without awareness.

— In order to see things the way they are, you must first become aware.

— I am not aware of anything. I just live.

— Great, but you say that you want something.

— I want to have money to pay for the seminar.

— And what will money give you?

— It will give me inner freedom.

To have in order to be, or to be and to have

— Are you saying that you want freedom rather than the money? This is an interesting trap. Everyone gets caught in this illusion. Let's review it in terms of: to be, to do, and to have. Ask any man on the street, and he will tell you he wants money. He is coming from the desire "to have". If you ask him why he needs money, he will answer that money will bring him happiness and freedom.

What if we were to investigate this situation from the point of view of "to be"? Let's say from your desire to be free, to feel the state of freedom? If we were to start with this state, you would have everything a free man should have.

— I don't feel that state.

— What does it mean to be free? All of you want freedom. What is freedom? We all want the same thing because our true natures are identical. In essence, we are free and eternal beings. By incarnating into a human body, we receive many limitations, and we start to fight them. This block was applied on our original state, on the state from which we withdrew in order to come here. Freedom is our initial state, the state we have always been in, are in, and are going to be in. We forgot about it here and started to occupy ourselves with having something that, as it appears to us, will make us free. We have lost touch with the state of freedom. We think we need money, cars, status, power, etc. Actually, we want to return to the state from which we came.

196

Ask anyone here whether he wants to be free, to love, to be immortal. This is what we have from the get go. This is our essence, our nature. Then why are we so afraid to talk about our real essence? Why were such heavy blocks applied? They are not coincidental either.

— *I would like to be less constrained in my communication with people.*

— What would you want to have instead of your constraint, and what don't you like about it?

— *I feel insecure.*

— And how would you like to feel?

— *I would like to feel self-assured, comfortable, and free.*

— You want freedom. How can you be free?

— *I need to understand the problems that force me to do what I don't want to do.*

— Do you do what you don't want to do? Ask anyone here whether he does what he wants to do. You will get a negative comment every time. Everyone here does something he does not want to do, and blames himself for it. This is a global problem.

So, why do people who do happen to have freedom, truth, eternity, and love, act as if they had fear, limitations, and pain? Why do they constantly talk about their problems? There is something in this.

— *They probably got used to it.*

197

— Where did this habit come from? If we are, in essence, love, eternity, truth, and freedom, where did fear, limitations, pain, and problems come from? Where did they come from, and why do people insist on them so strongly? There is meaning in all of this. God, being perfection, could not have created an imperfect creature. We are all perfect beings. So, why do perfect beings act so imperfectly? Why does a human being experience fear and pain, and why is he so unsure of himself?

— *Perhaps we are not capable of using the resources we have?*

— *This discussion about our divine origin is very theoretical for us, as we know that the body, in reality, hurts, etc. We want something else, but this is what we have.*

— There is a very deep meaning here. Which one of you wants freedom badly? You need to want it very strongly. You need to feel it.

— *It is probably those that suffered thoroughly, those who feel that they are not free, who really want to be free.*

We learn who we are through what we are not

— Yes. It is those who feel themselves not free who want to be free, because the notion and experience of freedom itself can only come from the opposite—through non-freedom. If you live and experience non-freedom, the desire to become free starts to build up. If you experience a lot of pain and fear, your desire to become love will get stronger. How can you discover what love is if you don't know the opposite state? How can you

198

find what infinity is if you have not had the experience of a limited life?

Here, we come to know who we are through what we are not. We have talked about many forms of fear. Why is fear so sustainable? Why does it manifest itself all the time, and why is it necessary?

Where did your desire to become free come from? It came from your experience of the opposite state—non-freedom. Without this experience, you would not have this desire; you would not search for it. The desire to become love comes from fear, which is the same as love. I just look at how things are constructed here. God does not create anything coincidentally. Everything here has a meaning.

The basic desire of a human being is to recall who he really is. We all want the same thing. We want to find out who we really are. The experience we receive here allows us to do that through the opposite. Yes, we know that we are love and truth, but we want to re-live it again. We can only relive it through the opposite side.

We live through the experiences we have chosen to receive. The experience of constraint is such an experience. This is experience. It is a certain state. In living through this state, you start to feel that you want something else. What can you desire while being in that state? In your case, it might be one thing, and in case of someone else—a completely different thing.

A human being can be compared to a plant. Every plant develops uniquely, depending on the soil, climate conditions, etc. Some people, in experiencing constraints, can exit to a completely different experience. Do you experience uncomfortable states that you want to change?

— *I frequently feel anger. I frequently desire things that I cannot get.*

— What exactly can't you get?

— *I can't find the balance between spiritual, material, and physical.*

— So, when you want something that you can't get, you experience uncomfortable states.

— *Whether I get the stuff I want or not, it is immediately visible.*

— Some of your desires get fulfilled when you have already forgotten about them.

— *But, currently, they are not fulfilled. There is only this uncomfortable state that I am experiencing every second.*

— Thoughts build our lives, but you have to remember the inertia of three-dimensional reality. When you desire something, it takes time to appear. Sometimes, it takes quite a long period of time. The impression appears that you are not in control of your fate; you are not its author. But, in reality, you are the author of your fate, no one else. You and only you determine what will happen in your life. Your thoughts are transmitted straight to the collective consciousness, but you are not aware of it. As a result, you don't feel yourself to be the author of your life.

— *These revolutionary changes inside me are stressing me out. I am here because I want to start to make aware choices in my life. Previously, the unaware choice constantly returned me to the circles of suffering. It appears that my desires are different at different times, but the same scenario replays itself, and I continue to accumulate the same experience.*

— I imagine myself to be a luminous sphere. I want to cleanse it from everything conditioned, so it can shine brighter, and be free and full of love. I am tired of being a bird in a cage.

— What do your limitations represent?

— "Good—bad", "Can—Cannot", "Shameful—Not shameful", "Love —Don't love". I want to do as I want to do. I don't want to do things as Cathy does. Cathy does what others expect from her. I don't like it anymore. I am bored with it.

— I came to understand that one needs to know what to do. One should continue to learn.

Create a new version of yourself

— I am going to announce a novel idea to you, that a human being knows everything from the beginning. Our school offers an opportunity for us to self-remember and to create new versions of ourselves. Everything that happens to us is the result of our own choice. Therefore, those who make unaware choices simply repeat the same old scenarios of their life experience.

We must start to become aware of ourselves. That's the first thing we need to do. When that happens, we choose another version of ourselves. This is not education. We don't need to learn anything. We simply choose a certain new version of ourselves, i.e. we recreate ourselves all the time.

You may think you need to learn. This might be of interest to you by itself. But this is just choosing a student version of yourself. You may choose an experience that you want to live through. For you to live through such an experience, you don't need to learn. You just need to choose to experience it, which is a completely different thing.

— It seems to me that as a result of this education, I can start to see the difference between my old self and the way I am now. This is very important for me. It is like being at a certain starting point and seeing what has happened to me during that time. That could not have happened without me receiving certain knowledge.

— Can we say that you have created a new version of yourself? Because of our discussion, a new version of you appears. A human being who lives mechanically simply repeats the version of himself he was given. He was assigned it, and he repeats it without even thinking about it. When you start to become aware of yourself, you start to create a new version of yourself. How many versions of yourself can you have?

— Billions.

— Yes. If I hold the idea that I can become someone only by completing an education, I may think that I must study a lot and for a long period of time. But what if I were to tell you that you don't need to study? You need to simply see the new version of yourself clearly and to choose this new version. Everything else will happen accordingly. Do you see the difference?

— The intention has been created, and it starts to work.

— Exactly. That's how it works. If you create an image of yourself as a student, you will follow that image—study here, then there, and then somewhere else. In reality, you are passing through a student version of yourself. But this is just one of the versions you have. There might be many of these versions.

— So, where is freedom? Is freedom only in choosing different versions of ourselves? Is that it?

— That's it. God has created many different creatures. A human being expresses one aspect of creation. God is the Creator. He is not just a teacher and a student. He is the Creator and therefore constantly recreates himself in multiple new versions. He created a certain aspect of himself here. This aspect, called a human being, corresponds to him in the characteristics of a creator.

What does this aspect of the Creator or this new creator do? Does he understand that the Creator has created him? He does one thing only, he constantly creates. Whether he understands it or not, a human being is created by the Creator and in his image, and, therefore, he constantly creates. He can recreate one version of himself for a very long time. That's what his creativity is in the given phase of development. But if he is aware of himself as a creator, he will start to create better and better versions of himself. This process is infinite. This is the freedom of the aware creativity. To understand what freedom is, you need to experience what we are discussing. When we discuss freedom theoretically, each one of us imagines his own version of it. So, what is freedom to you?

— Creation.

— Freedom is creation through aware limitations. Do anything you want, but be aware of what you are doing. A creator is totally free. No one limits him except himself. If he created something, he has created it. Later, he can create something else.

Where did the notion of sin come from? A system has been created here that holds a creator in very strict brackets imposed by commonly accepted, conventional notions of guilt, original sin, morals, and fear. The breaking of moral norms is accompanied by punishment. Is this a religion of a Creator? No, this is a religion of a slave.

— It is a certain creation of a slave. We created it ourselves.

God of a slave and God of a Creator

— Yes. Whatever we have here, we have created ourselves. We have created the religions, politics, and economy we have ourselves. This is what people call progress and evolution. In reality, everyone is kept in the same program. But we need this experience, if only to remember ourselves. We have created it to experience the opposite side of ourselves.

Out of this experience the next experience is going to be born. Out of the experiences of severe limitations, pain, and suffering, the desire to exit it and to become aware of ourselves is born.

Is that really me? Am I really doomed for eternity? Those are the basic questions people ask themselves here. Am I God's slave who must beg for God's mercy? And God is created similarly: if you pray to me—you will be taken care of, if you don't—you will be miserable. Who created him that way? This is not the God of a creator. This is a God of a slave. The God of a creator allows him everything, and his major goal is for a human being to have everything he needs and wants. That's God's major concern: to fulfill every desire of a human being.

— *A human being has a choice—to participate in this or not.*

— Okay. What other game can you participate in here if not in this one?

— *You spoke about other dimensions we can occupy.*

— Currently, we are here. I want to remind you that each one of us is God. What did God do? He divided himself to multiple fragments—us. And what does he do through us?

— *He becomes aware of himself.*

— Yes. He acquires experience. Therefore, each one of us is God in action. If that is the case, would God restrict us?

— *He had never restricted us. This is an incorrect understanding.*

— But this understanding is quite widespread here.

— *That's our misfortune. But we can get out of it.*

— That's exactly what we do here. To get out of something and to get somewhere else, we first need to understand where we are.

— *Where can we be if not in ourselves and in the reality that was given to us?*

— I have another question: who are we?

— *We are primordial divinity.*

— Who gave this to us?

— *The Creator.*

— Who is He?

— *Absolute, eternity.*

— How is this related to us?

— *We just coexist together.*

— We are It.

— *I do not experience that 'I am It'. I experience coexistence.*

— What is this coexistence in?

— *It is in the fact that I don't exist separate from Earth, Sun, and the universe.*

— Who are you?

— *A human being.*

— What is a human being?

— *It is an intermediary phase. It's a search.*

— Are you interested?

— *Yes. I simply live in it.*

— What have you come to understand about yourself? Who do you imagine yourself to be now? Those are very important questions. It appears that they are abstract and don't have a direct relationship to the things that make people suffer, but if we were to see them correctly, we would see everything.

This is very important, because everything that happens with you happens based on how you see yourself. That's what determines everything, nothing else. This is basic. Multiple consequences follow. The events of your life develop based on the way you see yourself and what you consider yourself to be at a given moment. This is not a philosophical but a practical question that determines what will happen to each one of us and all of us together. Therefore, I ask you: who are you?

— *I don't know who I am. I have a space through which the information about who I am can come.*

— So, you are awaiting the answer to this question.

— *I ask myself this question frequently, and my associative notions frequently change.*

— Why do they change?

— *I feel I am softness, tenderness, and femininity. I am not aggression and I am not hate, even though these states still manifest themselves through me. But they are not constant. I strive for balance.*

— I asked you who you are, and you answered that you are waiting for the answer to this question. But, now, in listing these notions you have about yourself, you say very tangible things.

— *I was talking about feelings. I have not gone beyond them.*

— You listed certain notions: softness, tenderness, femininity.

— *Are these feelings or something else?*

— Let's suppose that's the case. And what is freedom?

— *I think freedom is in one's experience of oneself.*

— What is the difference between tenderness as a feeling and freedom as feeling? We, as people, experience everything by living through it.

— *We are born without feelings. As children, we are totally unaware. We start to develop feelings later. Most of our feelings are not really ours; they are imposed on us by society.*

— Nevertheless , you experience them.

— What can we do?

— If they are not yours, whose are they?

— They are in me, but this does not mean I should stop searching for who I am.

— No one asked you to stop searching. I asked you a question, "Who do you see yourself as now?" You don't know the answer to this question, but you live. It means that you have the answer to this question, even though you are not aware of it.

— I come to the mirror and see an image. That's my notion of myself.

Who do you perceive yourself to be now?

— You have not answered my questions. You just said that this is not it and that is not it, and it has no relationship to you. But you live, and, therefore, there is something here that is related to you. Right now, you have a certain notion of yourself, in accordance with which you act. Whether you are aware of it or not, you have it.

We incarnate in order to experience different notions of ourselves and to recall who we really are. Who am I now? This question should be very specific, because if you don't see who you are now, you cannot create a new version of yourself.

People, including terrorists and serial killers, **always** act out of the best notions of themselves that they have. Everything depends on your point of view. Nothing is constant here and cannot be. Everything changes depending on how you define yourself.

— *What if I was coerced into doing something?*

— Whatever you did, you considered it to be good for yourself. You were coerced because this coercion was good for you, and whatever you did out of this coercion was also good for you.

— *Will I ever have enough power to resist this coercion?*

— Our entire culture is built on the ideas of resistance and conflict: we are all born sinful, the strongest will survive. Those are the basic myths of our culture.

We are born with the idea of original sin. We are born in fear, and we are fear. Religions offer different methods of how to get rid of fear, but these methods are the consequence of the initially accepted paradigm of our sinfulness. It is considered here that one should cleanse himself throughout his entire life.

The second paradigm states that only the strongest will survive. So, why are we surprised by the world's endless conflicts and wars? Why are we surprised to see the strong oppressing the weak? This is the basic tenet of this reality, the reality of a very low level of consciousness.

— *Is that the moral of society?*

— Yes. This society belongs to the lower level of consciousness. Consciousness of the higher level will never allow such notions. A society of the higher level of consciousness operates on the notion that we all are one. Jesus used to say, "Do unto others what you would have them do unto you." This is a statement of the high level of consciousness.

Everything here is built on the notion of how to get more for oneself, how to achieve greater success. People want to be rich and successful; in trying to achieve that, they step on each other's toes. What kind of peace and partnership can we have with such a paradigm?

We need to investigate the original axioms, i.e. the paradigms on which society's consciousness is based. Psychologists recommend not stepping on each other's toes to many times. But even if you don't step on somebody's toes now, the paradigm will not disappear. You will do it without understanding that you are doing it.

— A human being can be afraid of doing it.

— He might be afraid until he sees someone weaker than himself. In this way, the idea of separation is being constantly maintained. But in the highest version of ourselves, we are One Unified Consciousness, we are One God. But what do people do now? They bite their own noses; their right arm is fighting their left arm. What can you do in such a state? Nothing. Your arms are fighting. This is an illustration of the idea of separation.

What is going on now? More and more people start to understand the limitations of the myths they inherited. They want to build the new version of themselves and a new society. What will this version be based on?

— It will be based on self-remembrance.

— It will be based on unity. Originally, we all were one. We have forgotten that. We were torn from the source of love as children. As children, we did not have enough power to resist this oppression.

210

— Birth here is an invitation to hell. A child is introduced to the world of separation. A child is not fearful on arrival; he does not see the world as separated but he quickly becomes indoctrinated in the idea of separation. Unless society changes, children born into it will carry separation further and further. They will transmit it from generation to generation until what we discuss here happens: a certain number of people will arrive at the idea of Unity. This idea will spread, and a new society will start to rise based on the new paradigm.

— *Let's say this idea arrived. What kind of methods can help us to realize it? How can we recall our unity?*

— Do all of you see the difference between the way she speaks about it and the way I speak about it?

— *In her case, I can hear between the lines that this is impossible. She does not allow it. It's one thing to talk about it, and another thing to be it.*

— A seed sown into the soil will grow, germinate, sprout, and feel the sunlight. This is the experience of a growing plant. It is different when a seed, sitting in the soil, is occupied with the discussions that perhaps it will germinate and see the sun. Do you see the difference?

— *Of course, there is a difference. How do you feel about it? You are what you discuss. There is a great distance between words and actions.*

— Do you think so? By saying that, you create this perception for yourself.

— *I confirmed based on my own experience that a thought that comes and realization of this thought are quite separated in time.*

— It follows that you don't believe in what you say. There is a big difference between what you say and what I say. You are constantly fighting me, even though what I say doesn't presuppose any conflict. You need to see this.

— *How can I learn such a vision?*

— First of all, you need to have a desire for it. Presently you do not have this desire. You have resisted me through the entire duration of our conversation in order not to see it.

— *I have not heard of any definitive method yet.*

— And you will not hear it. What we are dealing with here is not about a method; **it is about intention.**

Unity and separation

— *If I am a creator, I am a creator who constantly asks, "How is that?" I am all about methods. The true creator simply knows and creates. In my case, I am occupied with childish questions: "Is it good or bad? How can I do something for it to be good?"*

— A creator knows "what", but he does not determine "how". He pretends he does not know "how". This is the question of methods.

— *What about the time gap between one's desire for something and its fulfilment?*

— The time gap is created by your resistance.

— *Perhaps, it is also created by our defense?*

— Resistance and defense is the same thing. **The most important thing here is your request to experience the new**

version of yourself. In the old version, you imagined yourself as something separated from everything that exists, and you experienced fear. You cannot experience anything else, because you are separated from everything and must fight everything in order to get something for yourself. This is a concept currently shared by most people.

Let's say you start to become aware of the states you happen to be in. In this case, you will recall that you are not fear, but love, truth, and freedom. This is not some theoretical discourse about something that was read, but a practical and real experience of yourself. You pass through the experience of separation, pain, fear, hatred, jealousy, and get tired of it. You have exhausted this experience, and now you are searching for the new version of yourself. You are not searching for any methods. You are not searching for the answers to the question "how? " You are searching for the answer to the question, "Who am I in this new version of myself?" That's what I want to emphasize.

— *Can it be found in the mind?*

— You manifest doubts all the time.

— *Yes. I am a human being that doubts.*

— That happens because you are in the concept of separation still.

— *Are not you there too?*

— I am speaking out of the concept of Unity now.

— *You say that, but are you in it?*

213

— Everything I say comes out of my own experience. Look, if something has a very strong impression on a human being, it is visible. You talk very easily about being either in separation or unity, but the impression is being created that neither one of them touches you. If something really touches you, it is visible to you and to others. You don't allow yourself to experience what you are discussing. There is a wall of distrust between you and me. You cannot shake the hand I offer because of your distrust toward me.

— *Do you trust strangers easily?*

— I behave in a certain way. It doesn't mean you should behave the same way. I want you to see what you want. I feel this desire in you and I offer you my hand. This allows me to see the wall between us, and I do everything I can so you can see it too. If that happens, it will disappear.

What I say to you comes from my heart, from my experiencing our unity. We speak about the way things are here. This is not a question of someone's personal achievement. Moreover, each one of you knows this. My task is not to teach you something, but to help you recall what you already know.

— *Are you trying to do this by using words?*

— *Well, words cause certain feelings.*

— *Words separate us from reality.*

— Something happens in you, and you experience doubts: "He says that, but does he feel it?'

— *I sense everything you say, but as soon as I start talking, this connection breaks.*

— You have a notion that words are lies.

— *Yes. People frequently say one thing and do something else. We live in this world, and in essence, I cannot get out of here. I would never commit suicide. That would not help.*

— This is your choice. If you decide to end your life, it is your right, and no one will condemn you for it. The question is whether you really want to or not.

—I want to sort things out. I am a product of this society, but I do not agree with it.

— *We don't agree with it either. That's why we are here.*

— We need to recall the state of unity, i.e. our real Home. If this state is forgotten, we fall into a state of separation, and everyone starts to protect himself and only himself. We will protect ourselves, because we live in the paradigm "I am being attacked—I defend myself" here. Nothing else exists in the system of separation.

I want you to see what we have here the way it is. You just need to observe which idea you take, which experience you receive out of living this idea, and where it leads. In this case, there would not be a war between bad and good, between right and wrong. There would be a partnership of the opposites inside of you.

— *This is not an idea. This is the state we live in. What is an idea?*

— An idea is something that a certain experience or feeling comes out of. If you live in the idea of separation, you experience separation. You may not understand it, but you experience separation. How do I know that? I know that based

215

on my own self-investigation. We have touched upon your inner experiences, and you have experienced the reactions that are habitual for you. You think that I, a man, attack you, a woman, and you need to protect yourself from me. I, on the other hand, tell you that it is irrelevant whether I am a man or a woman. We are one whole. You keep telling me that you want to hear answers to your questions, but you resist all the time.

— *Perhaps, I don't hear what I want to hear. I don't see me receiving what I need.*

— Take a look at what you are doing. You grabbed my hand, shook it, and threw it away.

— *Our hands have not touched yet.*

— They touched a long time ago; we are in this state from day one. This is the inertia of separation I am telling you about, "I will grab something for myself and leave." But that is not what can happen with the idea of Unity. You cannot take something for yourself and run. If that happens, you remain in the idea of separation.

— *For me, this is not an idea. It is a state.*

— An idea is something that leads to experience, to a state, later on. Take away your armor. Take away your defenses. The armor of separation cannot stand up to the idea of Unity. If you want to keep it, you remain in the state of separation. This is very important to understand. You feel it, but you don't show it. Unless you part with the armor of separation, you will not receive the state of unity. Everything will be the same again.

You have chosen an experience devoid of love

— Why don't you love your experience? Why do you treat it with such contempt? **A creator loves himself irrespective of what and how he is.** He loves all his sides. It's by loving himself first that he loves everything that exists. Do you have difficult time loving yourself, because you forgot what holistic love is?

— *Looks like this is the case.*

— It means you have chosen an experience devoid of love. That's where this melancholy comes from. Do you want to continue with it?

— *I am convinced more and more that I don't want to part with it.*

— It means, you have not received the entire experience.

— *That's why I am holding on to it.*

— But there is no love in this experience. Do you want to continue to accumulate this experience or choose something else? I push you to see where you are now and to make a choice. It can be done in an instant, but you have submerged deeply into this experience and have identified with it. So, I must come and remind you that you are a creative being who can choose another experience at any time. That's what I do.

— *The idea of separation torments me. I see people next to me who are separated. I want to come to them, knock on their door, and shake them up. But they don't want to listen to me. They tell me to go away. I came to this seminar hopping to learn how to do it from you. I want to share the work I did on myself of letting go of certain things, even if they are small,*

217

with other people. I want to share how beautiful it is, but I feel doubtful. Do I have the right to do it? What will other people think of me? What will they say?

— This is the basic thing we all have to do. Whether you can do it or not depends on you.

— All of this is totally new to me. I am told that I am god, but I cannot feel it. The idea that I can recreate myself is closer to me. Your words that we are gods sound arrogant to me. What kind of gods are we? We just sit here with our noses running, crying.

— Yes. You are gods whose noses are running and who presently are crying. God experiences that too. All of this is God, and he will not condemn himself for this. Multiple notions of God were thought up here: the condemning God, the revengeful God, etc. But those are human gods. In reality, God is everything, and God's main task is to create a space for human-gods, a space that would allow them to receive everything they want. If they want to cry, they can cry. If they want to love, they can love. He does not judge.

But a being that became aware of his divine nature moves to the next, more progressive version of himself. The next version for us is the version of Unity. And if you understand and feel it, you start to transmit it to others. In order to do that, you don't need to study anything. You don't need to master any new methodology. You don't need to graduate from a university. You need to feel it and transmit it as you transmit now.

— One probably has to feel the level of another human being, how he hears.

— You just need to say what you have to say. And trust me, you will meet people who would want to hear you. Nothing happens here by chance alone. I want to remind you that we communicate with ourselves all the time. There is nobody else here. The reaction of your companion can be different depending on the way you are at that moment: shy, aggressive, or calm. What's important here is your choice; it will guide you. How will this happen? You will find out yourself.

The basic thing here is choice. If you make it, it will develop differently in each one of you. And this is beautiful, because if you make a choice and receive a premade, known to you option of what is going to happen, it would be boring. It would not be a new experience. A new experience implies that you don't know what is going to happen next.

What does it mean *to know*? To know means to make a choice and to be in it, i.e. to accept what is going to follow your choice. And it will happen the way it will happen. You don't need any special education to do that. You have everything you need to be who you are. This is not a traditional psychological point of view that mandates that you receive an education and a diploma. I am telling you, you have everything you need already.

— *Because we come to ourselves.*

— Yes. That's what you try to convey to other people. There is no theory here, no methodology. This is creativity. It is yours, and it will be exactly the way you will create it.

— *Beautiful feeling.*

— This is how you start to manifest your nature of a creator. A creator does not run around asking which method was used before. If he does, he is not a creator, he is a craftsman. He might be a good craftsman, but he is a craftsman. The creator forms an intention, and it gets realized.

— *I came to school in order to learn to trust people and to trust myself through people.*

I did not come here to learn.
I came here to create.

— **You don't need to learn anything.** One must study and learn when one does not know something. **You know everything. You need to make a choice.** That's the most important thing. You are limiting yourself by the old, traditional scheme: I came here to learn. I did not come to learn. I came to create. It is the only thing we do here on Earth—we create. We don't study. We know everything. We create.

— *I said what I said based on your book called "The Present of Awareness". It is frequently said there that we study in school.*

— Everything evolves. Previously, we saw this reality as the reality of learning. Now, I offer you another idea that is much freer than the idea of learning—the idea of creativity.

The algorithm of creativity is thought, word, action. A thought appears in you about a new version of yourself. What do you do with this thought? You need to verbalize and pronounce it. When you verbalize new thoughts, you confirm yourself in a new version. The process of creation starts with you verbalizing a new thought. Then, you start to act. That's how the old thoughts leave and the new thoughts come.

Through verbalization of the new thoughts, you reinforce yourself in the new perception of yourself and start to act anew. You make choices, and you frequently get surprised: I did not think that way, I did not want it. But it was you who have made this choice.

A Soul is what we are. It is incarnated here in the body-mind. The body has its own requirements, the mind its own, and a Soul its own. Usually these three links are not aligned together. In reality, a Soul wants one thing only—to be what it is. It happens to be it anywhere it is: love, freedom, infinity, immortality. But entering the body-mind, it identifies with the collective experience. For now, the collective experience here is separation. Therefore, we all pass through it. But a Soul wants to manifest its true nature, i.e. the experience of limitless love and freedom. Therefore, regarding who I am here, a new thought is required.

That's what we are discussing here. This is not something unknown to you. This is well known to all of us, because that is who we really are. We are all one who know about it. But because this reality is still in the idea of separation, we lose and forget it in order to acquire the experience of separation. We do it to come to experience unity.

How can we do this? The appearance of a new thought should be accompanied by your verbalizing it and acting in accordance with this thought. What do I do? I have these thoughts. I express them to you, i.e. to myself, and act according to them. I act in accordance with the law of creativity of the Universe. There is no other law.

For you to choose between two opposite sides of a duality, you must accept them as having equal rights and equal importance. If you say that you see one and do not see the other side, you can't make a choice. It is very important to see the opposite sides the way they are.

The first necessary condition that will allow you to make a choice is in having something to choose from. In our reality, this is polarity. For example, you see yourself in the mirror and you say, "I am tenderness, and I am also callousness." Now, you have two opposite sides of a duality you can choose from. But being asleep, you can see your callousness without seeing your tenderness, and vice versa. That's why you can't choose.

Start seeing both in yourself and make a choice. Decide who you want to be at a given moment. And whichever state you would choose, it will be neither good nor bad. It will be what you choose now.

— *There is a heavy dependency on what others would think of you. Are you ready to hear from others who you really are? Suddenly, your notion of yourself can be destroyed, and you can experience pain. And the more painful it becomes, the more you want to be free of it.*

— Great. Life is change. Therefore, to preserve something as constant requires enormous effort and the pain associated with it. To preserve something is to go against life and against yourself, but everyone tries to do it.

— The most important thing I got coming here is an impulse to action. Everything we discuss during your seminars works. I think many people would agree that it works: if we believe in it, that's how it will be.

— If we stand, we will stand. But if we decide to go, we need to decide on a direction. **We need to have an intention.** And wherever the decision about the choice of direction came from, we chose it ourselves. We are unable not to create. We were created as creators. But we can also have an idea that we don't create on our own. And we create that too, and we have created plenty already from that idea.

The one who searches will continue to search, but a creator creates

— For me, the most important experience since yesterday is the experience of choosing a new version of myself. My thought is followed by a word and action. Creation of an intention: I want and I can. This reassures me and gives me power to direct all my energy to free myself and to awaken my Soul.

— What we discuss is very inspiring. If you create your life yourself, you don't need to learn anything. Your task is to form a new notion of who you want to be; it will start to work.

Let's look at those who search. They are not satisfied with something, and they start to search. They search for a long time. Here, on the other hand, we say that we don't need to learn anything, that we know everything. The question is, what exactly do we realize? Your life is what you realize in accordance with your notions of yourself.

This is the basic question. Everything comes out of it. Everything you have, all your problems come out of who you see yourself at a given moment. If you want to change your surroundings, you need to change your notions of yourself. That's it. You don't need to study anything. You just need to see the notion that you had, to feel it, and to choose a new version of yourself.

If something continues to recur and to repeat itself, that tells you that you are repeating the notions of yourself you have had. It can be repeated in multiple variations. This is an experience. This is neither good nor bad. This is what it is. But if you understand that you are a creator, you understand that you came here to realize your highest notion of yourself. You came here to experience this notion.

Every one of us receives a certain experience here. People come and they say they feel bad. They want to learn what to do to feel better. In reality, whatever you have represents the best thing out of what you currently represent. A human being always acts based on his best intentions, but these best intentions frequently lead to bad results. If a man is observant, he starts to understand that how he tried to achieve happiness does not work.

People are similar. They all want love, freedom, happiness. But they have different notions of how to achieve these goals. The question arises, "Can I achieve happiness if I continue to do what I am in the habit of doing?" Many people do not ask this question and continue to do things that do not lead them to get what they want. They either don't see it or they lie about the goals they set for themselves.

If you really want to be happy, loving, and immortal, you need to start to investigate your life from the point of view of what happens because of your actions. You create your life. You are unable not to create it. You were, you are, and you will be creators, and if you are not satisfied with your creation, you need to look at how you create it. Most likely, you will see that your goals and your actions to achieve these goals seriously diverge.

— *I saw clearly yesterday that when there is no seeing, there is no choice.*

— The physical reality we inhabit is made up in such a way that two opposite tendencies are present here at the same time. We call them dualities. Everything here is created for you to have a choice. We wanted to have a choice, and we incarnated in the reality where we have a choice. We just don't see it.

In order to choose something, you must learn both sides of yourself, i.e. you must investigate the side that is called evil here. Otherwise, you will not have a choice. We, as a Soul, know that we are love, immortality, and creativity, but we chose to re-experience this knowledge again. Our Soul cannot receive this experience where it is now. What does it need to do? It must fall asleep and enter the physical reality where it can receive this experience. That's what we did.

Without a choice, we cannot understand what is what. For example, how can you know what is good?

— *We need to know what is bad.*

There is only one constant thing in life—change

— Yes, we know what is bad, and we compare it with what, according to our notions, is good. How can we express our notions about anything? We can only do it through the opposite.

We are constantly changing beings. This is basic. There is only one constant thing in life—change. But we want to lead our life as if everything around us was stable and constant. People want stability. It is funny, but what they want so hard now, later they do not want.

To experience your version of something, you need to get to know what this version is not. That's the only way to understand yourself in duality. In order to manifest who we really are, we must choose to be who we are not.

— *Are you suggesting we fantasize? It cannot be that easy. We are walking hard earthly ways, while you are offering us an easy path. I feel an inner protest against your words, but maybe you are right, maybe it's easy and we just need to try.*

— It is easy, when you allow it to penetrate you. If you don't, it will be difficult.

— *First, we have to pass through "hard", to accumulate the experience. We cannot receive anything without having a certain baseline experience.*

— We can't say that we will not receive anything. We receive something in accordance with our notions all the time. The circumstances of our life correspond to our conscious and subconscious desires.

You have three options. The first option: you live in accordance with a chaotic number of thoughts present in your head. The second option: you follow the group consciousness that has been formed at a given moment and at a certain geographical location you inhabit. The third option: you live in accordance with your own notions. I invite you to choose the third option. This is not easy. It will require you to part with a number of thoughts present in your head and out of the group consciousness that currently, in this given reality, is oriented toward separation.

We already spoke about the myths upon which every culture is built: the myth of the original sin, the myth of the survival of the fittest, and multiple variations of these themes. It is impossible to have anything but competition, jealousy, and conflict while living in these myths. Everything here is built on these myths, but we, as Souls, are not these myths. To choose to be who we really are, we must experience what we are not. Everyone here receives this experience. No one in this reality can bypass this experience.

— *How do we accrue this experience?*

— Every mother and father download their child with a program that allows the child to receive this experience by forming his/her personality. A child does not come here in fear. A child doesn't know what fear is. A child is taught fear. We receive the perception that this world is the world of separation, here on Earth. This perception is transmitted from generation to generation.

What was formed in us as a personal program determines our perception, which in turn determines our thoughts, actions, and the experience we receive. A man says that it cannot be otherwise, because that's the way he sees things. Our culture is built on competition: who is the strongest? It is impossible to be in a state of holistic love while living in such a myth, because our perception of the world is based not on love, but on the fear to be left behind.

I offer another version of seeing the world and ourselves that is built on the awareness of our Unity. We are all a Unified Consciousness. What can you do when your left arm constantly fights your right arm? If you see the world and the people who surround you as your own parts, and seeing them as such you continue to be jealous of them, it means that your left arm is jealous of your right arm.

Jealousy appears in connection to what you praise more than anything, in connection to what you want the most. Love becomes fear. You want to be free, but you are also afraid that you are not going to be free. Originally, fear appears out of your love for something.

Look, love supersedes everything, even in this reality of separation. There is fear here and there is love here, but there is only love here. There are many of us, but we are one. If we were to accept that and to live our lives according to this idea, everything would change.

A human being is constantly thinking of how not to be cheated, not to be run over, and how to get more for himself. We live with the notion of limited resources. You want to get more, because everything is limited. But if you do get more, someone will get less. Therefore, we have a constant conflict.

Another world view is that we are all one. If that is the case, then by doing something for someone, you do it for yourself, and it will return to you. Whatever you give returns to you. When you follow this logic, you try to give away more. Irrespective of whether you understand it or not, you follow this logic and give away the best you have. If you consider fear, jealousy, and pain to be the best you have, that's what you share. You can only share what you have, and receive what you give.

— *What if I give something good, and in return receive something bad?*

The worldview of unity

— If you act based on the desire to receive a profit for yourself, you fall into separation again. You do not understand that others are you. If you pass something from one hand to another, it will stay with you. You had it, and you have it. But if you see one hand as yours and another as foreign, then passing something from your hand to this foreign hand, you will lose it.

You give to other people not because you want to receive something for yourself, but because otherwise you remain in the notion that we are not one. If you view other people as your left hand, you will pass from your right hand to your left hand, and it will transfer it back to you. This is another worldview. It is not sufficient to understand it intellectually. You must feel it.

229

If you gave something and expect to receive something in return, you don't understand that you gave to yourself. If you perceive another human being as a part of yourself, then by passing something to him, you leave it with yourself, because you have not passed it to someone else, you have passed it to yourself. This is a very important point to understand. This worldview is opposite to the worldview of separation currently accepted here, where people try to accumulate things for themselves, and the more they receive, the worse they feel. In living in this worldview, they are constantly occupied with how to take and get more. They don't understand that they take from themselves.

This preoccupation comes out of man's notion that he is separated from others, that the world is hostile, that there is no safety here except the safety he created for himself. The result of such a worldview is life in fear. I offer you another worldview, where you see other people as parts of you, where you understand that by giving someone the best you have, you give to yourself. You don't need to knock anything out of them, because you don't need to knock anything out of yourself.

— *Such a vision excludes any expectation of return.*

— You come from the point of view of the conditioned love where you give anticipating a return. This point of view is based on the notion that you are separated from the world and God. God is everything that exists, and you are a part of this everything. When a human being gets into the reality of separation, he turns off this perception and starts to see everything around him as foreign.

Such a perception does not bring him happiness, but he constantly talks about his desire to be happy, free, and to love. Everything he does is based on the separating and one-sided notions, and it does not give him what he wants. He continues to use the same methods that make him suffer.

— *We cling to this small love because we don't feel the big love. I am told, "Drop everything small and you will have everything." I want to experience love, but I am also afraid to lose everything I have.*

— I will drop everything I have, but will I find love? Fear gives birth to fear. You prolong what you are afraid of. You are afraid to lose love, and you don't have it. As soon as you are afraid of losing something, you have lost it. It does not happen sometime later, it happens instantly. Fear is a pointer that points to the fact that you do not have what you are afraid of losing. How can you lose what you don't have? But fear tells you that you have it, and if you are not afraid, you will lose everything. This is one of the illusions that you need to see. You got used to this state and say that there is nothing except that state.

— *We can confirm everything we discuss. It is very important to see things the way they are. You can repeat affirmation after affirmation, but you either don't see or don't want to accept what happens to you.*

— In order to create a new version of yourself, you need to see which version you are currently in. You can't make a step in a right direction if you don't understand where you are now. You need to know the version you currently have very well. That's what we are doing now by becoming aware of our personal programs.

Right now, you are exploring and getting to know the version of yourself that is being shared by most people. You start to see the myths upon which this version is built. You start to understand that based on these myths, you cannot have anything but the illusions of fear and suffering. You are not satisfied with this version anymore. You want to create a new version of yourself at the core of which lies a new worldview.

We are not throwing away our old experience. We are grateful to it, because we can move to the next experience only by pushing out the old one.

God has created us as creators, based on himself. It is precisely this aspect that He reflected in human beings—creativity, His own essence. He constantly creates. He recreates Himself in everything that exists. We can also recreate our lives.

Fear is contagious, but love is also contagious. Nothing can stand up to love, because it is the basic and ever-present energy. It is the original energy of any creation. A human being wants love, freedom, and immortality. He does his best to achieve it the way he understands it. But, as we can see, his actions do not lead to that, even though the aim is pronounced.

Every war ever waged was led with the aim of liberation, freedom, love of god and of motherland. All people, irrespective of who they are and where they were born, want the same things, but for some reason, whatever they do, cannot achieve it. If you were to look at your life and see that you want one thing and yet receive something completely different, you may start to think that your methods don't work. In this case, you may start to become aware of how you live and what your life leads to. You start to see that you create the same thing. You don't create what you really want. At that point, the notion of the evildoers who want to harm you starts to disappear.

— *Does evil hide behind goodness?*

— Out of which considerations does one human being kill another?

— *One usually kills out of fear, but always talks about common good.*

Stop praying to your own fear

— We have already discussed that what is hiding behind fear is love. There is one very interesting thing that we need to address: if there is a killer, there is also one who wants to be killed. This is not a commonly accepted point of view here. People think that to commit murder is to cause evil. In reality, all of us slowly kill each other, in so-called business, politics, and family life. People are not jailed for that. One side starts a war with another side, and as a result you have a thousand people dead. Someone comes from a war and brings home ten medals. Who is he? He is a hero. Kids are supposed to imitate him. But he is a killer.

Who is a killer? A killer who kills to protect his motherland is a hero. Someone who kills in a bar fight is a criminal. In both cases, we are dealing with murder. The difference is that in first case, it is considered to be a heroic deed, while in the second case it is considered to be a crime. No one kills anybody here without a reason. This is not the notion currently held by most people, but nothing happens here without a reason. Let's look

233

at the innocent victims of a terrorist act, for example. The people who were involved in it wanted to die. I repeat; nothing happens here without a reason!

God does only one thing. God realizes every desire of a human being: conscious and subconscious. God loves us unconditionally. If you love a human being unconditionally, you will fulfill all his desires, because they are your desires. That's what it means to love: to feel the desires of a human being and to fulfil them, irrespective of what they are. God does not condemn anyone.

The God that was created here is different. He condemns, punishes for not fulfilling his will, and rewards for fulfilling it. What kind of a god do we have here? Who thought him up? This is a god created by people in their own image. So, who do they pray to? They pray to their own fear.

A true God loves everyone. His love is in giving limitless freedom to any human being, as every human being is a part of Him. He loves people unconditionally and gives them an opportunity to realize everything they want, including the option to die the way they want to die.

It is very important for us to understand what death is. We view death as something horrible. The notion of the lapse from virtue is necessary for the church to rule and to hold sway over the parishioners. This notion is built on fear. Without fear, the church, the way it is now, is not needed. But it wants to be needed.

— *But people believe …*

— People believe because they are in fear. I offer you a worldview that is based on love. It will allow you to not be caught by anything that is based on fear. You will have nothing to be hooked on. You will not be hooked on lapse from virtue or on a need to confess. You will not need anyone's indulgence. You will not be hooked on anything that those who are afraid are hooked on. Church offers you a deal: you believe in what we give you, and we forgive your sins.

— *So, what do we do with forgiveness?*

— To be forgiven, you need to believe in your sinfulness. The entire church system breaks down if you stop believing in your original sinfulness. You don't need forgiveness. You are not guilty of anything. But if you accuse others, you will also accuse yourself. Why were we given relationships with other people? Why did God separate himself to multiple parts? You meet yourself in different images in order to manifest the next version of yourself in your relationships.

Suppose, you don't love yourself, condemn yourself, consider yourself not worthy, etc. You enter relationships with other people. What are you going to realize in such relationships? You are going to realize your version of your perception of yourself.

If you consider yourself sinful, the human being next to you is also sinful. How will you use relationships with other people, i.e. with yourself, if you are a kind and loving human being? You will love other people, and as a result, you will affirm yourself in this loving version of yourself. If you are jealous, you will affirm yourself in the version of a jealous man. If you have a competitive side in you, you will affirm yourself in the version of a competitor—people will appear to you as competitors.

Your relationship with other people is a mirror of your perception of yourself. The original question is who am I? Who do I perceive myself to be? You will assert your own perception in all your relationships.

— I consider myself kind, but others don't see me that way.

— We talked about the fact that every human being acts out of the best possible options he has. That's the first thing. Secondly, every human being strives for happiness, love, and truth. Therefore, he will insist that he does the best he can, i.e. that he does goodness. In the meantime, he always receives the reciprocal loop that he does not want to see in himself in return. If he wishes so, he will see what his "best" really is through other human beings. Everything here is built on oppression. The myth of separation by itself leads to oppression, i.e. you should force another human being to be good.

— We separate the internal and the external worlds artificially. In reality, these two worlds are one.

— Yes, this is an artificial separation, but it exists and it reflects the duality of this reality.

— I want to return to the statement you have made that I am not guilty, and I can do anything I want. Is not this a sly way to say that I don't care?

A permission to kill

— You are doing anything you want anyway. You can do the same thing but without guilt. In this case, you will not do many things you do while having guilt. We all do what we consider to be necessary. We start wars. We justify them by the act of terror committed by a small number of people. How will you kill other people, if you understand that all of them are you?

— *I understand now. This is far from what I initially heard as "I don't care." But someone may not understand you and hear you say that anything is fair game.*

— Everyone will hear what he wants to hear. Moreover, this someone will do what he wants to do anyway. If a man does not accept full responsibility for his actions, he will kill and blame others for his actions. It would not be me who gives birth to this desire to kill in him. This desire is in him already. He needs to defer to someone, who, as it appears to him, would allow him to do it. He does not want to be responsible for his actions.

— *Christianity found justification for the Crusades.*

— That's how humanity entertains itself living in the myth of separation, murder, and oppression. That occurred, occurs, and will continue to occur until the axiom of separation prevails. When we will start to see our unity, we will not be able to continue that.

— *What if I don't feel this unity?*

— You don't feel unity. What exactly do you feel?

— *I feel separation.*

237

— You feel separation and you behaved accordingly. Separation and unity are concepts. We can call them by different names, but it does not mean that if you don't feel something or are not aware of something, it does not exist. This is a mechanical existence: there is something inside you, and you behave in accordance with this something, without seeing it.

You will not be able to see unity unless you become aware of your separation. We come here to live through and to experience the versions of ourselves that are foreign to us in order to come to the version of what we happen to be.

We have entered something we are not. We entered the area of separated existence, and we experience this dream as real in order to reach a point where we will have to choose between separation and unity. When you have experienced separation to the fullest, when you kill everything you can kill in yourself and in others, when it fully nauseates you, only then will you be ready for something else—to choose the option of Love and Unity. Then, this choice will be suffered thoroughly by you.

It is impossible to convince anyone of this, and I am not trying to do that. I just tell you what works for me, but if a human being is not ready to perceive this point of view, he will start to fight me, insisting on his position of separation. And this is great too. I am not trying to put myself in a position of someone who knows more than everybody else here. I want to repeat: everyone knows everything here, and if someone doesn't want to move to the new experience now, it is only because he wants to continue with the old experience. This is his choice. I respect my choice, and I respect the choice of any other human being.

— *If you were to tell a man that he is sitting in suffering, that he chose this suffering himself, and if he were to start thinking about it, his whole world may turn upside down. He may not believe that he had chosen it himself. It's hard to understand mentally that I chose suffering, when I want to experience pleasure.*

— This is the paradox of this reality. We live in the paradox of opposite ideas. This paradox is inside us. We came here to acquire this experience. How can we receive it? Any experience is acquired through a certain point of view. To start acquiring a certain experience, you must have a particular point of view. What I say is also a point of view. This reality is created to receive such an experience. As we can see, the experience here is paradoxical. The conflict appears in connection with you choosing one of the dual points of view as yours.

— *Yesterday, while listening to you, I thought you were a man who has his own point of view. Today you are saying that you are forced to have this point of view because otherwise you will have to exit this reality. Yesterday, it cooled my attitude toward you, but today I saw something else.*

Point of view is an opportunity to receive a certain experience

— We cannot have anything but points of view in this reality. A point of view gives us a stepping stone, the pushing of which allows us to start acquiring a certain experience. Every human being represents a certain point of view that allows him to receive his experience in time and space. If he changes this point of view, he changes his experience.

What happens to you is determined by the point of view from which you look at one or another event that happens in your life. Every one of you has a certain point of view you see me from. You perceive what I say in accordance to these points of view. There are as many of me here as you, and at the same time you also care about other people's opinions of you. They will be different. There are as many opinions as people here. It is impossible to preserve the constant opinion of people about you.

— *Sometimes they coincide.*

— They coincide only because the same words are being used to describe different perceptions. People cannot have similar perceptions. People are different. It is impossible to create the same thing. To do that it is necessary to have great mastery or to be totally unaware.

I pronounce the word "love" and presuppose that you understand it the same way I do. We shake hands and then you do something that causes me to ask in surprise, "Is this love?" And I receive a confirmatory answer to my question. One word is being used here to describe completely different notions. Poverty of language does not allow us to explain certain things, but we must use it anyway. You say something and your friend shakes his head affirmatively, but it does not mean he understands what you have said the same way you do.

Regarding someone not behaving the way you expected him or her to behave, this is another interesting thing. We constantly require guarantees from other people. Everything here is built on guarantees. In politics, at home, at work: you have promised—so do it. What is this, if not a limitation? Can you guarantee what is going to happen to you? What kind of a guarantee can a human being who lives without awareness, in constant chaos of thoughts, give?

People constantly promise what they cannot deliver. A man promises something while harboring an opposite desire at the same time. His second desire also wants to be realized. However, it cannot be realized directly, as he is bound by a promise. As a result, a perverted realization occurs, and instead of fulfilling the promise, he starts to scream and yell at the one he gave it to.

Not being aware of ourselves, we consider that we can do what we really cannot do. We are constantly changing beings. This is the only truth. And this constantly changing being starts to offer guarantees in respect to what is going to happen to him. But we cannot know what will happen in the future. The only thing we can say is that we are going to change.

— *Loyalty, faithfulness, and stability are considered to be a virtue in any society. This is a lie.*

— Loyal is the one who asserts one point of view and insists on it as the Truth with the capital T. The point of view by itself is neither good nor bad. What's bad is one's insistence on it as the only Truth. And no politician will succeed here unless he postulates certain slogans and insists he will fulfill them. Try to come up with a program and say that perhaps in couple of days you are going to change it.

— *In our country, the politicians say one thing but do something completely different.*

— They cannot fulfill what they promise. This is an illusion of constancy. They promise what they cannot deliver, as otherwise they are not going to be elected. No one will elect them if they start discussing what we are discussing now. They are forced to lie, and the higher they get, the bigger the lie. Later, they even stop feeling that they lie. This is a nut house where the craziest one becomes the most famous.

— So, the point of view through time and space determines the experience I receive. Do I have to see, i.e. to become aware of this point of view, in order to receive a different experience?

Death as a change of a point of view

— Exactly. In such case, you receive this experience in full. Transfer to the idea of Unity is accompanied by becoming aware of the experience received in separation. Without this awareness, you cannot transfer to unity. It is impossible. You can transfer to unity only when you clearly see how you were creating the separation. In this case, you have a choice. Prior to this, you did not have a choice. The choice appears when you start to see clearly the opposite experiences in yourself. In order to choose, you need to know both experiences.

We knew that in the world we came from, but we forgot about it here. After incarnating here, we stopped seeing the world holistically and started seeing it from a certain point of view. This allows us to receive a certain experience. We may spend a few lifetimes acquiring one point of view. Then, we change it to the opposite point of

view and receive another experience. In this way, we thoroughly investigate the duality of this world.

When we, as a Soul, are in a state of total vision, we see everything at once. Here, we can only choose a point of view out of which we perceive the surrounding reality, and we receive a certain experience.

— *Is this what de-identification is all about, when one detaches oneself from what one is looking at and starts to understand the reality one happens to be in?*

— Yes. But, one must first acquire the experience. When you separate yourself from a point of view you happened to be in, you start to see clearly what was happening, how it was happening, and why it was happening. But as long as you are identified with a point of view, you can't see this. That's the peculiarity of our presence here.

As long as you are identified with your point of view, you simply acquire an experience. If you forcefully try to tear a human being who is not ready for it off the experience in order for him to see it, he starts to resist other points of view. That's why I repeat that no one should be forced to do anything here. Let a man identified with his perception receive his experience. It is neither good nor bad. When he fully receives it, he will be ready to step aside and to look at it from another angle. He will step aside, take a look, and move to another point of view. But this will not happen until he is ready to release the old point of view.

— *Is there a faster way to acquire experience?*

243

— Only awareness. That's what we are dealing with here. This is the fastest method to integrate your experience. Someone may spend many lives investigating one point of view. Someone can do it in one lifetime. And as God loves and accepts everyone the way he is and satisfies all our desires, God gives us as many lives as we want, so we can investigate different points of view.

I want to note that the change in a point of view is accompanied by very difficult states. It is perceived as a shock. It is death. The change in a point of view is death. And as the attitude toward death here is negative, the attitude toward changing a point of view is equally negative.

— *During the last seminar, I experienced fear. The state I was in at the time suddenly lifted. I let it go, and the new state appeared. It scared me. Back then, you said that the mind gets used to whatever it happens to be in. The state it is in might be bad and unpleasant, but it is used to it— it is habitual.*

— Any change in a point of view is a shock. The loss of habit is a shock.

— *One does not want to lose what one has. The habitual is always important, even if it does not bring pleasure, even if it is painful.*

— You have a dime in your hand. I am giving you a hundred-dollar bill, but you say you don't need it. You want everything to remain the same. To take this hundred-dollar bill, you need to release the dime. But when you learn to manage the changing points of view, you will not be afraid anymore. Yes, you don't know what is going to happen next, but it is going to be very interesting. You know you are going to exchange a dime for a hundred-dollar bill. When you release something, something greater always comes along. Later, you are going to release that too, and something more interesting will replace it.

— *This is a jump into the unknown.*

— *Where is one to get the energy when one is on his own, face to face with one's states?*

— You get the energy from inside of you. When a student is ready, a teacher appears. If you are prepared for a change, the one who will reflect your readiness is going to come. I come to reflect your readiness for a change and to confirm my own.

— *Is this an exchange?*

— *This is love.*

— Yes, this is love. Whatever you give returns to you. If you want to have more of something, start to give it away. Only the one who has something can give it away. What kind of an act is it—to give? You cannot give what you don't have. If you give something, it means you have it.

How can one switch one's mind to the new thinking process? For example, one considers himself poor, but I ask him for money. He replies that he does not have it. I insist that even though he does not have a lot of money, he has some to spare. If he gives away what he has, he starts to feel rich, because only the rich man can give, i.e. the one who has something. What will you give if you don't have anything?

— *He starts to feel rich, and he becomes rich.*

— This is the way to change one's state. You cannot lie here. You can only act. If you want to become rich, start to act like a rich man. The rich man is the one who has, and the one who has—gives away.

What will you do if you are rich with love? You will give this love away. You will not count how much to give and to whom. Your supplies are limitless. You give it away, and it returns to you hundred times over. You don't give it because you are trying to get a return on it. No. You give it because you have plenty of it. When you come from the state of plenty, you want to share it. When you come from the state of scarcity, you want to hold on to it.

Why do you want to hold on to something? You want to hold on to something, because you believe you don't have enough. And the more you think that way, the less you want to give. That's how you lose what you have.

("Whoever has will be given more, and they will have in abundance. Whoever doesn't have, even what they have will be taken from them." Matthew 13:12) This is not only about material wealth. Wealth is everything you consider to be wealth. It might be love, beauty, mind, awareness—everything you consider to be important. We are trying to create value here and save it for ourselves. If you can consider yourself smart only in relationship to stupid people, you will gather dummies around you. If you want to appear happy, you will gather misers around you. But this is just how things appear to you.

But what if you see yourself in others? In that case, you do not see the difference between you and them, but to see your unity.

Three in one: soul, mind, and body

— So, the most important thing is for us to become aware of our past experience.

— I asked every one of you to speak up in order to create a better opportunity for awareness. Announce your intention. We are creative beings. Whatever we announce gets realized. You may feel fearful that something will remain unsaid, get stuck, and will continue to recreate itself. Everything you pronounce will lead to the right results. If it is fear, you will start to see it. If it is your intention, it will be realized.

— I have a strong desire to feel that we all are one. It is very difficult to understand that we all are one, while the physical vision still sees everyone separated. I experience quite a difficult state in connection with this dilemma. I have difficult time grasping all of this.

— Yes, it is impossible to do that using the old, habitual-for-you-mode of perception.

— Initially, I felt the resistance of the body and the soul. Then, I imagined the soul separating from the body and flying around the world observing everything that is happening. I saw myself in every human being. I felt very light. I don't want this state to end. I don't want to be separated anymore.

— Our difficulties and our greatness are based on us being made of three parts: soul, mind, and body. The soul happens to be in love and unity. It is immortal, and it has its own desires. The mind and the body are in different states, and they have their own desires. These desires do not always coincide.

— Is this misunderstanding?

— This is a different understanding. Each one of these parts lives its own life, and each one of them has its own desires and tendencies. They may not coincide. In that case, the inner separation occurs. This separation is perceived as a heavy state. Our task is to unite. When the soul, the mind, and the body start to work as a unified organism, the mind and the body will start to realize the choice of the soul.

The soul transmits to us what it wants to achieve in this reality. The mind is the creating mechanism that uses thoughts to create reality. The body acts in this reality.

When we connect the Supreme "I" with the creating apparatus and manifest it in action, we will receive the experience that was chosen by our Soul. I call it God's Kingdom on Earth. Until it happens, we are going to experience difficult states connected to the different tendencies of each of these three parts. If we verbalize each one of them, we can see. If we see, we can change things. We can only change what we see.

— *When we spoke, I sensed the simplicity of the pronounced words about love and unity, but they were also difficult to comprehend. I also felt the greatness of these words. I felt the surge of energy. I realized I can do it.*

— It is very important to feel yourself as such greatness, as it is created by all of us together and each one in particular. On getting here, we feel lonely, unhappy, and lost. But, in reality, we are the greatest being who creates reality. We are both at the same time. One does not exclude the other. I am God who creates everything, and I am a human being who feels very unhappy. Both facts are true.

— *I feel a very strong desire to live.*

CHAPTER 6

TO WANT OR TO BE?

•◆•◆•◆•◆•◆•◆•◆•◆•◆•◆•◆•◆•◆•◆•◆•◆•◆•

A man lived in a house without windows and always complained that the sun never visited him. One day he found Nasreddin and said:

— You are very smart, Nasreddin. My house is devoid of sun. Even the smallest ray cannot penetrate my rooms. What can I do?

Nasreddin contemplated for a while, and finally asked:

— Does the sun visit your field?

— Yes, it does.

— In that case, — Nasreddin answered, — move your house there.

Choose who you want to be, not what you want to have

— *My body reacts to what happens during your seminars. I cannot explain it.*

— Where is your mind?

— *It's in my head.*

— Your brain is in your head. The brain consists of many cells. Your body also consists of many cells. But where is your mind? The mind is in every cell of your body. Every cell behaves consciously. Your personal program has been inculcated into every cell of your body. You are now experiencing the process of the restructuring of the cellular programs of your body. What happens to the body when you change your point of view? The consciousness of each cell of your body, not only of the brain cells, starts to go through this restructuring process. In connection to this process, you are experiencing certain sensations in your body.

— *We talked about unity. I know and feel it. However, separation also appears in me. I feel as if my body is being split into two equal parts.*

— *I felt relief when you spoke. Tension associated with the question, "What to do?" that I constantly ask myself has left me. Now I know that this law exists. I know that this opportunity exists, perhaps not for everyone, but it exists. I feel calm.*

— It existed, it exists, and it will always exist for everyone, but not everyone is ready to use it.

— *Something prevents me from allowing it in. Some distant parts of my brain still doubt. I want to thank you for this news. I heard you say that everything will remain the same, that we are going to remain in it, and a question arose in me: "How long can a man fight himself?" I feel a strong desire to change something in myself, but then, after another unsuccessful attempt, I understand that I am exactly the same as I was before. Of course,*

I feel certain changes, but I am not sure whether I am doing what I need to do.

— Let's sort your desires out. For example, you want to have money. Where does this desire come from?

— *It's based on the fact that I don't have it.*

— What kind of state do you experience if you continue to desire money? You continue to experience the state of the absence of money. If you want to be free, your desire is based on you not being free. When you continue to desire something, you maintain this state. You do not receive what you want. You sweat and puff trying to achieve something, persistently asking the same question, "How? ". This is not the way to do it.

If you want to be happy—be happy. This statement is perceived as a joke, but this is a fact. That's why we say that we need to start not with a state of "have and do", but with a state of "be or being", and then do and have what you have in connection with it.

You don't have to search for anything to be happy. You need to become happy, and then you are going to have everything that a happy man needs. But people do the opposite here: they try to have in order to achieve the state of "being". You need to be, and then you are going to do what is necessary and have what you want to have.

The basic misunderstanding here is in trying to pass into a state of "being" through "having" something. But you can only have something through "being". When you choose a new version of yourself, you choose who you are going to be, not what you are going to have. This is very important to understand. If you think about what you want to have, you only order what you already have, increasing it quantitatively.

— *The desire to be happy is probably the strongest desire of a human being. Whether it is easy or hard to accomplish this, this is my choice. It's important to feel that this choice is available.*

— We spoke about the fact that everyone strives for happiness and freedom but tries to achieve it through "to have". People are totally identified with the physical plane, and consider that happiness will come to them as the result of, for example, having money. They run around searching for money, but they do not become happier. One man has money, another does not. Yet, both are unhappy. This was Hamlet's question, "To be or not to be?" The basic question we are dealing with is "Who to be? ", not "What to have? ".

— *One has to be himself.*

— What does that mean? "Let's have a simple life", "Let's have a friendly life", etc. Those are just slogans that don't lead anywhere.

I repeat: we come to this physical plane to experience what we are not, in order to recreate the version of ourselves that corresponds to what we really are. That's why we accumulate the experience connected to what we are not, i.e. fear in many varieties, to come to feel who we really are.

If you were to talk to the Soul about fear, it would not understand anything. The Soul does not experience fear, jealousy, and separation. It happens to be in the Eternal Love. It experiences no limitations. But it cannot experience what we experience here. We must compare ourselves with what we really are. It is only through this comparison that we can recall who we truly are.

The fear that we experience in all its different manifestations is a necessary element that allows us to come to the realization of who we really are. People who experience fear as the only reality will consider our conversation to be total nonsense. They simply accumulate what they came here to accumulate—the necessary experience. They will come to this when they are internally ready to make the next step.

— *All our problems are due to desire. When I desire something, I give birth to a situation in which I experience the lack of something.*

I want to be happy vs. I am already happy. The mechanism of desire

— Exactly. To desire something, you should not have it. Then, you must create a situation where you don't have it, and to experience your desire. That's what people do. Let's say they want to have money, and correspondingly, they have a situation where they don't have money. They *want*, and God answers them, "Do you *want*? Great! Experience this *want*". They don't have money, but they experience the desire to have money.

It is very important to understand how thoughts and desires get realized. Are you trying to get up from a chair or do you get up from a chair? Those are different things. Do you want to be happy or are you happy? Is there a difference?

If you want to be happy, it means you are not happy. You are going to be unhappy, but at the same time you will desire to be happy. Look, that's how most people formulate their desires, while at the same time remaining in situations where they have an opportunity *to desire* something. You cannot desire happiness if you are happy; if you are happy, you are in happiness.

A human being identifies with a dream about something and does not want to part with this dream. He does not want to have what he is dreaming about; he wants to desire. Most people want to be happy and rich, while being unhappy and poor.

If you choose to be happy, it's a totally different thing. This is a choice. In this case, you start to do the work we do here. You see both sides of a coin, and you make a choice. You must discern between two sides. This is not easy, as you can see. It is easy to say, "I want this and I want that." But this is superficial, as one has not done the work of discernment. One does not understand what it means to be happy; one simply says that he wants to be happy.

To be happy means to perceive others as a part of you and to do things for them that you want to be done for you. Everything has been said already. I am not saying anything new here that you do not already know, but I say it from a new angle so that you hear it as something new.

Everyone understands and sees everything clearly yet continues to do the same thing. Therefore, something else is needed. To say "I know" is not enough. It is not easy to change a thinking process. We have said that people want to be happy, but at the same time they are not happy. How can we change that? That's where the notion that others are you kicks in: in doing something for another human being, you do it for yourself, realizing your choice—who to be.

You choose love. Great. How can you realize this choice? Start to manifest it toward yourself, i.e. toward other people. If you build your relationships based on love, you are love. You are your relationships. You and your relationships are the same thing.

— By not accepting a certain part of myself, I constantly fight other people. But sometime, I get into a state of no judgment, a state where fear and anxiety are absent. At those moments, I feel the influence of the Soul. I also observed that this state is followed by the state where things start to manifest themselves. Do I need to accept this part of myself and see how it will manifest itself?

— Yes. Whatever you don't accept in yourself and don't see will manifest itself externally. It will realize itself in certain situations and attract people who you are going to fight, experiencing fear. When you accept this part, you will start to relate evenly to what another human being says or does. It does not mean you agree with his words or actions. Your point of view may not agree with his point of view, but you will not be afraid of him and you will not need to fight him.

Both points of view have a right to exist. Moreover, you will start to experience gratitude for this human being for allowing you to sharpen your point of view and to see all its nuances. It is impossible not to have different points of view in this reality; we will have opposite points of view. They will appear in the form of other people and situations. We have a choice. We can fight them if we don't accept them in ourselves, or we can accept them as a much needed assist to see what we consider to be right.

— *Bystanders may see it as a fight.*

— If someone sees conflict in it, it means that the same duality is not balanced in him. What happens here allows you to look at yourself from multiple points of view. By changing your points of view, you change your relationship to what is happening. You are not changing what is happening, but you are changing your relationship with it. This change occurs when you start to see something you did not want to see or were afraid to see in yourself.

— *You want peace, but at the same time you don't see that you are afraid of war. Our fears provoke dangerous situations.*

The paradoxes of this reality

— Yes, that's how wars are provoked. To fight for peace, you need war. To fight for health, you need sick people. That's what the ministry of health is occupied with. It is not interested in health. The same can be said about the police and military: both are fighting for safety. If there is no danger, they are not needed.

This has to do with any role that is built on conflict. The paradox is that everyone who speaks of peace wants war. Everyone who speaks of health wants disease, etc. That's what the economy, department of defense, political parties are built upon. All of them work against the aims they consciously declare.

— *Why can't other people understand what we discuss here?*

— Be careful. We are discussing facts here. But you can create problems if you try to explain these facts to people who are not ready to understand them.

— *That's what I see in my family.*

— **Why are you next to people who do not understand you? What do they mirror in you? They mirror your own not understanding. You project your own not understanding onto them, and they return it to you.**

— *But I don't see my not understanding.*

— As long as you going to use your understanding as a cover, you will not see holistically. You can say whatever you want. If you want to accuse someone of something, you can use anything you want for it, including my words. Words and facts can be used in different ways, depending on how we look at them.

I tell you about certain facts. How you use them depends on you. If you feel that the world is one, then when you come home at night, you are not going to reproach your wife for her not understanding. You understand that when you call her stupid, you call yourself stupid. You understand that when you humiliate her, you humiliate yourself. This is a deeper understanding of a question.

When you start to look at the situation from this perspective, you try to sort out why a human being who does not understand is next to you. You will do everything you can to not relate to her in a way you don't want others to relate to you, irrespective of what she is doing. People who crucified

257

Jesus laughed at him. They screamed, "Why don't you save yourself if you are God?" He did not create a miracle in front of everyone, but when he was left alone, he ascended. His task was not to astonish those people. He did not have to prove anything to anyone.

— *Both the personality and the Soul have certain desires. The desires of a personality: you want and you remain in what you want. Nothing happens.*

— I would like to be more specific. Personality is a dual structure that consists of the opposite points of view or tendencies.

— *A human being, while in the body, can experience the influence of the Soul—he becomes a living Soul. His state becomes his Soul. I want to ask about unity. Let's say a certain situation occurs, and I experience fear. What if I change my point of view? Does it mean that this situation will not cause me to be fearful? There is also a question of my acceptance of myself. Different states might be felt. I need to observe them. I should not try to push these states away. I should try to observe them, accept myself in them, and then calmly discuss them.*

— Stop hiding what you hide. It is normal to feel what you are feeling now. If you feel hatred, you can talk about it. You need to express it. The average human being feels hatred. While he does not talk about it, he manifests it, nevertheless.

A desire that appears in us strives for manifestation. When we suppress our desires, they manifest themselves in a perverted fashion. What are we doing here? We open the doors and start to manifest feelings and desires that were locked in us. We will experience hate and aggression. We will express and manifest these tendencies. We will do it with an understanding that we harbor many hidden, unrealized desires and that we all are one.

When you approach someone here and say that you hate him, you do it only to see your state. In reality, you are approaching yourself and you are saying it to yourself. You are manifesting what you have in order to transform it. If you are afraid to talk about it, it will remain in you and eventually find a way to express itself.

It's one thing to express a negative emotion to someone in order to see and to transform something in yourself, and another thing to express it to continue it and to reinforce it. The meaning of your action depends on its intention. You can approach someone and tell him that you hate him in order to start a conflict. On the other hand, you can say it as you would say it to yourself in order to transform it. Is there a difference? The second road does not lead to the recreation of the old, habitual pattern; it liberates you from it.

Master's prayer is not a petition. It is gratitude

— How often do you thank God for what is happening to you, for this amazing process called life? What do you strengthen when you pray to God and ask to receive something or complain about something? You strengthen and maintain the state regarding that for which you pray.

God is not a high rank manager who investigates complaints of his customers. God has created an amazing universe that is based on the laws of Love. But when we forget these laws and separate ourselves from God, we succumb into a state of separation, darkness, and inner not understanding.

What is darkness? Darkness is not understanding that you are a part of this enormous Whole that we can call God or some other name. When you arrive at this understanding, you start to experience enormous gratitude. When you forget that, you experience loneliness, fear, pain, hatred, and jealousy.

A man who understands how the Universe is made and that we happen to be part of the Whole is always grateful. He knows that the Universe reacts to everything that happens inside him. It realizes all his thoughts and feelings. Because of this knowledge, his prayer is not a petition, but gratitude. He knows that whatever he is grateful for will happen. He is in a state of eternal gratitude. There is nothing better than that.

But how often do you thank God for being a part of Him? How often do you thank God for Him loving you dearly? His love is manifested by him offering total freedom to each of his parts. Is there any state that a human being experiences that would correspond to this understanding besides love?

— *It is love.*

— Love is gratitude. When you love someone unconditionally, you are grateful that this human being is the way he is. Love is constant gratitude. It is open to everyone. It is not a privilege of someone who was chosen. The one who is chosen is the one who chose it. The chosen one is the one who chose to be it. No one choses anyone here. Man choses something and his life proceeds based on what he has chosen.

So, what do you choose, and what do you receive because of that choice? Every moment of our life is an opportunity to choose.

— *Are you saying that we have chosen suffering and pain?*

— Yes, you have chosen suffering and you receive it. You have chosen to experience suffering yourself. While making this choice, you forgot that you are God. You chose something that is not Love.

We have already discussed that this reality is built on the principle of duality: there is love and there is hate. Hate and fear are necessary in order to feel love. When you choose suffering and fear, you submerge into them to feel them thoroughly, to get tired of them, and to choose love.

When you choose love and when you are grateful, you feel your connection to God. You feel yourself as a part of Him. In choosing fear, you don't feel that connection. The question everyone should ask himself is a question of choice. Whether you like it or not, you have created your life the way it is now yourself.

— *We experience flashing moments of love and understanding, but we also experience fear and other negative states. What happens when one state transfers to another? Will we ever be able to see the whole picture and to make this state of love permanent?*

— You will experience both fear and love here, and you will always have a choice. When you forget that you have a choice, you choose fear and go through situations that you have already experienced.

You want someone to help you. In forgetting that you are a creator who can choose, you don't turn to yourself, and you lose connection with love, with God. This is an illusion. You cannot lose your connection with God, because you are God—you are an eternal part of God. During the heaviest and darkest times and states you have experienced, you were God. And you continue to be God. You can renounce God, but God will never renounce you.

— *Our problem is that we don't see God in ourselves during those states.*

— We search for what we had and what we always have, because each one of us is a derivative of Love. There is nothing here but Love. Even fear is Love.

— *If I am God, where does fear come from?*

— What happens when you try to avoid something? What you try to avoid follows you. You become afraid of something, and in being afraid you attract it. The question is how masterfully you use what you happen to be in. Our reality is created in a great way, but in not knowing its laws, we resemble a man who sticks his fingers in the electrical outlet trying to figure out what electricity is.

Anything that leads to fear initially was a desire, a desire that you did not realize. That was the original desire. It originated out of your interest. The basic thing here is interest. When you are interested in something, you don't need any conditions to do it. Duty and responsibility are required to do something you are not interested in. Desires get separated here into good desires and bad desires, correct desires and incorrect desires.

When a certain desire appears in you, defined by someone as bad, you block it. It does not disappear. It starts to attract a situation for self-realization. When a desire does not get realized, fear appears. The best way to get rid of a desire is to yield to it. The best way to get rid of fear is to yield to it.

"I am afraid of being deceived..."

— *I am afraid of being deceived.*

— How does a situation in which you feel deceived appear? A small child wants to get something, but his parents refuse.

— *Adults apply certain conditions. They tell him that he would receive it if he does something in return.*

— Yes. He understands that he cannot talk straight about his desires. He needs to be sly. He needs to find out what his parents prefer in order to receive what he wants. If a child can't get what he wants directly, he needs to understand the system of his parent's beliefs. This is deceit.

A spontaneous desire that appears in a child is not satisfied, and a child starts to look for alternative routes to satisfy his desire. Later, he gets so mixed up that he either forgets about his desire or starts to be afraid of them. This is the situation in which most people happen to live.

— *What if one tries to fool the situation that was created and says, "I want to be deceived." Will the wheel turn another way?*

— You need to allow the possibility that whatever you try to avoid will happen. For example, are you ready to be deceived? Are you ready to see your husband or your wife taken away from you? Are you ready to be robbed? Are you ready to experience this sort of situation and to accept what you are afraid of as your hidden desire? You also need to allow the opportunity for something that you dearly want to happen to not happen. That's the way to untangle the ties created by the suppression of your desires.

— *When I allow the situation that I don't want to happen, I experience fear. I become afraid of attracting this kind of situation.*

— Let's figure out your fear of being deceived. The words themselves are deceptive. When you call something that happens to you a deceit, you start to experience that situation as a deceit.

But words are just symbols. Feelings are primary in the process of acquiring life experience. Feelings are the language of the Soul. You call something a lie when someone says something that **you don't consider** to be the truth. He, on the other hand, considers you to be a liar, because you say something that he **does not consider** to be the truth.

We can look at any given fact from many different points of view. If we look at the situation from one point of view only, all other points of view will appear to be a lie. It is very important to see unity in plural points of view, because multiple points of view of one fact create an opportunity to perceive it holistically. In other words, these points of view do not contradict; they complement each other.

There are many of us, but we are one, and each one of us has individuality. Each one of us expresses a certain perception about what is going on, and this perception is not an incorrect perception. This is an equally correct perception for another human being. Will your relationship to the events that occur in your life change if you accept this multiplicity of equally valid points of view?

— *It will probably change. If one accepts deceit, one will probably stop deceiving others.*

— In that case, you would stop fighting those who express opinions opposite to yours. This reality is illusory and deceiving. It's a dream. If you understand that, your relationship to the events that happen to you will change.

This dream can be experienced as a nightmare or as happiness and gratitude. When I say that this reality is a dream, I mean that every one of us happens to be in this world, but not of this world. If you think that you are a body-mind and that nothing but this reality exists, your life will be a nightmare. Would your attitude toward events that happen to you change if you were to know that you are the one who was, is, and will always be, and that your presence here represents a certain experiment conducted by your higher self to receive a certain experience? You chose to be here prior to your incarnation here. After so-called death, you will transfer to the state of pure Love, Truth, and Freedom.

— *Will such notions as deceit and anger stop to exist?*

— These notions will remain, but your relationship with them will change. You can change your attitude toward them. The same event can be viewed by you from opposite points of view without inner conflict and condemnation.

What don't you like in your life? If you don't like it, you will fight against it. But this fight will just escalate your condemnation and the feeling of guilt that accompanies it.

Can you accept something you don't like as a fact, as something that simply exists? If so, you will not have to fight it. You will simply accept it as something that exists. Such an acceptance will change your state in relationship to the actions that previously were seen by you as a humiliation or insult. The same facts will allow you to receive another experience.

When you are afraid of something, you receive exactly that. You may continue to be afraid of it, or you can see it from a different angle. If you see it differently, it will not hurt you anymore. If it will not hurt you, it will not recur.

— *How does it work in terms of pleasure? I like certain things. For example, I like to have a drink in the company of a beautiful woman.*

Why do I want to have a drink?

— Let's figure out why you want to have a drink. What does a drink give you? You want to have a drink not just to lower the quantity of alcohol on the planet. You receive a certain state as the result of this action. So, what state do you get into when you have a drink?

— *I reduce my anxiety.*

— So, you don't want to have a drink. You want to get rid of fear and to be calm. Alcohol is a substance known to you which currently provides you with this result. Let's say you had

266

your drink, and you have received the desired result. How long does it last?

— The duration of its action is very short. The opposite state appears very fast, and it gets stronger.

— You remove something, but it gets stronger later on. You receive the opposite effect. Then you start to look for other methods to receive and maintain the desired state. But what if you were to start to see both of these states simultaneously. If you have a drink and feel good as a result, no one will ever be able to force you to refuse this drink. But what if you have a drink, feel good, and then, for the same reason, start to feel bad?

We just came to understand that a human being drinks to get rid of a heavy state in which he happens to be. This method is used subconsciously. If you have an aim, you can use many ways to achieve it. Why do people drink so much, especially in Russia? There are not as many psychotherapists here as in the US. Psychotherapy here is a glass of vodka. A human being tries to get rid of the limitations he got entangled in by using a commonly known method. Perhaps you use a different method?

— Drinking is starting to be a problem for me.

— This is a swinging see-saw. You swing up and down. You may swing it to such an extent that your see-saw will break. A human being gets used to the state of swinging: I feel bad now, but I want to feel good. The worse he feels, the more he wants to improve his state, i.e. to have a drink. He gets a drink, gets his so-called "good" state, and then he starts to feel bad again.

He wants to have another drink to feel good. Every single dependency is built upon this scheme.

— *It looks like pleasure is not in pleasure.*

— You stop feeling pleasure after a while. Pleasure turns into something questionable, but what comes as the opposite to it is very real. The habit, however, is so strong that you cannot get rid of it now. If a human being were to objectively observe what happens to him, he would search for something else. But most people hold on to this scheme until the see-saw breaks.

For example, you like a woman. After a while, you look for another woman, and then another woman. This situation escalates. What do you get at the end?

— *I look for a variety of experiences and I find them. Different situations play themselves out, and I experience pleasure. The sensation of novelty eventually fades, and then it becomes habitual. I lose interest, submerge myself in a state of dissatisfaction, and remain in it until another opportunity comes along.*

— Take a look. This is another see-saw. What is your original desire? Why were you looking for a woman? You wanted to love her. You wanted to experience love, but instead you got into a circle of recurrent situations where you don't experience love. You experienced a certain pleasure that slowly diminishes with each new woman. What's habitual here is your search for love.

We have just investigated two tendencies. First, you want to get rid of fear. Second, you want to find love. These two tendencies are primary in all our aspirations, but few people see it that way. People consider a man who flips women frequently to be a womanizer and condemn him for such behavior. The mechanism of condemnation, punishment, and guilt gets turned on.

We are searching for Eternity, Absolute Love, and Truth, but instead get trapped in a duality and get locked up in these dualities like birds in a cage. A partial solution to the problem is not the solution. You search for love, but you only find fragments. You try to get rid of fear, but you cannot do it.

— *I search for it outside.*

You search outside for something that is hidden inside

— You search outside for something that is hidden inside you, i.e. you do not search where you have lost that something. If a man were to observe what happens to him, he would see that he does not get what he wants. He would see that he applies the same efforts all the time that lead to the same results. Perhaps then he will view what he creates as something that he wants to create. But if he does not see it, he will continue to do the same thing again and again.

A human being encounters a certain recurrent situation; he cannot bypass it. He searches for a solution in the external world, but the common-sense methods he uses do not work. They lead to the opposite of what he wants. He wants to get rid of fear, but he continues to experience fear. He wants to receive love, but he receives hate.

If you don't dig deep and come to understand what's going on, you will continue to do what you are in the habit of doing.

It seems to you that you know the answer. You experience fear. It means you must have a drink. You want to have love—you need to search for a woman. But in both cases, you receive the opposite of what you were looking for. You received what you wanted, but it offers only temporary relief. After a while, you accept that this happens to everyone here, and you give up.

— *I live in this stereotype. I consider it to be normal because that's how everyone here lives.*

— Yes. But in this case, you don't realize your main desire for Unconditional Love. This desire will never leave you, because your Soul knows what it is. But your personality always falls into traps. It tries to fight those traps, but it gets even more entangled. You forgot who you are. You got stuck in the dualities of your personal program.

Can we attain Unconditional Love here? Some people lose faith in it and satisfy themselves with a surrogate, i.e. sex.

— *You wrote somewhere that sex is a spiritual bridge between a man and a woman.*

— Yes, one has to believe in this. If you lose faith in Unconditional love, you will not get it. "You shall receive according to your faith". If you want to have the maximum, you will get it. If you want minimum, you will be satisfied by it. Look at how many questions people ask about sex. Actually, our entire communication can be seen as sex. Everyone and everything enters a sexual relationship with everyone and everything here, but it is one thing to have a one-night stand,

and a completely different thing to communicate at the level of heart, mind, and soul. You received the physiological orgasm, but did your heart get turned on during it? Did your soul open? That's the question.

You experience dissatisfaction that pushes you to search for a man or a woman, but your search ends with your falling into a trap of another fragmented relationship; mutual claims, grudges, and feeling of guilt follow.

What kind of claims can there be if two people are happy and love each other? What else can they ask from each other? If you feel another human being as yourself, you will offer him everything you have. You will not accuse him or her of not providing you with something. So, why can't we achieve such a version of ourselves?

— *We live with the notion of limited energy resources.*

— What do you spend your energy on? You spend it on mutual blame. You spend it suppressing and not to allow multiple fears of your sub-consciousness to rise to consciousness. Your fears are your parts, and they require manifestation. But you don't want to see them, you block them. Envision a house that has thousands of doors. You run around trying keep these doors from opening, to prevent your prisoners from getting out. All your energy is spent blocking these doors and keeping these prisoners inside. But what if you were to allow yourself to be who you are?

— *If I were to do that, no one would understand …*

— We have already figured out that no one understands anyone here anyway, because the moral created here prevents us from understanding ourselves. As long as you are afraid of other people seeing you as bad, you will eternally run away from yourself.

— *Is there a way out of this mess?*

— **Yes, there is a way out. The way out is to open all the doors and to allow yourself to say that you are who you are. We are both positive and negative at the same time. In reality, we are everything. Someone who is afraid to be called a prostitute is already a prostitute.**

People are afraid of words, but they don't try to figure out what these words mean. What is prostitution? It is selling one's body for money. What do people do in their so-called families? They do exactly that. They sell their bodies for security and money. I don't see any difference. Who wants to see the difference? Everyone here is scared, and everyone is preoccupied with word manipulations. Let's be sincere and see that every one of us has everything in him. Then, we are not going to be afraid to show ourselves to others.

Aggression is a cry for love

— You do what you want, but you don't understand who is it in you that wants it.

— *You are right. I do it, even though I am afraid of it.*

— What does it mean to be afraid? When you are afraid of something, your original desire is present in this fear. **If you are afraid of being under someone's command, it means that you have a desire for someone to command you.** At the same time, you are afraid to consciously accept this desire and you deny it. This is neither good nor bad. This is a fact. Everyone commands everyone here. What's wrong with that? But a man says that he is afraid of being under someone's command, i.e. he cannot acknowledge his desire. At the same time, he satisfies the desires of other people. People ask him for something, and he does it. As you can see, one fact or act can be viewed differently.

— *But I don't find it pleasant.*

— Then why do you do it? If you do something, it means it agrees with you. Until you acknowledge that you want to do that, you will continue to see it as a problem. You must do it with a full understanding that you want it yourself. It does not matter what you do; your attitude toward it matters.

— *If we were to accept that a human being is love, then who can command him? Can we see anything as a command in that case?*

— A human being does what he does only if he wants to do it. But words are used afterwards to define something as good or bad. People react to words. If you do something or do not do something, you like it. Look inside and try to understand this.

— *I like when people ask me for help.*

— You experience pleasure in that case. However, when someone asks you for something and you judge it to be an order, you do it without experiencing pleasure.

— *Yes.*

— So, what makes you dissatisfied in that case? Your perception about where a human being, who asked you for something, is coming from is what dissatisfies you. Is he asking or demanding? If you see it as a demand, you feel displeasure. So, what do you want? Do you want to be in a state of love? How can you remain in a constant state of love?

— *I have to change my attitude.*

— Stop seeing and calling something an order. Someone can call something an order or he can call it a favor. Who appraises that? You do. Who has the keys to the door of your happiness?

— *I do.*

— Do you use them? These keys are universal and can be applied to any situation. Your attitude toward any situation is determined by how you see it. Who is assessing it? You are assessing it yourself, and you can assess it the way you want. For example, someone is screaming at you. You will not get angry if you feel that you are being screamed at out of love.

What is a command? What is a manipulation? Who tries to manipulate others more than anybody else? It's the one who needs something. What do people need? Love. Everyone needs love here. But when you assess it to be the manifestation of power, an attempt to control you, whether you do it or not, you experience fear and dislike. What do you see in someone who attacks you? Do you see an attempt to manipulate you or a plea for love?

— *I am in the habit of seeing it as a manipulation.*

— A master understands that aggression is a cry for love. It's one thing to see an enemy in the aggressor and try to defend oneself from him or her, and another thing to see an aggressor as a human being who is desperate for love. Will you defend yourself, attack him, or give him what he so desperately wants?

— *Are you saying that the aggressive people have a minimal supply of love?*

— They are deeply unhappy because of the absence of love in their life. That's the reason they manifest aggression. Look at it this way and your attitude toward them will change drastically. You will not perceive them to be your enemies anymore.

— *I asked myself why I don't always do what other people ask me to do, and I realized that I live with the notion that I don't have anything to give. I consider myself deprived. I experienced a feeling of guilt. It was followed by anger directed toward myself and toward those who ask me to do something for them. I realize that I need to find and create a new version of myself, in which I have something to give people. I feel that this is happening already. There is a different kind of love, and it is not necessary to completely submit to everything other people want from me. I can give what I have at that moment, and that can help someone else. I can do something sincerely, from the heart. That will change the situation.*

— In order to become love, you simply have to make a choice.

No one can kill anyone

— When other participants shared their experiences, I observed myself thinking that they were describing my own states. But now I think these thoughts were transmitted to me from them.

— About thoughts: your own and others. The mind is a receiving apparatus. It was created to catch thoughts. As a radio receiver tunes to different channels, the mind receives the energy of thoughts. In the process of doing that, it considers some of them to be its own, and some to belong to somebody else. Actually, all these thoughts are yours, because you caught them and you can recreate them. However, these thoughts are polar in nature, and as a result you experience a problem of choice, which can be formulated as, "Which thoughts are mine and which thoughts belong to other people?"

When you choose an intention, you start to sift through the thoughts that you need from the thoughts that you don't need. Without an intention, you are a garbage can for all sorts of thoughts. Someone approached you, said something, and you are in a state caused by his thoughts. Someone else came, and you submerge into his thoughts. So, where are you?

Without an intention, you are a reflection of different thoughts and the corresponding states of the people with whom you are dealing. Later, you become surprised. What is happening to me? Both positive and negative thoughts come together, as they are two sides of one coin. But because you want to be conscious of only the positive thoughts, the presence of negative thoughts causes you to experience fear. You may be surprised by the thoughts that appear in you. You may blame someone for them. In reality, you were simply ready to catch them.

— *Were these thoughts really mine?*

— What is mine and what is not mine? This is a question of your ego. It asks this question because it can't understand itself. For your Supreme "I", all the thoughts that appear in you are yours. But to understand that, you need to accept yourself as a whole. In other words, you need to accept both your negative and positive sides.

Everything is interconnected with everything else here. We have discussed One Unified Soul that gives birth to multiple manifestations of itself in the form of human beings. So, who navigates your life? Is it the mind, the body, or the Soul? Until you see yourself as these three elements combined, you will be constantly bothered by these questions.

How can a human being exist in the presence of such inner disharmony? How is it possible for our organism not to break into pieces? What keeps our cells together in this structure that we call a body?

— *Is it the energy of the Soul?*

— Yes. When the Soul sees that a certain body has exhausted the experience it was supposed to receive, it simply exits the body. This process is called death. Death is a return to yourself. Look at death this way. No one can kill anyone here. This is impossible. "Die you will not, but change you will". We are constantly changing forms. We are always alive. We are life itself.

So, what keeps a human being and human civilization together as one whole? How can we explain this if we don't look at it as one whole? If we are simply a collection of certain pieces, each one of which acts the way they want, why are we still alive? Something is present here that keeps all of this together. We are kept together by the power of the Unified Soul or the power of God. But if this is God, then everything is interconnected with everything else. The same process that occurs in our body, with cells dying and regenerating, occurs with human civilization. Some people come and some go, but the organism remains.

We are parts of God's body. Some say that a human being is a microcosm. What is a microcosm? A microcosm is God. He created human beings in his image and likeness. That means that in investigating ourselves we can learn who God is. This opportunity exists because God gave a human being what is basic for him, i.e. the ability to create. But currently, most human beings create without awareness.

How does spiritual evolution occur in a human being? We have all heard of the seven chakras buried inside a human body and of Kundalini that must be raised from the first chakra to the seventh chakra. Some call it enlightenment.

These chakras, even though they cannot be seen with physical vision, determine the perception of a human being. If your attention is concentrated in the sexual center, you will see life as the interrelationship of sexes. If your attention is concentrated on the first chakra, you will see life from the point of view of safety and survival. You will be preoccupied with the fear of death and will attempt to get rid of it. The third chakra is responsible for the control and manipulation of other people. This is a short excursion into the first three chakras.

Next, we ascend to the heart chakra. When a human being elevates his energy to that level, he starts to interact with the entire world. He starts to feel Unconditional Love.

Your perception depends on which chakra your attention is directed toward, i.e. which chakra you happen to be in. The changes we await will appear in the fourth chakra. A human being who is not in touch with the heart lives in the world of separation.

So, our self-remembrance is connected to the ascent of energy through the chakras.

Now, let's imagine how God lives. If we were to use an analogy, the scheme is the same. Who elevates their life energy from the lowest chakra to the highest? We do. Going through the evolutionary circle, we enter this reality and forget that we are the eternal, loving Soul that exists in Truth. We enter this world to receive a certain experience and to realize who we really are.

We know everything, as being in the multiple spheres of being; we are outside time and space. Over there is only here and now, where the multidimensional and eternal happen. From over there we see, know, and understand the unity of everything that is called past, present, and future here.

When you want to enter the physical plane and to experience something physically, you enter a certain situation in the conditions of which you cannot see everything. To live through this experience, you have to forget who you really are. It is only by forgetting who you are that you can become aware of who you really are. To walk through the path and to recall who you are, the mechanism of forgetting gets turned on.

— *It looks like we descend here in order to ascend.*

Evolution is not a staircase; it is a spiral

— We can compare our evolution to a spiral. That's how we move. How does energy move in the enlightened human being? It travels in a spiral. The same thing happens in the Universe. We go through circles while working on self-remembrance. Actually, everything is known. We already know everything as spirits and souls. Every one of us is a creating spirit. We need to remember that. In remembering that, we move through chakras or through the spheres of being. A human being elevates energy in his own body, while humanity does it in the body of God.

God is a creator, and a human being is a creator. We create ourselves, and God creates Himself through us. We possess the same creative ability, and we create ourselves. When we get back to where we came from, we can choose what to enter next. We can decide to enter the physical plane again and to experience another life here, or we can enter a different reality, a different world. This is total freedom. There is no competition there. Over there we are free to do anything we want. There is no notion of top or bottom there. There is no notion of higher or lower spirituality there.

— How should we relate to the energies of the lower chakras that we start with? Can I simultaneously feel the energy of the second chakra when I am in the heart chakra? Can I use this energy?

— We do not exclude anything. On the contrary, we include everything. So, when the next chakra is turned on, you receive a broader vision. As a result, situations that used to create problems on the level of first three chakras resolve themselves. Let's say you are attracted to someone. You have physical contact with him or her that brings you sexual pleasure. However, aside from sex, your relationship with this human being is bad. When you get to the level of the heart, everything changes. If both of you get to the heart, you start to see each other in a totally different light, and your intercourse will be superior to any physical orgasm.

— While on the lower levels of consciousness, we can only see the problems we are in: problems at work and at home. Until we move through a certain invisible border, we continue to live in these problems.

— There is nothing else in the lowest vibration. Everyone competes with everyone there. Even when people unite, they unite only to fight somebody else. For example, a family is formed. It must fight for existence. It fights the whole world, and as a result, it feels united. But there is also separation inside it. The institute of marriage has not proven itself livable. Look at the number of divorces around you. People do not get what they want from marriage.

You experience a totally different state when you reach and enter the heart chakra and start to see your interconnectedness with everything around you. You start seeing everything in a different light. You start to understand that the kids that you gave birth to are the souls who came here to acquire a certain experience.

— *It seems to me that the way to the heart is a difficult path. Sometimes I think that I already live by the heart, but the people next to you don't want to understand you. Then I look deep inside and see that someone just mirrors my own side to me that I have not seen. When I see it, I accept it irrespective of how difficult it is. I feel a surge of energy, and in this state, I understand that the people who surround me, even though they are in the same state, do not cause me to feel contempt toward them. I sense that I know. I feel I was in it and I remain in it.*

— There are no chosen here. We are all the same in this respect. We are all god-like. When you develop such a vision, the competition stops.

— *You start feeling what other people feel.*

— What role do the people, who happen to be in, let's call it illusion, play for the one who acquired a broader vision? They play the role of someone who you are not. We have already discussed that we came here to experience what we are not and get to what we really are. They live in fear, but you can feel love, leaning precisely on this fear. That's how the process of self-remembrance goes. Therefore, these people perform a very important and necessary role for the Whole and for each one of you in particular. They maintain what you are not, but based on this, you can see who you are.

— *When I think that they are not me, I fight, scorn, and try to avoid them. It turns out that I scorn a certain part of me that I don't understand, and this part keeps bugging me. It appears that I got myself surrounded by friends who think the same way, so I go to the seminars, but as soon as I come back home, I return to my old circles.*

— You don't accept them because you don't understand why they behave the way they do. Now you can look at it from a different point of view. When you accept this, everything will start to change in your life. You will not need to lean on who you are not anymore, to be who you are. But during the period of your becoming true to yourself, you need those people as a supporting foundation. As you progress in self-remembrance, you will no longer require their presence to such a degree.

We are dealing with the eternal conflict between good and evil. It is impossible to uproot evil. But your understanding of what evil is changes. You start to understand how to transform evil into goodness. You don't need to fight evil anymore; instead, you need to see it in yourself and transform it.

Live out of inner interest, not out of external duty

— When you start to live out of interest to the experience you receive, you start to get interested in everything. In this case, common influences accepted here, such as duty and coercion accompanied by condemnation and guilt, stop influencing you. You will not experience fear anymore.

An impulse appears on which you start to base your actions. This impulse is you, and it is endless. When you exhaust one interest, i.e. experience, you move to the next. This new way of life contradicts the old one, the one which was based on separation and fear.

When you start to live out of this interest, people will call you an egoist. The old system is based on obligations that do not take into account a human being himself. When you start to manifest what we discuss here, you start to contradict the old system.

Imagine a society that is based on a different approach to life, where no one imposes anything onto another, where each man chooses what he considers to be necessary and does it the way he considers it should be done.

— *Will this lead to chaos?*

— It will, if you consider breaking the currently existing system to be a chaos. But it will create a new system, where what is considered chaos here will be the order. That's why transfers to the different levels of consciousness are associated with chaos, out of which the new orders are born.

If we were to take kids as an example, we would see that they don't want to be limited in any way. Limitations force them to follow a certain path, and at the end, kill the interest in them. Limitations kill that basic creativity in them that is characteristic in all of us. They are forced to memorize and absorb outdated knowledge. They resist. In the end, kids repeat what their parents did. This is a vicious circle.

It is not easy to recall who you are and to start to follow your own path, because the entire system here tries to make you forget who you are.

The intensity of your changes is connected to the change in your point of view

— Life is filled with constant change, but our perception is tuned to constancy. From the outside, a human being appears to be something unchangeable. But if we were to look from the inside, for example, from the point of view of physiology, we would see that human being constantly changes. We are dealing with endless changes every second.

So, what is a human being? Is he something constant or something that constantly changes? A human being is a constantly changing creature, but our harshly fixed perception only catches what is permanent in him. If a man is bored, wherever he goes, he will experience boredom. **By changing our perception, we change our state.**

Someone said yesterday that he was bored. His mind was torturing him. What does it mean? It shows fixation on one point of view that creates the impression that nothing changes. Everything is constantly changing, but you don't see that. You are fixated on something that appears stable to you. That's why you are bored.

Another man who can change his views, sees the diversity of things, and his life is completely different. If you want your life to be the same, fixate your attention on something. When you start to change your point of view, changes will start to occur, and life will become fun.

The intensity of your change is connected to the changes in the points of your perception. If a human being is willing to change them frequently, someone may say that he leads an unquiet life. Someone else lives a very quiet and monotonous life, using only one point of view.

— Last night after the seminar I experienced severe pain in the area of my heart. I could not sleep all night. What was that?

— What is pain? We call everything we don't like pain, but in reality, your heart is asking for attention. Dead people don't feel pain. And most people consider a pain-free state to be the ideal state. As soon as they have the slightest ache, they rush to a doctor and do everything to turn into cadavers again. If something is hurting you, it means it is alive and asking for your attention. In defining your sensations as disease, you take pills or run to the hospital. I don't get sick. I change. This is a different point of view. We are constantly changing creatures, and it is only our fixation on our constancy that forces us to throw away everything that is not congruent with our notions. As soon as we allow ourselves to change, we turn into something new.

One can change instantly. What is God's Kingdom on Earth? It's a state when you instantly change everything, from your appearance to your surroundings, in accordance with your thoughts. We are living in the material world, where it takes a thought a certain amount of time to realize itself due to inertia, where you don't see the connection between your current thought and what happens now. Over there, this connection is immediately visible.

A human being can be oblivious to the fact that everything he has here he has created himself. Over there, his thoughts lead to instant results. If he transitions from here to there with the thought that he is sinful, he will arrive in hell. He will go to hell not because hell objectively exists, but because his mind has created it. But then he will see that everything changes very fast there. He will see that reality follows his thoughts instantly over there; if he continues to create nightmares over there, it means he likes them.

— *I used to be irritated by people and the situations they would get themselves into. I thought that one must search for all the answers inside himself. I thought no one could help me sort out these questions, and it is better to be by myself. That's how the mistrust that I kept reinforcing was born. Now, I am interested in other people.*

— **You can only see outside what is inside you. When you build a relationship with another human being, you build a relationship with yourself. If someone keeps bugging you, it is your inner part. The part that you don't see comes to you in the form of the external human being. The inner fears you have, will come to you in the form of people and situations.**

You can continue to hide from yourself, to dive into solitude and depression, and to repel the external world. But in that case, you will not see, investigate, or change yourself.

Why do you shy away from people? You do that because everything is the same and boring, and there is no trust.

— *I consciously chose a solitary path of self-investigation. I was not in the group, and I was comfortable for a while, but something has changed in me now.*

287

— That was a point of view. You have experienced yourself as a solitary seeker. You have moved on your own. But the people who have gathered here want to receive a new experience. We keep talking about what we need to do to receive it. We can continue to accumulate the experience we are fed up with. When we have something, it means we wanted it—we chose to have it. We can continue to experience it, but we can also choose to experience something new.

— When one comes to a point when one is ready to change something, the question of "How?" appears.

Intuition is the language of feelings

— This question of "How" frequently comes up. It comes from the mind. As soon as the mind discovers that something new exists, it immediately asks how to achieve that. If you listen to your heart, you will not hear that question. There are no questions there. This is a different territory. Most people don't even touch it. The mind tries to suppress it.

We have discussed the fact that we are multidimensional beings who were given certain instruments to explore and to get to know this world. Our major instruments are feelings. God expresses himself and communicates with us through feelings.

Everything is different in the province of feelings. We must start to understand the language of feelings. This is a different language. This is not the habitual everyday language of ours with its linear, harsh logic. Intuition comes from feelings. You intuitively feel where you need to go without turning on the thinking machine. One can sit there for a long time, calculating and doubting while using logic or quickly do what he needs to do by using intuition. This is a different sphere with different laws and different logic. That's what I am trying to pass on to you, and for me to do this, I need to use the mind apparatus.

—*We are going into the territory where the mind is useless, and we have to use the mind?!*

— Exactly. We receive experience based on knowledge. Knowledge, experience, and being. Knowledge comes first, and I transmit it. You don't yet have this knowledge. You have not yet recalled the state of unity. You will not experience unity unless you have this recollection.

You have acquired the experience of separation, hatred, and conflict. You were in a certain state of being during this process, and you continue to be in it. We can call this state of being separation or survival. You know how to live in the world of survival, but you don't know how to live in the state of the consciousness of unity. I provide you with the boosts of energy to recall the different knowledge, the knowledge of the state of unity. This knowledge is originally present in every soul. When you start to recall and experience this knowledge, you will start to see the situation in the new light. You will start to receive the new experience of unity, and you will get into the corresponding to this experience existence.

We all want to have a certain quality of existence. We suffer and feel anxious because our existence does not satisfy us. But because we use the knowledge of survival we received, we have separated existence. So, we must recall the knowledge well known to us that has to do with our unity. This knowledge will provide you with a different perception of reality.

We don't try to change the external world. We don't march through the streets screaming protests. Our work is the inner work. We start to see things and situations differently. As we start to recall the knowledge forgotten by us, it starts to determine our existence. This recall leads to the leap to the qualitatively new level of being.

It is impossible to achieve happiness on the level of consciousness of survival. It is possible to get there in the new state of being, and we want to experience it. We don't want to just know that happiness exists, that everyone is united, that God loves us, and that we can do anything we want, we want to experience it. We will not experience it right away. As we follow this knowledge, we will acquire our own experience and get to this state of being.

— *I felt love today. I did not expect it. I did not plan for it. I did not analyze it. Everything happened the way it should have happened.*

Where do you need light?
You need it in the darkness.

— What you have felt was immediately reflected by the outside world. Nothing is impossible here. Your most fantastic performance may be realized by you. You can be anything you imagine yourself to be, and you may experience it. Where do you need light?

— *We need it in the darkness.*

— Jesus was accused of socializing with the lowest classes of society. He answered that it is a sick man who needs a doctor. Light is seen in the darkness. That's why our path lies through the darkness. We receive our experience of who we are by being who we are not. The darkness will get darker, and not understanding will get heavier. **We must remember who we are.**

We are the light, and when it gets darker, we shine brighter. Remember that. We are experiencing the state of a very bright light now, but we can experience different states. We will be free of darkness only when we exit this reality. The fact that darkness is present here is not bad. It allows us to experience ourselves as light even more.

Tomorrow you will get into a different state. The state of self-remembrance you have experienced today will become blurry, and you will experience fear and suffering again. But you will recall what you felt today. This knowledge will accompany you from now on irrespective of what happens, irrespective of how dark it gets. Escalation in darkness will provide you with an opportunity to better feel who you really are.

Without darkness and light, everything is gray. You need to make this inner discernment. When Jesus said, "Not peace, but a sword brought I to you," he spoke of discernment between dark and light. He brought the sword that will help you to separate good and evil in order to see and to connect them later.

All cats are grey in the dark, but light allows you to see their different shades. That's the only way to see something the way it really is. Light allows you to see everything clearly; darkness hides things. You must enter your shadow zones and to shine the light of awareness on them.

Fear and pain are hidden deep within us. We can't see them. We should not run away from them. We need to get very close to them and investigate them. When you are afraid of something and call it dirty and horrible, you are afraid to look at yourself.

Shadow zones hide big presents for us. When we change our relationship with them, we open and see them in details. Insight and awareness come as a result.

— *I am listening to you, and I realize that I know everything you say. Is this self-remembrance?*

— This is the initiation into self-remembrance. The key to self-remembrance is love. When you catch this wave, you immediately experience a resonance. Every one of us knows everything. The question is how to use and realize this knowledge.

— *I thought about this. How can I realize this knowledge? I think, I need to experience this new state at least once, and then the events that you have described will start to occur. Is it enough for us to just recall this in order to get into the new state?*

— There is a difference between the state a human being is in and the state he chooses to transfer to by asking the question "How can I do that?" Those are different spheres, and it is impossible to transfer there step by step. This is not a short walk from one room to another. This is another house, and you can only get there by transferring to the new state of consciousness.

— *This is a jump. The question "How?" will just slow us down.*

— The question "How?" is a slow walk. We, on the other hand, need to jump. I cannot jump for you, but I can push you to jump. We are all pushing each other toward the borders of the unknown in order to jump. Some of us approach this border but return to the same old circles.

"What kind of harmony can I find in my being stung by a bee?"

— In using our consciousness, we can enter anything we want because everything is One Unified Whole. The Unified Soul gave birth to a multiplicity of forms, but the building material is the same. Therefore, we have access to everything. We see the world of animals, plants, and minerals all around us, but can we feel how their representatives live? For example, how does a bee or a flower live?

— *A few days ago, a bee flew under my shirt, and I really felt it.*

— You perceive a bee as something that flew under your shirt and bothers you. Can you enter a bee with your consciousness and see yourself from the point of view of a bee? We all are One, and when we are talking about unity, we are not only talking about the unity between people. We are talking about unity with everything that exists: trees, grass, etc. We are everything that exists.

How do trees look at us when we walk through the woods? How do they perceive us? To understand that, we need to transfer into them using our consciousness. Look at the

293

multiplicity of forms and ways of life. There are billions of life forms on Earth alone.

Take a stone, for example. It is immobile, but how many processes occur in it? The external form is immobile, but billions of atoms and molecules are moving inside it. Using our habitual mode of perception, we only see an immobile stone.

— *We can enter and feel any human being this way.*

— Yes, because you are this human being. This can't be done if you are coming from the point of view of separation. This can only be done in the world where We all are One. We can feel and perceive everything.

God simultaneously perceives everything because He is One Harmonic Whole. But our perception of ourselves is fragmented, partial, and disharmonic.

What kind of harmony can there be in my being stung by a bee? But what if I am simultaneously me and a bee? This is a totally different way of looking at the situation. When our attention is focused on what we call problems, our perception of the world is very fragmented.

Sexuality: exchange or a throw away?

— For the lower levels of sexual attraction, total indifference to the reaction of a partner is characteristic. My desire is above everything else. The other human being is not seen as a part of me. He or she is just an opportunity to satisfy myself. What don't you accept in sexual relationships?

— *I don't accept many things that I have experienced.*

— How long can you experience something and not accept it? If you accept something, you don't condemn it anymore. If you don't accept and condemn something, you are attracted to it. This attraction is based on the attachment that is connected to condemnation. If you have experienced something and accepted it, you can look at it calmly; you understand that someone is going through his lessons.

You get to know yourself through what you are not. Not accepting who you are not, you cannot see who you are, i.e. you don't have a choice.

— *I don't accept one-sided sex, sex that is not built on the desire to exchange sexual energy with a partner.*

— Do you have this desire in other spheres of communication? Will it be present in other spheres, if it's absent in this sphere? If you allow yourself to be oppressed in bed to avoid conflict, you do it in all other spheres of your life. Consider this—the sexual sphere is not separated from other spheres of life, everything is interconnected and one.

— *It is difficult for me to accept a situation when one does something for another human being without getting anything in return.*

— In the victim—oppressor situation, a victim receives his victimhood, while an oppressor receives his oppression. Both parties receive something. But if you, in receiving something, say that you don't receive anything, it means you don't see what you receive. In this case, you are attached to something that you don't see. You can be attached to what you are getting out of this situation either positively or negatively.

Someone forcefully takes, while another retains by using force. A victim insists he is being oppressed, but the force that a victim uses to be a victim is equal to the force applied by the oppressor. The only difference is that one manifests this force actively, while another manifests it passively. We can see this manifested in everything, not only in sexuality.

What we have just discussed relates to everyone; every one of us participates in this game here.

To cheat without changing

— The root of the word "cheating" in the Russian language comes from the word "change". Usually, a human being cheats without changing. Change! Build a new version of yourself. It appears that cheating is betrayal, and betrayal is horrible. But who betrays whom and why? What is a betrayal?

You think that the human being you love should only be with you. If you are with him, he should only be with you. How many people do you know think they can only be with one human being, while he or she is free to be with others? Those specimens are hard to come by.

So, you select one specimen out of many and promise to love her. It is assumed that she will carry the same obligation, and if she manifests something else, you claim that this is cheating. You scream that your truest feelings were betrayed.

The Soul has no limitations, but by entering the body-mind, it receives many of them. Does a requirement to love just one human being represent a limitation? Of course, it does. This is the limitation that contemporary marriage is based upon. What will the Soul that faces such a limitation do? It will rebel.

Where did the idea of loving just one human being come from? An object was chosen, and the words "I love you" were pronounced. This is a business deal, a contract. That's why there is so much talk here about not fulfilling a contract.

Can you love two or three human beings? Can you let other men and women who manifest different sides of you into your life? We consume a variety of products, movies, music, and books. But in the sphere of intimate relationships, we don't allow anything new to come in.

This is a fixed type of love. You fix something and announce, "I will stop loving you if you make a step to the left." In this way, you make yourself very narrow and specific, like a specific brand of cheese, and request from your partner not to consume anything else. How long can one eat only one brand of cheese?

— *Marriage is totally unnecessary. People can cohabit in threesomes or by four or five.*

— I did not say that, but if you are married, it does not mean you have to exclude all other people from your life. But you are not even allowed to look in their direction. The more salt you are going to eat, the more sugar you will want.

We cannot know the higher feelings unless we know the lower feelings. We can't get to the higher version of ourselves unless we know our lower version. That's how things work in our dual world. We live in the world of dualities, where we find who we are by getting to know who we are not. To make a choice, we need to see both sides. We sort out who we are based on the experience we received being who we are not. Without this experience, we will not come to this understanding.

— *We are dealing with dualities. What kind of power allows us to become aware of these dualities?*

— The holistic perception and choice are available only when you are aware of yourself, when you are in this third power. If you see what you are not, you can also see what you are.

—*What if there is no awareness, but just a vision that you are not it?*

— In that case, it is impossible to make a choice. You are living based on what you are not. That's where all the suffering comes from. If it is hard for you to deal with people, if something constantly irritates you in people, it is something you reject in yourself.

— *Do I have to dig out all the ugliness of the world, take a good look at it, and accept that everything is in me?*

— You call it ugliness. You will find out that what is ugly for you is beautiful for other people. It is your perception that creates beauty and ugliness.

Sexual attraction is a strive for unity

— Sexuality is always positive. Duality is present in the mind and in feelings, but not in sexuality. Attraction is either present or not. It is not dual and is always colored positively. The essence of sexuality is to get closer and to connect. Duality is brought up by the mind when it calls something good, and something bad.

Without sexuality, the dual pair "man—woman", one of the strongest dualities here, probably would not even come into existence. Men and women would not interact. A certain power appears that attracts you to a human being of the opposite sex. What kind of power is this? What does it do to you? It calls you to unite.

The essence of sexuality is unity, but at the level of the second chakra, complete fusion is unattainable. Everything changes when the heart gets turned on. Everyone here strives to unite, to get to where we originally came from.

— *Sexuality leads to pleasure which later on transforms into disgust. Is it possible to not depend on sexuality?*

— How can we connect a duality? A man and a woman is a duality. Sexuality is a power that performs the connecting role. You cannot connect if you don't accept something, let's say in a woman.

When you feel sexual attraction, you feel an impulse toward unity. But the mind with its separating notions steps in. How can you accept your inner man and your inner woman? You must accept every quality they have. This is a final test.

You will have to pass tests on many dualities, but this will be your final test. The total fusion of your inner man and your inner woman represents a happy enlightenment. When two bodies connect without the soul and the heart, a physiological orgasm can be experienced. The true orgasm, however, can be experienced only when the full connection between the body, the mind, and the Soul is present, i.e. in a state of unity.

— *Do I have to exit the borders of dualities, and to accept what I don't accept, in order to accept my husband?*

— First of all, you have to accept what you don't accept in yourself. I don't know whether you will achieve it with your husband. Let it happen to at least one man and one woman. Without doing this inner work to your heart, you may exchange thousands of partners and never experience that.

— *I see passivity during sex as a resistance. That means I do not accept my own passivity, which my partner mirrors me. I want to be active, not passive.*

— We are dancing here. You are staying on a certain spot, and you are surprised that your partner does not take the same spot. But you are standing on it. In this physical reality, it is impossible to stand on the spot that has already been taken. You must move away from this spot. Only then will your partner be able to occupy the spot you have left.

Other people just fulfil your desires. But when they fulfil them, you change your desires to the opposite desires, and as a result, you experience displeasure. When you accept both sides of your desires as equal, you start to perform a harmonious dance. You start to understand that other people fulfil your desires, and you thank them for it. But if you don't understand that, you continue to condemn and hold a grudge against them; you continue the game "victim—oppressor". A victim is passive, while an oppressor is active. Two bad dancers are dancing the dance of the oppression.

The usual sexuality does not lead to spirituality. You cannot get to the heart through it. The heart turns everything up. Sexuality that is manifested through the heart is a way to yourself. In the world of unity, sexuality offers you a stronger union; there is no conflict in it.

The material and the spiritual—two sides of one coin

— The bird Phoenix gets burned and is reborn in a new quality. We are not bored with a human being; we are bored with his image. Let this image burn. Let yourself be reborn. You leave in the morning and return at night completely different. But your mind holds onto the perception that everything is stable, constant, and unchangeable. This is not so; we are changing all the time.

Allow yourself to see that the human being next to you is different. You got used to seeing him in a certain way, but he has changed. He is different now. How different is he? This is the first feeling and the first love.

— *Yes, during my adolescence I experienced strong passion. My relationship with my husband is different. I don't want to lose him.*

— You cannot lose anything. It is impossible to lose something that exists. You can transfer to another quality of love—wisdom. You can transfer to a wise heart and a loving mind. There are no claims there and no fear of losing anyone.

— *I am upset by his indifference in respect to what needs to be done around the house.*

301

— He balances your anxiety related to housekeeping. When someone occupies one side of a duality, another will take the opposite side. There is no other way. He was taking responsibility for the spiritual side, and you were taking responsibility for the material side. Both sides are equal sides of one duality. You need to see the habitual separation between spiritual and material as one duality. You are equally responsible, but in different spheres of life. But because you were looking only in your own direction, he appeared to you to be completely irresponsible. Actually, this is not the case. You possess the necessary qualities, and you express them very strongly. You are equal partners here. You just need to see that. Each one of you has accumulated an enormous and priceless experience in the spiritual and material spheres. You just need to exchange them. When the situation straightens itself out, the drama that appeared based on separation and antagonism of the material and spiritual sides will disappear.

But you needed this experience to approach this partnership of the opposites. You had to accumulate this experience in the state of separation. You have fully accumulated it, and now you can integrate it. Allow yourself to be happy, and everything will happen as it should.

Being in love is a state. If you are constantly in this state, many things that were habitual start to open up to you in a new and amazing light. The world reflects what you feel. What if you were in love with life? What if you were to feel drunk with this feeling?

A human being always needs someone to love. It is not the other human being who is important but the state of being in love. Every time you meet him, meet him as if for the first time. Every time you see him, see him as if for the last time.

Usually, everything happens in correspondence with the old, habitual images you have, and everything looks the same. Why does this state of being in love disappear? It disappears because you did not allow the old image to die and the new image to be reborn.

Gratitude is the key of a master

— Gratitude is extremely important here. The power of gratitude is enormous. Be grateful for everything you want to have. Gratitude is the key that opens all the doors. When you experience happiness, be grateful for it and it will get stronger. Be grateful that you exist.

One woman did not like me being thanked for what I say and do. It appeared to her that I was rubbing my vanity in this gratitude. But as you can see now, gratitude is necessary primarily to the one who verbalizes it.

I invite you to see me as part of you. Let's say I am the part of you that moved further than any other part in understanding itself. By expressing gratitude to me, you thank yourself.

The state of gratitude is very natural. But from the point of view of the conditional mind, this is not the case. It believes that to express one's gratitude is to encourage someone's vanity. That's exactly what the conditioned mind wants for itself when it positions itself against others.

When you thank me for the new knowledge I carry, you thank yourself, but only if you understand that we are one. In that case, your understanding of yourself gets broader. If you were to broaden your notion of yourself to the level of a group, you will have a completely different perception.

— *When I accept myself, I accept the situations that occur now and situations that will occur in the future. That is very important for me, because my fear of a new experience is still buried somewhere in me.*

— You used the phrase "fear of a new experience". How can you be afraid of something that you don't know? You project your old fears onto the new experience; it is fear of the old experience, not of the new one.

Fear appears as the result of your unwillingness to part with something with which you currently identify. This is a fear of fear. You can't experience fear of a future that you don't know. But you can be afraid to lose the fear you currently have.

Words are symbols.
Learn to use them properly.

— You can concentrate your attention on many different things. For example, you can fix your attention on stepping on dog shit, and you will have a corresponding state. You will think about why you got dirty, and how to clean yourself. Then, you will step in it again and think about how to get clean again. On the other hand, your attention might be attracted to the sunlight, blowing wind, or murmur of tree leaves.

Whatever you concentrate your attention on starts to become your life and to create a corresponding state. You should observe the changes that occur in you and express gratitude for them. It is very important to feel inner harmony inside.

This is a process: you move in the direction of your Soul. You must try not to lose this direction. The direction of the movement of the Soul, the mind, and the body may be different. The mind and the body may tear away from the Soul and only accept the signals from the conditional mind. This is one life. When you hear your Soul and what it wants, you will have a totally different life. In this case, the mind and the body act congruently with the Soul. This is what intuition is all about.

— *I got into a very strong current of love during this seminar. I want to become a part of this current. I want to love, to be in a state of awareness, to feel myself to be a part of everyone, and to accept my fellow human beings as my own part.*

— When we live through something, we acquire an experience. You may read many books but only perceive words and thoughts. Words are just symbols, and if feelings do not enrich them, they are just empty bottles.

When feelings get turned on, you acquire the experience that is yours and yours alone. You will never forget it. These are not words that can be learned and forgotten. When you have lived through a certain experience with feelings involved, it becomes yours.

New knowledge determines new vision. The conflict between yourself and others is a normal phenomenon in the matrix of separation. The knowledge transmitted by the matrix of separation maintains and reinforces this conflict.

But if you are ready to experience a partnership of opposites, you must have new knowledge. The unfolding of the new experience occurs through new knowledge. Your knowledge determines your perception. When you know that everything is united, and when you start to use this knowledge not just as a new theoretical paradigm, but as a way to look at yourself and the world, you start to experience unity.

I want to repeat that everything I say is already known to you, but you went through a period when your attention was fixed on something that was not you, on separation and fear. I invited you to see who you really are now. To do that, you need to recall who you are. By absorbing and experiencing the new axiom, by starting to look at everything from the point of view of unity, you will start to receive the new experience, the experience you actually came here to receive. In this case, your perception will become connected instead of separated.

You die fixated on your habitual problems and convictions. You recreate them again and again. In this process, you are afraid to die, but you have already died. You have whatever you are afraid of.

You are offered an opportunity to accept your death and to be reborn. Yes, this was death, and you recreated it again and again. Imagine your funerals that occur day after day. This scene gets recreated year after year. You've gotten used to it, but you must get up, step out of the coffin, and announce that you are alive.

When you want something but receive the opposite

— A man who is not aware of himself falls into the trap of opposite desires. He thinks he is afraid of something, but in reality, he wants this something to happen. This is a paradox. He acts based on his desire but receives something he considers to be undesirable. As a result, he experiences suffering.

Let's take a look at what irritates you. You will feel irritated until you start to see what exactly irritates you. This must be something tangible. For example, you are irritated by the fact that people do not yield to you and a certain situation constantly repeats itself: someone does something that you don't want him to do, and you get irritated. Try to understand that it is you who wants to get irritated, and this "someone" must play along and resist you.

So, you are living in this paradox: on one side, you want people to yield to you, but on the other side, you don't want that to happen, because you want to relive the experience of irritation that you have already experienced. You constantly provoke other people in order to experience irritation. When someone yields to you, you search for another player who will not yield to you. In this process, appearances are taken for reality. The appearance is that you want to do something without anyone interfering with your plans, yet what is real is that you want to get irritated.

This is the world of illusions, where appearances are taken for reality. When you start to see the underlining, you start to see reality. In your case, it is your habit to be irritated.

You start to change when you start to see what you are constantly recreating. If you don't see it, it means you have not accumulated enough of this particular experience. No problem. Continue to accumulate it. Until you start to see that you want to experience discomfort, you will not want to experience anything else. You realize your subconscious desires here. Everything is dual in this relative world. To maintain something, you need to be afraid of it. You are dealing with a frozen moment that you must re-live again and again.

CHAPTER 7

FROM FEAR TO LOVE

A woman brought a suit against Nasreddin. He vehemently denied all her accusations. Finally, the judge asked:

— Tell me just one thing, Nasreddin, did you sleep with this woman?

— No, your honor, I have not closed my eyes for a moment. Nasreddin answered.

Are you ready to give freedom to your partner?

— My problems go all the way back to my childhood. I never liked my dad. I thought he was bad. I did not want to talk to him, and when asked, I answered all questions pertaining to him as if he was dead. I was jealous of families where both parents were present. I live feeling guilty for not appreciating him. From early childhood, my sister and I were told that we were beautiful. I was stuck-up and behaved arrogantly. I thought I would be able to achieve anything with my looks. When I was unable to do so, I would feel pain and freeze, because I was empty inside. I also felt guilty,

309

because I did not meet mom's expectations. Four things used to scare me: jail, prostitution, drug dependency, and poverty. Now I do the things I used to condemn. I have tried every drug I could. I started to drink heavily. Condemning prostitution, I sold my body quite a few times. I met a man, fell in love with him, but then I betrayed him with another man. That's when I understood that I can love a man for no reason—just for love's sake. And then I decided to sort out my inner world. I want to figure out what drives us to do the things we do. What power directs us? I feel guilty for doing the things I used to condemn. I am scared of other things on my list that I have not yet experienced.

— You always receive what you are afraid of. You did exactly what people you have condemned did. You have experienced that. Was it scary?

— *I experienced fear afterwards.*

— You experienced fear later, thinking that you should not have done it. But was it scary by itself?

— *No. While I was doing it, I did not ask myself whether I was ready to lose everything I had.*

— And why do you have to lose what you have?

— *I am afraid to lose what I have out of fear of loneliness.*

— There is a commonly accepted notion here that a husband should not have fun without his wife, nor a wife without her husband. We are dealing with limitations here; this is one of them. Many people experience their lessons in these limitations. They do what is forbidden, and then they experience guilt. That's what you will experience if you stay inside these borders. You will be afraid, and as a result you will do what you

310

are afraid of doing. You will blame yourself and do it again. Can you see that these are just the borders?

— *I see that, but fear does not leave me.*

— Are you ready to give freedom to your partner?

— *No. Externally, I tell him, "Do what you want," but internally I don't allow him to do that. If he is to do anything of that nature, I will leave him or avenge myself by doing the same.*

— And this will continue eternally. Why did you get together? Did you get married to keep each other in chains?

— *We married in order to be free and happy.*

— If that's the case, what prevents you from achieving that?

— *These limitations.*

— Exactly. The more you forbid a human being to do something, the more he will try to break this prohibition. It is the fear of breaking a prohibition that will push him to break it. Would he even try to break a prohibition if we were to remove it?

— *He would not even think of it.*

— Yes. Every child receives certain prohibitions while his personality is being formed by the process of upbringing. When something is forbidden, a child fixes his attention on it and starts to fight it. He fights with himself. That's how we are taught to fight the world and ourselves.

But you can only fight what exists. Therefore, it is necessary to create certain situations in order to fight them. We have approached the earliest prohibitions that were inculcated into a child. You can only remove them by removing them from others.

Other people are me. We enter relationships with other people in order to manifest ourselves the way we perceive ourselves. You have certain notions about yourself, and you want to realize them in practice.

Let's say you don't love yourself. That's being inculcated from childhood on through condemnation. For example, you don't love yourself because you are a prostitute, drug addict, or a loser. Those are different forms of not loving yourself. How will you manifest yourself while entering into a relationship with other people?

— *The same way.*

Your relationship with other people is your relationship with yourself

— Yes, because you want to confirm that you are you. You think that you are a prostitute and a drug addict, and therefore, you will behave in a way that shows others that you are a prostitute and a drug addict. Your relationship with other people is your relationship with yourself. You need to sort out your relationship with yourself. Otherwise, you will not be able to sort out your relationship with others.

You can only change something through yourself. When you look inside yourself, you see prohibitions, condemnation, and guilt. You see that you don't love yourself, and as a result, you cannot love others.

You feel guilty because you think you are bad. This internal mechanism is inculcated into every child, and it works for lifetime. This mechanism constantly causes you to feel guilty, because you are doing things in a way that they should not be done, not the way your parents demanded you to do things.

Guilt is a consequence of condemnation. You condemn yourself, and that condemnation makes you feel guilty. We need to see how we make ourselves unhappy, because in reality, we are other people. By incarnating on Earth, we receive programs of separation and programs of not-love. To see these programs and the way they operate, we need to start seeing them inside ourselves.

— *Sometimes I feel that I am fooling myself. It seems to me that I see something, but in reality …*

— The basic notions downloaded into every program are the notions of what is "good" and what is "bad". These notions determine your perception of yourself. For example, knowing that prostitution is bad, you start to think whether or not you are a prostitute. These thoughts create the corresponding situations and cause you to experience them.

— *Yes, when it happens, it seems to me that this is totally normal, and I can do that. But at the same time, the other side steps forward, saying that this is not okay.*

— You are both the defendant and the district attorney. When you do something that is bad, your district attorney accuses you, and your defendant feels guilty.

— *I want to get rid of the feeling of guilt, but I am afraid of not being able to do so. I am afraid that what we discuss now will not work.*

— Your program defends itself. How does it do that? It does it in a dual way: one side says that you will be able to do that, another says you will not.

— *I will be able to do that, because I want to do that.*

— Who is this I?

— *My inner world.*

— What is that?

— *My Soul.*

— We are not discussing your Soul. We are discussing your personal program.

Any Soul that incarnates here in the form of a human being gets into the world of separation and forgets itself. It falls asleep and starts to see a dream in which it is fighting itself and trying to survive. We are trying to remember ourselves as a Soul and to return to a holistic perception. To do that, we need to see the limitations and borders of our personalities, stretch them, and to get out of them.

— *It is hard and painful to live in these limitations.*

— They push us toward the road of self-remembrance.

— *Sometimes, when it gets very dark, I feel very frustrated.*

Fear and guilt—the defenses of the old programs

— I can say the same. I understand everything you say, because I have experienced these states. Those are the steps on the road to yourself.

— *Guilt stops everything to the point that one can't do anything. Why?*

— Guilt and condemnation extract the energy of fear that your personal programs work on. When you start to observe your program, it starts to resist. It does so by causing you to experience guilt and condemnation. The goal of your program is to survive the way it is now.

— *I feel afraid when I find myself lying to myself.*

— This is normal if you are not in an aware state. We constantly lie to ourselves. You have started to see your opposite parts, and you have started to understand that each one of them has its own, opposite truth. This vision reinforces fear. Even though you were always in this situation, you have never seen it as clearly as you see it now.

You have described the facts that you have noticed. As you continue this self-observation, the level of your guilt and condemnation will decrease. You will simply observe your condemnation of yourself and your fear that appears as a result. This self-observation will allow you to become aware of how your personal program works. You will start to see the intricate working mechanisms of your program. You will see them without condemnation.

You will face a situation you were once afraid of. When you see the mechanisms of its appearance and choose not to continue with the conflict of your opposite parts, you will transfer to another level of consciousness. You need to pass through every situation you were afraid of, meet your fears, and see their illusory nature.

— *This does not happen often.*

— Real is what you consider to be real. Fear and conflict is real for someone who believes in them.

— *But my body feels real pain in certain situations. I have experienced a situation when I was afraid not of the physical pain, but of the distorted and ugly reflection of my face in the mirror. The physical pain followed.*

— Do you think you have experienced the fear of being ugly? No, this was the fear of losing the habitual method you use to achieve your aims. You are using your physical appearance as a tool to achieve your aims.

— A few months ago, *I experienced fear because something I wanted to hide became known. I was depressed for a couple of days, and then I became hysterical. I cried all my tears out, and I felt better. Actually, I became happy.*

— You did something you were afraid of doing, and you saw that this was not so scary. You increased your fear to the maximum, and it manifested itself, allowing you to see and experience it. That made you happy.

— *At the time, the feeling of guilt disappeared. Now, in recalling that situation, I feel bad.*

— You did what you did together with a human being who was in the same situation with you. So, who is guilty here and who is not?

— *But it was I who physically did it.*

— You did it together. Both of you had to experience it.

— *It was necessary to give me a push.*

— That's how it happens in life. To move to the next step, you need to experience what you currently have. If you want to be free, but at the same time do not allow your partner to be free, you will not be free. You are changing yourself through other people, because others are you. You can only get rid of what you are bored with by sincerely seeing it as it really is and by telling another human being about it.

— *That will lead to his liberation.*

— People are totally controlled by their limitations. If we fully accept who we are, we can do anything we want without guilt and condemnation. People pressure each other here, "I will do what you want, if you do what I want." They live in constant fear of each other.

What kind of love can we even talk about here? There is no love here. We are dealing with the illusory word and mutually applied limitations. We talk about love, but there is no love here. There is only fear here. What can you promise here? If I want to be with you, I am with you. If I want to leave, I will leave. If I want to return, I will return. This is sincere.

— *Are you saying that both the husband and the wife can leave?*

— They can do whatever they want. When limitations are lifted, people start to live in the state of limitless freedom, and whatever they do is sincere. No one knows what is going to happen next, but as long as they want to be together, they are sincerely together. Their desire to part will also be sincere.

Marriage, the way it currently exists, represents an illusory guarantee of safety; it provides a woman with the means of existence and a man with a house and safe sex. This is an arrangement similar to prostitution.

You are afraid to have what you already have. You think it can happen, you get afraid of it, and you have it. Look and see that whatever you are afraid to have, you already have.

— *It looks like I already have everything.*

Why does a man do drugs?

— Yes. Each one of us has everything: positive and negative. But when we are terribly afraid of something, we realize it. If you are afraid of becoming a drug addict, you will become a drug addict. Why does a man do drugs?

— *Initially, one is interested. Then one defends this interest by saying that everyone does it.*

— Perhaps you want to fit into a certain crowd, but why do drugs? You can choose something else. What do drugs offer? They offer kaif and freedom.

We all try to return to what we originally are. We want love and freedom, and we start to use different means to get them. These means frequently lead us to a dead end.

In desiring freedom, you start to take drugs, but in the end you become dependent on them. Drugs lead to physiological changes and habit formation. That leads to degradation. We are discussing a totally different way to obtain freedom. Is what we got to in our discussion freedom?

— *Yes.*

— In that case, you don't need drugs or alcohol. What do you need alcohol for?

— *I like the taste of good wine.*

— What kind of state does it offer you?

— *I become free in my communication and movements.*

— You can satisfy your desire for freedom by removing your inner limitations. In that case, you don't destroy, you heal yourself. Previously, you had to have a drink to lower your stress and to have a relaxed conversation. Now, after you have removed your inner limitations, you do not experience this stress.

— *I could never bring my friends home, because my mom drank a lot, and I was ashamed of her. I asked her not to do it, but she continued to drink. She drank every day, but I was forbidden to drink.*

— This is a paradox. Parents forbid their children to do what they do themselves. By the way, she also drank to be free.

— *I have everything I used to condemn in me, but I see it all differently now—I have it, and that's okay.*

— Yes. It simply exists. You don't need to condemn it.

— I would not be able to do what I did. I feel the inner prohibition to do it.

— Every actor of your show did what he wanted to do.

— Yes, I understand that now.

— Will you condemn yourself for your desires now? Haven't you accepted them in yourself yet?

— I frequently fantasize about being in bed with other men.

— You do not allow yourself to realize this fantasy. If you imagine it, it is in you. By imagining this, you increase your desire, but at the same time you don't allow yourself to realize it. This desire does not disappear. It gets stronger and stronger. Finally, it gets realized. That's what happened to you. You have created this situation yourself. This is neither good nor bad. This is what it is.

— When I recall what I did, I feel disgusted.

— Every single interaction in this world is sexual in nature. There is nothing bad in sexuality. Society paints sex as something bad and ugly. As a result, people do it and blame themselves. They do not experience happiness that true sexuality offers.

A human being is a very complicated creature that is made of seven chakras. The second chakra represents sexuality. Two human beings experience attraction in order to connect, which by itself is beautiful. But they do not go further. Let's say you feel good with someone in bed, but you share no other experiences with him outside of the bedroom. You connect with him partially, only on a physical level. This is neither bad nor good; this is just an incomplete contact. The full contact that we all are striving for is something incredible.

— I experienced fear before our meeting. I thought you would force me to do what I just discussed.

Freedom is to realize yourself without fear

— This is not a fear. This is a desire. You can see it as fear, but you can also see it as your own desire that you condemn. A desire appears, and it is followed by condemnation. That leads to fear. Certain desires are present, and your attitude toward these desires is also present. If your attitude is condemnation, fear immediately gets turned on: this happened, it's bad, and therefore scary.

Inner freedom allows you to realize your every desire without fear. You achieve true freedom when you stop condemning yourself for what you do. If you do something without condemning yourself for doing it, you realize a certain impulse, a certain desire.

You condemn yourself for your desires, but every desire is natural. It is condemnation that makes it unnatural. You promised something. People always promise something. But this is crazy. You cannot promise anything, because life, and we as part of this life, constantly changes. Your notions about yourself change throughout each day, and because of it your desires change. But if you promised something in the morning and break your promise at night, you consider yourself to be a liar. Why did you promise?

321

— *I promised, because I thought that I would not do it.*

— That's what you thought then. Later, you started to think differently. Now you see that you can think differently. Therefore, to promise something is to lie.

— *I experience dependency on the opinions of other people, because I think that they see the situation better from their side.*

— This is the consequence of not knowing and not trusting yourself. If you don't see that your actions are the result of your desires, you condemn yourself for them and start to follow what other people say, removing responsibility from yourself for what you do.

— *In order to condemn someone else.*

— Yes, the mechanism of guilt starts to work again. If you accept full responsibility for what you do and allow yourself to manifest everything that is in you without condemnation, then you don't need to ask anyone for permission.

— *I want to move to another theme. I have a very difficult time refusing someone a favor. If I don't, I feel guilty.*

— We all have certain desires. If you allow another human being to be free, you allow yourself to be free. Until you free other people, you will not free yourself. In this case, you don't allow yourself to do certain things that you call "bad". You depend on other people's opinions in order to remove responsibility from yourself.

— *I am afraid people are going to think badly of me, and so I go against my own desires.*

— Why are you so dependent on other people's opinions?

— I want others to be good to me and to love me.

— And what do you get?

— I receive something completely opposite.

— So, it does not work. By holding on to what you were holding on to before, you receive the opposite result. As an investigator, you see that this does not work. Therefore, you need to look for another method.

— So what can I do? Should I do something that will result in my not being loved by other people?

— This question comes out of the notion that you can be loved only for something. Is this really love? You love someone irrespective of what he does. He is a part of you, and if you love yourself, you are unable to not love him. Therefore, all these programs we have been discussing are the result of our not loving ourselves.

— But it seems to me that I love myself. Is this another illusion?

— You use one word to describe two totally different things. You can love cheddar cheese and you can love a human being. The word is the same, but we are talking about two different things. We use the same word to describe completely different states. When you love someone for something he does, it is not love. You love cheddar cheese because of its taste and because it fills you up, not because it simply exists. You love someone conditionally when you love him for something he does. This is a business arrangement. This is prostitution.

— I will stop doubting that when I see that it works.

— You should always confirm everything by experiencing it.

— I had a choice: career, money, nice life or life with someone who could not provide these things. I chose the second option, because I love him and want to be with him.

— You always have a choice. Sometimes it is clearly visible and sometimes it is not. If you were to choose option one, you would have entered the well-known path. You would get everything on this path except freedom.

— No one understood me except him, because he studied with you.

— That was a huge change for him too. You got together to realize a new version of yourself. This did not happen for you to have more comfortable life. It happened so that you could move toward yourself.

— I see many programs that I inherited from my mom. I don't want my kids to suffer the way I did.

The end of the family's program of separation

— First, you need to correct these programs in yourself. If you do that, your kids will not inherit them. You can only give them what you have. When changes occur, they touch everyone in the family and are transmitted throughout generations. If that happens to you, you complete your family's program of separation and move to the program of unity. Whether you want it or not, everyone around you starts to experience its influence.

— *My sister does not understand me. She does not want to see me. She does not want to talk to me.*

— No one should be forced to do anything here. If she wants to know, you will transmit it to her, if not—not. You should not try to convince anyone of anything.

— *I want to meet with my father. I feel guilty for not giving him love and for humiliating him. I want to ask him for forgiveness*

— Do you want to come to him with guilt, in order to exacerbate in him what he has?

— *I can come to him and tell him that I love him. Would that be enough?*

— Yes. If you ask someone for forgiveness, it means you experience guilt. This is quite widespread here.

— *But another human being is waiting for it.*

— He is waiting for it, because he experiences guilt himself. Do you want to reinforce his state of guilt?

— *No, I don't. I just want to see him.*

— It will be natural to see him the way he is.

— *I did not say goodbye to him when he left.*

— Back then, you had different notions and acted out of them. We are constantly changing beings. Back then, you were different, and you acted based on what you considered to be the best, and that was the best. We always do the best we can do, but in the end, we get the worst: fear, guilt, etc. The situation recurs and recurs until we see it and move toward what we are presently discussing. Then, we don't need fear and guilt. If you want to go and see him, do it. You don't need to blame yourself. You don't need to ask him for forgiveness. You don't have to be forgiven for anything.

— I feel jealous when my girlfriend goes out with her friends instead of coming to my place.

— This is the perception of separation again. When you start seeing that everybody else is you, then, when your girlfriend, as one of your parts, goes to another part of you, you feel happy for both of them. Jealousy appears out of the desire to receive love and attention only for yourself. You try to obtain love by using the wrong means, means that do not lead to love. You get jealous in order to receive more attention for yourself.

Feel happy for the one who does what he wants to do, because it is you who is doing it. This can be applied to family life. If your partner went to someone, he had his reasons for it. If you are afraid of him betraying you, this will happen. We get what we are afraid of.

This fear is your desire. There is nothing here except love. Fear is another manifestation of love, albeit a perverted form of it. When you are afraid that something will happen, you simultaneously desire it to happen.

— I don't want to think about it. That can't be true. I can't desire it.

— But that is exactly what happens. Nothing happens here without your desiring it. If you are afraid of something, you think about it. You imagine it. If you imagine it, you want this to happen, and you will do everything for it to happen without seeing or understanding it. For example, you see a man and you imagine yourself being in bed with him. You want that to happen and simultaneously condemn yourself for it, i.e. you are afraid of it. By being afraid of it, you subconsciously want it to happen.

We give promises that we cannot keep

— You want to have kids. You are simultaneously afraid of the opposite, of not having kids. The fear of not having kids appears as the result of your desire to have kids. These two things are interconnected. Fear appears as the consequence of love. Originally, you feel love for children, but you immediately feel afraid that you will not have them. The original desire you had was the desire to have children, i.e. love. If you were to investigate the appearance of any given fear, you would see the same pattern. A certain desire comes first; it is followed by the fear of it not getting fulfilled.

Let's return to the previous example. You see a man and you want to be with him. This is a desire of love, and it works toward expansion. You limit yourself when you promise someone to be only with him. It means you cannot be with anybody else. The desire to be with someone else appears; it is followed by your condemnation of yourself for the inability to keep your promise. But again, love was primary.

— *Based on what you are saying this trip to City Hall is just a game.*

327

— The way it currently exists it is a *bad* game, because people give promises they cannot keep. The worst thing you can do here is to suppress the love that you have inside you. If the impulse to love someone appears, and you don't manifest it, it is the worst thing you can do.

— Do I have to approach him and to express my love?

— Yes, because this is the truth.

— People can be loved differently: some love is stronger, and some love is weaker.

— You will always love people differently, and the question is not about love being stronger or weaker. This is just an appraisal. We are talking about your own part. You meet a man, and you like something in him that you like in your own self and you love it in him. This idea cannot fit your habitual, conditioned mind, which tells you to keep the promise you gave and to be with one man only.

If you, seeing yourself as one with everything, meet someone you like, you can allow yourself everything you want. When you suppress your desire, it does not disappear. It will surely find a way out in a perverted form. Allow yourself to do what you want to do.

You have many unfulfilled desires that were suppressed. They did not disappear. They are inside of you, and they are waiting to manifest themselves. They are not allowed to be manifested. They search for an exit to express themselves, and they manifest themselves in a perverted form.

A woman who thinks that she should not be with anyone but her husband experiences many desires in relationship to other men. These desires manifest themselves in the form of jealousy. If she were to act based on the premise of freedom, her desires would not be blocked and would not need to search for an alternative exit.

People who offer freedom to each other respect their own desires, because they understand that every desire is important. Unfulfilled desires ask to be realized. One can start to drink or to use drugs to realize these desires in the state of loosened limitations offered by chemical substances. Later, when asked why he did it, he defends himself by saying that he was drunk and is not responsible for his actions. But he had to get drunk to fulfil his desire. He could not realize it while sober.

— *Why don't we remember anything when we are drunk or stoned?*

— One gets drunk, realizes his hidden desires in a drunken state, and forbids himself to remember what he did. At the end, this can lead to a total loss of memory. This is degradation.

Whatever is prohibited gets forgotten, but enormous inner tension is created. It can lead to psychologically abnormal states. This happens because people don't allow themselves to realize their desires, considering them to be bad. People go crazy because they experience a severe imbalance between conscious and subconscious desires. They lose adequacy in their relationship with other people. They are considered crazy, because they don't behave the way other people do, even though others are equally crazy. I don't see a difference between them.

— *Sober-minded people do things sometimes, that …*

— How are they *sober-minded?* They think, but they think in the category of separation. A crazy person just lost touch with this reality. When your unrealized desires can't find an exit, they take on forms of craziness.

— *I don't want that to happen to me. Perhaps this is the reason I started to think aloud lately.*

— People usually don't talk openly about the most important things, because they are afraid of not meeting the expectations of the people around them.

— *I had once expressed my dissatisfaction with the fact that I did not feel his attention or caresses, and he told me he had the same experience. As soon as we verbalized it, the situation changed. Prior to that, I kept grudges for weeks.*

When two human beings really love each other, they can say everything to each other

— If it does not get expressed, it accumulates and starts to search for an exit through some kind of a perverted form, such as conflict. True love is when two people can say everything to each other. This can also be said about health. Disease appears as the result of a blockage of your desires. As soon as you forbid yourself a certain desire, you block the organ of the physical body connected to this desire. Physiological changes follow.

When you verbalize your desire, it gets realized, and then it leaves you.

— *There are certain things that I would not allow myself to verbalize.*

— This comes from your notion that you are bad. If you know that you are love, then whatever appears in you will be good. Originally everything is love. Even fear is love. Fear is love that was not allowed to manifest itself. Most people live under the pressure of multiple prohibitions. They live in fear.

— *I feel pity for my mom because she was unable to realize herself. She is very unhappy.*

— You have experienced the turning point in your life as the result of some unpleasant events. And it is precisely these events that led you to see things from a different point of view. Will you continue to pity yourself for entering the path that leads to yourself? Your mom follows her own path. Everything that happens to a human being here is right. What is there to pity?

— *I feel the pain she feels in connection to me.*

— **She does not suffer on your behalf. She does not see you. She suffers because of herself. A human being cannot experience anything for another human being. If a man experiences a feeling of pity, he experiences it not toward someone, but toward himself.**

— *What if someone broke his leg. Do I suffer for him? Perhaps I pity myself for the pain I would have experienced in a similar situation.*

—When someone breaks his leg, he gets what he wanted to get. This is very important to understand: everyone gets what he wants. But we have different notions about what is good and what is bad. Many people think that it is good to receive flowers and gifts, but to break one's leg is bad. But you get exactly what you want in both cases. Why would you pity someone for receiving something he wanted to receive?

From this level of seeing the world, your mother gets what she wants. We have discussed the separated perception that comes out of the axiom of survival. In such a state, a human being wants to get as much as he can for himself and to give away as little as possible. This happens because he feels separated from other people.

How can such a perception be changed? It can only be changed through the kind of suffering that forces people to ask why certain things happen to them. That can lead some people to discuss what we discuss here.

The principle of life in the world of unity is to share with each other, and to not separate yourself from anything that surrounds you. When you are in such a state, you constantly try to transmit to others something that is important to you, and you are transmitted in return.

—*I was shocked when I heard that we have everything in us, from angel to a serial killer.*

—We recognize and come to know ourselves through something that we are not. Our life is a method that allows us to find out who we really are. Someone may live a life that from his point of view is stupid, meaningless, and useless—a life of someone who he is not. But it is precisely through that sort of life that he can find out who he really is. How can you find out what love is if there is no fear? The Soul that happens to be in the world of love has nothing with which to compare it. We have been given an opportunity to compare here, and as a result we have a choice.

— *Can I love and hate at the same time?*

— You are free, and you can do anything you want. The presence of polarities creates an opportunity to choose. Let's say you consider yourself to be ugly and experience everything connected to that experience. Later, you experience the opposite point of view. Now you can choose the experience you want to have from these two opposite experiences.

— *There are people out there who tell you how you look.*

— These people are you. For example, you hate someone and you are jealous. After a while, you find that this does not make you happy. Everyone here wants to be happy, free, and immortal, but people have different points of view on how to get there. You act the best way you can, according to how you currently see a particular situation. However, you see that what you do does not lead you to get what you wanted to get, or it leads you to get something opposite of what you wanted to get. Perhaps this experience will prompt you to start asking questions related to the dual nature of your personality.

— *I want to be free and happy. I did not believe that was possible until I met someone who told me about your school. I saw that he was happy. I felt how great it was. I still have certain limitations, but they will go away*

333

with time. I used to live to make money. I got depressed just from the thought of losing it. Now I want to run up and down a street, screaming about my love.

— The primary thing here is to choose who you want to be. You want to be happy? Be happy. Don't look for money or anything else. Don't live your life based on the principle "to have". Live it based on the principle "to be, to do, to have". You must start by choosing your state, and everything will come with that.

"I used to manipulate him by using my physical appearance…"

— We had a completely different relationship prior to my trip. We just used each other. I used to manipulate him by using my physical appearance. He used to go crazy with jealousy, but at the same time, he was pushing me to do what I did. I gave him an opportunity to be jealous. Something was pushing me to do that.

— He wanted to be jealous, and you made him jealous. Both of you were playing this show. You were the actors and the screen writers.

— Why isn't everyone on this path?

— When a student is ready, the teacher appears.

— I used to think I would never be able to live in such a small town. Being on this path, I understood that I could live anywhere. I did not think I would be able to satisfy my desires here.

— Desires change. New desires replace old desires, and you start to see the situation differently.

— *I am quite haughty, and I am afraid of the humiliation that I experience sometimes.*

— If you stop being haughty, you will stop receiving the experience of humiliation. A haughty human being shows to other people that he is higher than them, but by experiencing the opposite state, he comes to know that he is very low. He has a very low self-worth, and as a result, he wants to show the opposite. If haughty and lower states are balanced in you, you don't worry about them. By the way, your limitations in communication are also connected to this duality.

— *I feel free talking to you. I don't need to think about what to say.*

— *I frequently experience a fear of loneliness. At the same time, I want to be loved by everybody.*

— Let's take a look at the state of loneliness. What is behind it: love or fear?

— *It is fear.*

— You separate yourself from others. Then you get afraid of being separated from people and you ask them to pay attention to your persona in order not to feel it. But irrespective of how much attention other people give you, you will continue to feel lonely.

— *Theoretically, I understand that, but when I feel it, I can't comprehend it.*

— When you separate yourself from others, you feel exclusivity, or exclusion.

— *Why does a fellow human being act towards me in that way?*

— He acts that way because he experiences fear. Every negative act that people do is connected to their experiencing fear. This fear comes from their perception of the world as something separate and hostile. In having this perception, you don't need the people who surround you; you need confirmation of your existence, which comes from them. But you are afraid of not getting it, and you become angry with them as a result.

— *It follows that when I say I am afraid to lose him, I also hate him.*

— If the fear of losing is present, love turns into hatred pretty fast, especially when something that you don't expect to happen happens. What would you experience if you were to come home one day and find him with another woman?

— *Hatred and humiliation.*

— Here is a good example for you.

— *I can admit that my man can act this way because of my fear that this may happen. He accepted me after I was involved in a similar situation.*

An obligation is always connected to the fear of not-fulfilling it

— Okay. Let's look at the situation from another point of view. It is one thing to love a man conditionally, and a totally different thing to love him unconditionally. Conditioned love is always associated with the fear of losing the object of this love.

You will always be afraid to lose your partner in such a relationship.

— *I am talking about losing him specifically to physical cheating. This is what I am afraid of more than anything else.*

— What exactly are you afraid of?

— *I am afraid I will not be able to understand that.*

— Do you always understand everything?

— *I always try to understand.*

— You try, but you don't understand everything. Should we be afraid that we don't always understand everything? For example, you do not know exactly what awaits you when you visit a foreign country. Should you be afraid to go there?

— *I think we should be afraid of it.*

— If you choose love, there is no fear.

— *I experience pleasure just from being at the University and from studying what I like. I am not fearful of not passing the tests or of not fulfilling someone else's hopes. I am just interested.*

— You are doing those things for yourself, not for anybody else. As soon as you orient yourself with someone, fear appears.

— *Fear can appear secondary to the thought that someone paid your tuition, but you did not match their expectations.*

— That means you consider yourself obligated. If there is an obligation, there is also the fear of not fulfilling it. Everything here is built on obligations and debt. This is what conditional love is about. I love you, so I will give you money to go to school. You just have to study well. If you love me, you would

337

give me this money with no strings attached. I am not obligated to you in any way. It's great that you love me, but we are free. This is difficult for the conditioned mind to understand.

— *But one can understand this.*

— Everything becomes clear and understandable when you come to experience it yourself. The new knowledge is an opportunity to experience something new.

— *What if one does something himself and feels good because of doing it?*

— If you like something, you do it because you like it. You experience pleasure because you do something that you like. But if you are obligated to do it, you start hating it precisely because you are obligated to do it. It is fear again in a different manifestation.

If you want something, you are afraid of losing it. If you don't want something, you are afraid of meeting it. The system of education is built on the sense of duty, guilt, and fear. Nobody asks you whether you like or don't like what you are offered. A school accepted you, so be a good student and study well. What if you don't like a certain subject?

— *What if I have to pass it?*

— As soon as the phrase "have to" appears, so does fear. The entire social system is built on fear, including the system of education. If you accept this system, you get into fear, i.e. into guilt and condemnation.

— *Should we try to push this fear away?*

— You need to see the mechanisms that give birth to fear. Everything depends on where you are coming from. Are you coming out of sense of duty, debt, or interest as a self-investigator? If there is an interest, you do what you want to do and you don't give a damn what other people think of you. But to do that, you need to exit fear and all its consequences.

Interest is an inner tendency to experience something. You experience it and you want to experience something else. In the process, you always deal with yourself and only with yourself. Therefore, everything you do here is directed toward acquiring an experience.

— *I don't like when people praise me for going to school.*

— That means you don't appraise what you do yourself. You transfer this call to somebody else.

— *Yes, that's what I do.*

— You give your power to somebody else. Later, they may give you a bad grade, and you will not like it. These are two sides of one coin. You like when people praise you, and you don't like when they berate you. In both cases, you are not coming from your own self. If you are coming from your own self, these questions will not even appear. Then, you are either interested because you are receiving a new experience, or the experience has exhausted itself and you search for another one.

"I felt perplexed. At the same time, I felt jealous of you..."

— It appeared to me that Kathy did not succeed in seducing you. I felt perplexed, but at the same time, I felt jealous of you as a man and anger toward her. She was doing something without being aware of what she wanted to achieve. Next, I started to negate you as a teacher. I started to question your methods of work. I came to this meeting experiencing these feelings. When I started to sort it out, I came to conclusion that I confirm my opinion of her as hopeless. I was afraid that everyone would read my thoughts. I tried to suppress them. I did not want to admit my jealousy. After the break, I found my strength and approached you. I verbalized my fear, but I did not admit the jealousy. I left you feeling that I had not finished something, and was experiencing a fear of the unknown. I was sitting here asking myself where my self-investigator was. The feeling of jealousy I experienced was very strong. I have not experienced it for a long time. I felt as if an old wound was reopened. Later, at home, Kathy asked what was going on with me. I answered that I was angry. At that time, my feelings had already changed. I felt angry with myself for my emotions. I started to understand that it was not you who was guilty or that your methods were not working; I could not get into a working state. I understood there was nothing between you and Kathy, and that I could not blame her for anything. I got angry for nothing. But the state of anger did not leave me.

— We are dealing with condemnation again. You continue to re-experience the old experience that you have not fully experienced.

— At the moment when I felt jealousy and self-pity, I caught a thought that I was trying to control her, and she would do something that I did not

340

like. I got scared. I tried to review the entire situation from the beginning, but I could not do it: everything was frozen with fear. I was afraid that our relationship might end. I asked myself what our relationship meant to me, and I heard the word kaif. I returned to the past again and experienced my oppression of her and her freedom to do what she wanted to do. Strong emotions, loud laughter, and tears accompanied this. During the night, I let everything go. I felt enormous lightness, and I told her I refuse jealousy and choose love. Afterwards, we experienced intimacy that could not be compared to anything we have ever experienced before.

— Can you admit that there could have been something between me and her?

— *I can admit it because I have a choice. I can talk about it now, and above me there is my jealous "i", and the "i" that hates. But I know that I have a choice. I can turn on the "i" that is jealous and full of hate, or I can bless you. I feel light not because of what is going on here, but because I have a choice.*

— **The question is not even whether this has physically happened or not. If you thought about something, it already happened in your imagination.**

— *Jealousy and guilt are two of the strongest experiences.*

— What lays at the core of these experiences? It's the feeling of ownership. This is mine, and it should not belong to anybody else. But in that case, it does not belong to you either. That's the most interesting part. If you are jealous and believe that someone belongs to you and to you alone, you are losing him or her. As soon as you have imagined a betrayal, it becomes real for you.

Let's look at this from a different angle. Let's say you are jealous of your wife. You imagine her with someone else. Hence, this is your desire. You want that to happen. In reality, no one belongs to anybody, and when you create an illusion that someone belongs to you, these thoughts get stronger, and you see her with someone else. You like that. You experience kaif.

If you did not have this desire, you would not put a prohibition on it. I assert that you want it. If you are jealous, you want this to happen but do not allow yourself to see it and insist that you want something else. You are crushing your own desire.

Jealousy is a perverted form of a true desire. Moreover, the greater your jealousy is, the greater is your desire to confirm the betrayal. Your primary desire does not get satisfied and gets sublimated into jealousy.

— *But one does not necessarily have to imagine that. One does not necessarily have to be jealous.*

— But jealousy does exist, and it is based on your own desire. You satisfy this desire of yours through jealousy. You can receive this pleasure through me. At the base of your jealousy is your own desire. But you do not see it.

— *I got it.*

— You carry a prohibition at the core of which lies your own desire to be betrayed. The one who is jealous always provokes his partner to betray him.

— *Later on, I got into another extreme. I felt guilty for pushing her toward it. I was pushing her to betray me. I understood this mechanism, but I got into the opposite side of it.*

You blame yourself for what you forbid yourself to express

— People blame themselves for things they prohibit themselves to do. Jealousy is a limitation: you don't allow your hidden desire to manifest itself. If you were to allow it to manifest itself, you would experience pleasure. By prohibiting yourself from something, you receive what you receive.

— *If I were to allow this to take place, she might not do it.*

— You would not be interested in it. It would not be important. By letting go of jealousy, you allow your desire to manifest itself. This is a classic situation which blocks the understanding of unity, where everything is interconnected, and if a desire appears in someone, it appears in all of us as one whole. We all belong to one whole, as two arms belong to one body. Do you have a problem with your left hand shaking your right hand?

— *In reality, all of this is free and aware choice. I choose my reaction to what happens.*

— You need each other in order to be aware of each other and to move further in a particular direction. Everything that happens here is part of the scenario chosen by you to broaden your consciousness. Everything that happened between two of you will be used to see and to become aware of your old image. When you start to build your relationships on the axiom of partnership, they become endless and limitless. Everything is right in such relationships. Irrespective of what happens, everything is used as firewood to maintain the fire of awareness. You meet your shadow sides, and you become aware of them. It is important to review everything that comes your way, and you work to help each other.

Manifest your desire as soon as it appears. Allow it to manifest itself. Imagine everything you want. Allow yourself that. Enjoy it.

— *In that case, your partner will stop feeling your aggression.*

— Yes. Otherwise, he or she is feeling pressured by you and starts to resist. In that case, she will do what you are so afraid of, i.e. what you want. What is the difference between me shaking her hand and us getting in bed together?

— *There is no difference if one is jealous.*

— Would you refuse her if there was something between me and her?

— *No. Not now.*

— What is the difference between sex and what we have discussed? The contact we experience during our conversation is much deeper than superficial sexual interaction people usually enjoy. All communication is sexual in nature. Why aren't you jealous of our conversation? We had a very intimate conversation.

This happens because of the materialistic perception, where physical sex is considered a betrayal. If you forbid sex, then go all the way and forbid every communication.

— *So, when people lament and ask why they get what they did not want to get, they don't understand that their own desires were actually satisfied.*

— Yes. WE are trying to complete the logical chain all the way down to this thought. If a prohibition is present, it can encompass everything. What state are you going to be in if everything was prohibited?

— *Do I understand this right, that there are no prohibitions?*

— There are no prohibition for the Soul, but there are many prohibitions for the personality. And until we see all of them, we will not be able to feel ourselves as the Soul.

* Kaif or Kif – from Arabic kayf pleasure. Any drug or agent that when smoked is capable of producing a euphoric condition. The euphoric condition produced by smoking marijuana.

9 781944 722036